ANGER, ALCOHOLISM, and ADDICTION

by the same authors

Letting Go of Shame

Shame, Guilt, and Alcoholism
by Ronald T. Potter-Efron

edited by the same authors

The Treatment of Shame and Guilt in Alcoholism Counseling

Aggression, Family Violence and Chemical Dependency

A NORTON PROFESSIONAL BOOK

ANGER,

ALCOHOLISM, and

ADDICTION

Treating Individuals,

Couples, and

Families

Ronald T. Potter-Efron

Patricia S. Potter-Efron

W. W. Norton & Company • New York • London

The text of this book is composed in Elante. Composition by Bytheway Typesetting Services, Inc. Manufacturing by Haddon Craftsmen, Inc. Book design by Justine Burkat Trubey.

Library of Congress Cataloging-in-Publication Data

Potter-Efron, Ronald T.
  Anger, alcoholism, and addiction : treating anger in a chemical dependency setting / Ronald T. Potter-Efron and Patricia S. Potter
-Efron.
     p.   cm.
  Includes index.
  ISBN 0-393-70126-3
  1. Drug abuse—Treatment.   2. Alcoholism—Treatment.   3. Anger.
I. Potter-Efron, Patricia.   II. Title.
  [DNLM: 1. Alcoholism—therapy.   2. Anger.   3. Substance
Dependence—therapy.   BF 575.A5 P869a]
RC564.P67   1992
616.86′0651—dc20   91-39083   CIP
DNLM/DLC

W.W. Norton & Company, Inc. 500 Fifth Avenue, New York, N.Y. 10110
W.W. Norton & Company Ltd. 10 Coptic Street, London WC1A 1PU

1   2   3   4   5   6 7   8   9   0

This book is dedicated to Norma Potter
and the memory of Esther Efron and Anna Hansen.

CONTENTS

LIST OF EXERCISES

LIST OF TABLES

ACKNOWLEDGMENTS

Many individuals have contributed their thoughts, time and energy in helping this book come into being. Among them are Stan Friedman, Earl Heuer, Dave Leicht, Ann McKinley, Charlir Rumberg, and Sandy Smith, readers of a previous version of this volume that subsequently was divided into a segment for general readers and this effort. In addition, Susan Barrows has been an enthusiastic and thoroughly competent editor on behalf of W.W. Norton & Company. Her suggestions have been uniformly valuable. Three persons who typed substantial portions of the book are Liberty Ayrres, Jenny Potter-Efron, and Mi-Lou Trask. Not only was their typing excellent but so were the ideas that they suggested while at their work. Finally, we wish to acknowledge our debt to our clients, those alcoholic and chemically dependent anger avoiders and chronically angry persons who taught us about the many forms and variations of anger and addiction.

ANGER,

ALCOHOLISM, and

ADDICTION

1

INTRODUCTION: DEFINITIONS, APPROACHES, and GOALS

This book is intended primarily for counselors and therapists who work in chemical dependency treatment settings or who see alcoholics, addicts, and affected family members in the course of their practice. It is designed to help professionals understand the complex relationships between anger, aggression, and chemical use/abuse. The focus is practical and includes many exercises and ideas that relate to the question: "OK, I'm not using (or drinking) anymore, but what do I do with my anger?"

Major themes in this book include understanding what each client's anger means to that person, how one individual's anger affects others (its functions), and how anger issues can be addressed in therapy.

THEORETICAL/PHILOSOPHICAL APPROACHES TO ANGER

Three main approaches to anger have emerged over the last several years. Each has its advantages, disadvantages, and appropriate uses.

The first school of thought is the *ventilationist* approach. The premise of this approach is that anger is a good and useful emotion that many individuals have been taught to ignore or avoid. Ventilationists argue that ignoring one's anger often backfires,

1

leading to physical illnesses such as ulcers and other stress-related problems. Furthermore, they note that people who never get angry often get trampled, becoming doormats to more aggressive individuals. They suggest that we should fully accept the emotion of anger and that anger needs to be expressed vividly, sometimes through yelling, shouting, and physical exertion.

The ventilationist approach makes most sense for individuals who have greatly repressed and denied their anger. These persons need assurance that they can survive their anger. They need to recognize that it is normally possible to express anger without endangering others. Some may even need to pound a punching bag a few times to learn to recognize the physical signs of their anger.

Many chemically dependent persons and affected family members have trouble recognizing and expressing their anger. Indeed, some expressly use alcohol or drugs to disinhibit themselves enough to allow anger. The focus in treatment settings upon "showing your feelings" probably helps these individuals learn to express their anger more often and more appropriately.

It is vital, however, to realize that ventilation of anger is not a useful tactic at all for those who already carry a lot of anger with them. These people already know how to express anger—in fact, they are experts at it. Every time they yell and scream they only train themselves, and everybody around them, to get more and more angry (Tavris, 1989). Encouraging them to ventilate reinforces an already dysfunctional pattern.

In general, ventilation is not an effective way to deal with anger. The ventilator confuses using anger as a signal that something is wrong with trying to solve problems with it. She does not understand that anger is a cue rather than a means to an end.

The second school of thought can be called the anger *reduction* approach. Proponents of this approach, such as Albert Ellis (Ellis & Harper, 1975), believe that anger generally raises more problems than it solves. They note that most angry people are unhappy and suggest that we should work to reduce the total amount of anger we experience through varied techniques, such as forgiveness, challenging negative thoughts, and relaxation.

Anger reduction is often an excellent approach with many persons treated in chemical dependency settings. Many of these individuals are too sensitive to their anger and insensitive to other feelings. Later in this book, for instance, we will present some research results (Potter-Efron & Potter-Efron, 1991) indicating that many alcoholics and adult children of alcoholics suffer from chronic anger problems. Some of these persons seem to be "angry all the time," often over trivial incidents that others would ignore. These individuals already ventilate their anger. They do not gain by "communicating" that anger to others through endless arguments. If they could realize that most of their anger comes from inside themselves, they might learn how to reduce their daily experience of anger.

While it would be a disservice to encourage anger avoiders to reduce their anger, since their problem is that they have already attempted to reduce it below useful limits, it would also be a mistake to encourage the chronically angry person to ventilate, since that behavior increases one's overall amount of anger.

The third approach to anger is to focus upon the process of anger *management*. It is based on the theory that when anger is experienced in moderation it is a valuable human resource. The goal is for clients to learn how to express their anger in moderate and socially acceptable ways. Assertiveness training is an example of the anger management approach, with its distinction between aggressive and assertive behaviors (Alberti & Emmons, 1986). Anger is perceived as a normal emotion that can be harnessed for the good of all, even improving relationships when used correctly. Those individuals who get into trouble with anger are taught social skills so they can control their outbursts without becoming completely docile.

The anger management approach is best for chemically dependent persons and family members who can accept their anger but need to learn what to do with it so that nobody, including themselves, gets hurt. Techniques such as fair fighting and learning to listen without interrupting can help these persons go through a natural process of recognizing, using, and then letting go of their anger.

Throughout this book suggestions are presented about using anger well. An anger management model is often utilized with this material, stressing the use of anger in moderation. Of course, this is exactly what many people who are recovering from addiction need to do with their lives—learn how to live in moderation.

In the long run, most clients will benefit from the anger management model. However, anger management is less useful for those who are either terrified by or fascinated with their anger. These persons might learn some valuable skills about anger in communication lectures; however, they simply will not put those skills to use. The anger avoider says: "I just can't do that. I'm too scared of my anger to be assertive." Meanwhile, the compulsively angry individual argues, "That's just the way I am and others will just have to take me this way."

This book is intended to be pragmatic. Therefore, we have tried to take what is most valuable from each approach: the ventilationists' appreciation of the strength and power of anger; the wisdom of the reductionists that too much anger can destroy a person's life; and the emphasis on skill-building and careful use of anger stressed by the anger management approach. All three will be needed in any chemical dependency or mental health treatment setting. What is crucial is learning when each should be applied.

DEFINITIONS

Certain definitions are helpful when dealing with anger. Here are six that will be used throughout this book:

- *Anger:* An immediate emotional state that can range in intensity from mild irritation and annoyance to fury and rage (Spielberger et al., 1983).

- *Rage:* The strongest form of anger, very physical, threatening the individual with possible loss of control over his or her actions.

- *Aggression:* Actual behavior that is intended to harm someone. Anger does not automatically lead to aggression although often the two occur together.

- *Hostility:* An attitude toward specific individuals or the world that includes readiness to see others as enemies and to be angry with them.

- *Resentment:* A process in which anger is stored rather than released, usually accompanied by a belief that the individual has been harmed by others; the opposite of forgiveness.

- *Hatred:* The end product of the resentment process, hatred is "hardened" anger that results in an intense and unchanging dislike of another.

OUTLINE OF BOOK

The remaining chapters of this book are as follows:

- Chapter 2 covers the relationship between anger, aggression, and chemical use and abuse. The chapter, a review of literature and research in the field, illustrates the complex interactions among these variables.

- Chapter 3 presents models of normal anger, anger avoidance, and chronic anger, showing how individuals characteristically handle anger.

- Chapter 4 discusses anger avoidance concerns among chemically dependent persons and affected family members. Anger avoidance occurs when someone habitually ignores, denies, or evades his anger. We will describe how this behavior is related to chemical use patterns, the effects upon family members, and how change can be initiated.

- Chapter 5 describes two brief devices for assessing chronic anger, which can be used during chemical dependency treatment or at the beginning of a therapeutic relationship.

- Chapter 6 discusses the functions of chronic anger, including several gains that people receive from their use of anger. This knowledge is useful for both assessment and treatment purposes, since it specifies the often hidden reasons why individuals cling to their anger.

■ Chapter 7 offers general principles for treating anger problems, as well as specific applications of these principles for a chemical dependency population.

■ Chapter 8 describes work with chronically angry clients within a chemical dependency treatment setting. Specific guidelines for connecting chemical dependency concerns with anger management issues are presented here.

■ Chapter 9 covers treatment of selective aspects of anger and aggression, including explosiveness, anger-inducing thought patterns, and long-term resentments. These problems have been selected because of the frequency of their occurrence within a chemical dependency population.

■ Chapter 10 includes information related to helping affected family members survive living with an angry (and perhaps addicted) person, to working with angry couples and families, and to therapy with adult children from angry and addicted homes.

■ Chapter 11 addresses the need to treat self-directed and self-destructive anger as part of therapy with chronically angry individuals.

■ Chapter 12 covers professional anger issues. Counselors may discover that they have their own problems with anger avoidance or excessive anger, in both their personal and their professional lives.

2

ANGER, AGGRESSION, and CHEMICAL ABUSE

There is no single or simple relationship between the use of alcohol and other mood-altering chemicals, on the one hand, and anger and aggression, on the other. Rather, the two are interwoven in complex and often mysterious ways. However, one principle seems clear: *Any mood-altering chemical is capable of promoting anger and/or aggression.* This happens routinely with some drugs, such as alcohol and amphetamines, more rarely with others, like marijuana and the hallucinogens. However, there is no such thing as a "safe" drug in this regard. Any mood-altering chemical increases the risk, at least for certain persons in certain circumstances, of anger and aggression. On the other hand, no drug is invariably "criminogenic" (Cohen, 1985).

This chapter is a review of the relevant literature. It is primarily a summary of three previously published articles (Miller & Potter-Efron, 1990; R. Potter-Efron, 1990; Potter-Efron & Potter-Efron, 1991). Readers who want more detailed information may turn to those articles as well as to the other references cited here. The primary topics of review are: (1) the relationship between chemical abuse and anger/aggression; (2) the connections between chemical abuse and anger/aggression with possible complicating physical or psychiatric diagnoses; (3) the theme of

7

"angry personalities" among alcoholic and adult child treatment populations; (4) social and cultural factors that influence the connection between substance use and the appearance of anger or aggression.

CHEMICAL ABUSE AND ANGER/AGGRESSION

Alcohol and drug use have often been associated with child abuse, sexual abuse, and spouse assault. For example, Flanzer (1990), in reviewing this subject, cites numerous relevant studies. These include Labell's (1977) findings that 72% of abused women in a shelter reported that their mates had a drinking problem; Flanzer and Sturkie's (1987) data indicating that the actual severity of child battering increases as the perpetrator drinks more, but that moderate and severe drinking parents were at higher risk to batter than alcoholic parents; and Gelles' (1972) important observation that people use alcohol as an excuse to become violent. Jesse (1989) notes that addicted or alcoholic families tend to be violent, even in recovery, especially around issues of control. She also cites sibling physical abuse as a specific problem in alcoholic or addicted families.

A history of physical or sexual abuse has often been linked with alcohol and drug problems. For example, Schaefer, Evans, and Sterne (1985) compared women going through chemical dependency treatment programs with a control group. Although over 50% of each group reported a history of sexual abuse, the incidents began at an earlier age, lasted longer, and were less likely to be reported by the women in treatment. These researchers also indicate that these women were more likely to have physically or sexually abused their own children. Covington (1986) states that alcoholic women are more likely to have experienced physical and sexual abuse than other women; and Black and Bucky (1986) found, in their study, that daughters of alcoholics were twice as likely as other women to be victims of incest. Barnard (1990) adds that there is a "significant correlation" between alcohol abuse and perpetration of incest.

Studies of spouse battering also link this behavior with substance abuse. For instance, Eberle (1980) collected descriptions of four battering episodes from each victim in his study. Of these, all four involved alcohol 16% of the time, and alcohol was involved in at least one episode among 65% of the victims. Kantor and Strauss (1986), and Leonard et al. (1985) have also documented a correlation between drinking and spouse abuse.

Child neglect is also associated with alcoholic families (Black & Mayer, 1980), perhaps as a result of the parents' distraction from the children as they concentrate on drinking-related crises. While the parents may not themselves be physically violent, they may fail to protect their children from their mutual aggression. Jesse (1989) suggests that anger is expressed indirectly in such families by leaving the children, pouting, or withholding. Additionally, anger may suddenly erupt when parents are asked to meet their normal responsibilities.

Anger and aggressive behavior can rarely be attributed solely to the effects of taking a mood-altering chemical. Usually violence results from a combination of the drug, the situation, the user's and others' expectations, and the personality of the user. However, certain drugs of abuse do seem to increase the likelihood of anger or aggression. Also, some drugs, such as phencyclidine (PCP), regularly propel individuals toward anger and aggression, producing "disruption above a certain dosage level [which is] consistent and to some degree free from social determinants and expectations" (Morgan, 1985).

Cohen (1985) clearly describes many of the ways that drug ingestion is connected with anger and aggression: (1) specific actions of particular drugs may induce belligerence and hostility; (2) drug-induced aggression varies by dosage, often following a curvilinear path as maximum dosage incapacitates the user; (3) aggression is more likely to occur on the ascending limb of the blood/drug concentration than when blood level of a drug is decreasing; (4) the setting of the drug use modifies and can even overwhelm the pharmacologic effects of the drug; and (5) there are a number of pathways that drug-induced violence can take, including: (a) the drug might diminish ego controls and release submerged anger; (b) it might impair judgment; (c) it might induce restlessness, irritability, and impulsiveness; (d) it could produce (or exacerbate) a paranoid thought disorder; (e) an intoxicated or delirious state might result in combativeness, hyperactivity and violence; (f) a user's drug-induced feelings of omnipotence and bravado might promote dangerous behavior; (g) unpredictable and uncharacteristic behavior might be associated with amnestic and fugue states.

Detailed information has accumulated on the effect of many drug categories. Much of this information is summarized in Tables 1 and 2. Below we review information about the effects of particular mood-altering substances upon anger and aggression.

TABLE 1

Covariance of Substance Abuse and the
Behavioral States of Aggression and Violence

DRUG NAME OR CATEGORY:	Intoxication	Intoxication Delirium	Withdrawal	Withdrawal Delirium	Idiosyncratic/ Paradoxical Response	Substance Induced Dementia	Chronic Substance Induced Paranoia	Drug-Procuring Violence
Alcohol	c		c	occ	occ	occ	occ	occ
Other Sedative/Hypnotics			c	c	occ	occ*		
Phencyclidine (PCP)	c	c					c	
Cocaine	occ						c	occ
Other Stimulants	c						c	occ
Opiates								c
Hallucinogens						occ		
Cannabis							occ	occ
Inhalants		occ						

c = common   occ = occasional

Designed by Dr. Michael M. Miller; previously published in Miller and Potter-Efron, 1990.
*only gluthethamide

TABLE 2
Covariance of Substance Abuse and the Emotional/Psychological States Associated with Irritability and Anger

	Production of Irritable "Short-Fused" State	Induction of Acute Paranoid Thoughts and Behavior	Exacerbation of Underlying Paranoid State	Disinhibition of Intrinsic Anger
Alcohol or Sedative Intoxication	2+ – 3+	1+	0 – 2+	3+
Alcohol/Sedative Withdrawal	3+ – 4+	1+ – 2+	1+ – 2+	0
Stimulant Intoxication (includes cocaine)	*3+ – 4+	3+ – 4+	3+ – 4+	0
Stimulant Withdrawal	0	0	0	0
Opiate Intoxication	0	0	0	0
Opiate Withdrawal	3+	0	0 – 1+	0
Hallucinogen Intoxication	0 – 1+	0 – 1+	1+ – 3+	1+
Cannabis Intoxication	0 – 1+	1+ – 3+	2+ – 4+	1+
Phencyclidine Intoxication	2+ – 4+	4+	4+	0

The numbers in the table are for comparative purposes, with "0" = no known association and 4+ = a very strong association.
Designed by Dr. Michael M. Miller; previously published in Miller and Potter-Efron, 1990.
*includes caffeine

Alcohol

There is general agreement among researchers that alcohol is the drug most commonly associated with violence (Cohen, 1985). One reason is simply that alcohol is used to such a great extent in our society. Alcohol can trigger violence during intoxication, during withdrawal, and in other specific clinical states.

There is little doubt that alcohol is a dangerous drug in that it does foster anger and aggression. What is debatable, however, is

CASE STUDY: Alcohol Withdrawal

A 44-year-old accountant with a peptic ulcer condition and frequent headaches comes to a family therapist complaining of difficulty tolerating conflicts at home. He says his 16-year-old son is becoming more oppositional, with heightened verbal conflict with mother. The accountant's 41-year-old wife has been drinking more, and despite her attempts to hide this from her husband, he is concerned about her drinking. When he comes home, his wife is often sobbing, complaining of how she just can't control the boy anymore.

But the accountant says that what really upsets him is the amount of fighting in the mornings when they're trying to get the children off to school. He's trying to calmly gather himself for his day ahead, and his wife has intense shouting matches with the son. Her yelling seems to escalate her son's oppositionality, and she's been so irritable lately that there have been times that she's thrown a coffee cup across the kitchen, either trying to hit the boy with it or just crash it against the wall.

What may be happening is that, before beginning her daytime drinking again (out of a sense of frustration and exhaustion) after her husband and children have gone off for the day, this woman is experiencing alcohol withdrawal. She drinks throughout the day, will usually have a nightcap after her husband has gone to sleep, but experiences alcohol

how alcohol promotes violence. Is it attributable to the drug itself, interactions of alcohol and personality factors, social expectations (including particularly the conviction that alcohol "makes" a person violent and the tendency in many societies to excuse any violence associated with alcohol as not really the fault or responsibility of the intoxicated user), or some combination of all of these things? It seems likely that a combination model is generally most valuable. Although there may be times when the

CASE STUDY: continued

abstinence in the mornings. She dismisses her tremulous-
ness as nervousness about the family tension, but she is
particularly irritable and prone to getting into conflicts with
family members because of her hyperaroused central nervous system from her alcohol abstinence syndrome. Ironi-
cally, if she were to have had a drink at dawn to abate
her withdrawal, mornings around the house would be more
peaceful, with less anger and potential for violence — though
such breakfast-time conflicts are currently serving as one of
the more conspicuous signs of her illness, thus increasing
the likelihood that her husband will force an intervention
to usher her into treatment. ■

drug itself is clearly the culprit (for instance, in the rare case of
idiosyncratic alcohol syndrome, in which a person who takes
even a minute quantity of alcohol becomes fiercely hostile), usually numerous factors interact.

Could alcohol itself produce violence? At least one apparently
sophisticated study (Taylor & Leonard, 1983) has found that individuals generally become more aggressive as the dosage of alcohol increases and that this increase cannot be attributed to cognitive or environmental cues. Still, approximately one-third of
participants in this study did not become more aggressive, even
at high dosage levels. Once again, it is safe to conclude that the
relationship between alcohol and anger or aggression is positive
but not precise.

Other Sedative-Hypnotics

Withdrawal from sedative-hypnotics, in particular the barbiturates, is strongly associated with both interpersonal violence (Levenson, 1985) and suicidal intent (Grinspoon & Bakalar, 1985).
Cohen (1985) rates these drugs as second only to alcohol as con-
tributors to assaultive behavior. Although these chemicals are

supposedly sedating, they tend to produce argumentative, irritable behavior, perhaps because the affected individual is released from normal inhibitions while intoxicated (Cohen, 1985). Spotts and Shontz (1984) note that heavy barbiturate users tend to provoke senseless fights with family and others, and that the anger of the chronic barbiturate user is associated with strong self-destructive urges.

Phencyclidine (PCP)

PCP is regularly associated with the appearance of aggression, most commonly among chronic, heavy users who develop a psychosis that mimics an episode of paranoid schizophrenia (Allen, 1980; Peterson & Stillman, 1978). PCP users often switch quickly between normal sociability and hostility (Grinspoon & Bakalar, 1985), making their behavior difficult to predict. PCP psychosis is characterized by insomnia, tension, hyperactivity, and intermittent unexpected aggressive outbursts (Luisada & Brown, 1976).

PCP does not trigger psychotic-like episodes only in those who are already vulnerable in that direction. Instead, it appears that above a certain dosage level PCP can produce these disruptive effects in most persons (Morgan, 1985). This indicates that the drug itself is responsible for the tendency toward aggression.

Chronic PCP use is associated with gradual personality changes. Many users become more angry, irritable, and violent over time (Fauman & Fauman, 1980). Without question, PCP is one of the most dangerous drugs currently available with regard to the eruption of aggression and violence.

Cocaine

There is no doubt that cocaine use is highly associated with irritability, guardedness, and suspiciousness. One study of a cocaine hot-line found that 99% of callers described these symptoms (Crowley, 1987), while another indicated that 82% reported irritability and 65% paranoia (Washton, Gold, & Potash, 1984).

CASE STUDY: Phencyclidine Intoxication

As a chemical dependency counselor for the Community Corrections Department, you are asked as part of a pre-sentence investigation to do a chemical dependency history on a 19-year-old college student. He is known to have a history of regular marijuana smoking, heavy drinking of alcohol on the weekends, and experimentation with psilocybin mushrooms. He has no criminal history whatsoever, but one night, he broke into a record store, assaulted the clerk, and gathered into his arms a half-shelf full of albums of his favorite "heavy metal" band. Upon questioning the jailer about his behavior the night of his arrest, one learns that he was banging his hands on the walls of the cell, but saying that it didn't hurt, and talking incoherently, with very rapid emotional shifts, sometimes laughing hysterically, other times yelling in intense rage, and saying he felt as if his arms were ten feet long and getting entwined in the bars of the cell.

This is a case of intense, otherwise inexplicable, violence in a patient with no past history of criminality. In trying to understand what happened that evening to bring this on, several factors are salient. One is that this young man had a history of drug experimentation. The other is that marijuana was his drug of choice. The other is his unusual behavior at the time of the violent crime, including reports consistent with anesthesia in his extremities and a sense of distortion about the length of his extremities. Such symptoms are consistent with phencyclidine intoxication, which commonly occurs when marijuana has been laced with phencyclidine in an attempt to make inexpensive marijuana seem as potent as the most expensive imported varieties. ■

However, angry mood and irritability do not automatically lead to aggression, and researchers have not documented a strong correlation between cocaine use and physical violence, although many cocaine users describe such events. What aggression that

CASE STUDY: Amphetamine Psychosis

A 31-year-old male security guard has been brought to a chemical dependency counselor by his superiors because of concerns of marijuana use on the job. Superiors report that he is noticeably paranoid and that recently he confronted a new worker with whom he was not familiar. Upon coming around a corner and bumping into this other guard in the dark, the guard grabbed the new worker and began choking him until a third guard came to his aid. When the guard calmed down, he said that he had thought that this new employee was someone who had been sent there to rub him out as a part of a Mafia hit. The supervisor says this guard has been a good employee overall, but that he wonders if marijuana use is making him more paranoid.

On collecting the history, one discovers that this man had injected "crystal" methamphetamine daily for two years while in the service ten years ago. Upon discharge from the military, he continued to use oral speed, up to 16 "hits" a day of "white cross" amphetamine tablets for four years. He had been psychiatrically hospitalized for what was reported to be paranoid schizophrenia, and though never rehospitalized, had had continuing paranoid experiences episodically ever since.

It's impossible to determine from this data how much the patient's cannabis exposure exacerbated his paranoid state, but the underlying paranoid state is one of residual psycho-

has been described is most often associated with the smoking of crack cocaine, a mode of ingestion that seems likely to produce violence as well as significant psychiatric symptoms (Honer, Gewirtz, & Turey, 1987).

There does seem to be a probable correlation between the use of "upgraded" drugs and the potential for violence. This applies to cocaine, "ice" amphetamine, and perhaps even marijuana. However, much more research needs to be done in this area before this connection can be definitely documented.

sis, induced by heavy chronic amphetamine exposure. A residual syndrome has been produced, involving paranoid delusions, and a tendency toward excessive suspicious-ness—a paranoid condition continuing in the absence of amphetamine exposure. Psychiatric referral may be necessary to place the patient on maintenance antipsychotic agents to treat this chronic amphetamine-induced paranoid state. ■

Other Stimulants

Amphetamine use is definitely associated with irritability, hostility, and psychosis (Grinspoon & Bakalar, 1985). As with PCP, a psychotic pattern can develop in essentially normal persons when they use amphetamines, even with relatively short-term administration (Morgan, 1985), implying that the drug itself is a causal agent. Amphetamine psychoses may persist for months or years after an individual quits ingesting amphetamines. Cohen (1985) links large doses of amphetamines with hyperactivity, paranoid suspiciousness, and impulsivity.

Intravenous use of amphetamines has been linked with violence, as has withdrawal after "speed runs" of up to two weeks' duration (Moyer, 1976). In addition, "ice," smokable amphetamine, has been gaining popularity. Although research documentation is limited, popular reports seem to indicate that this form of substance abuse is quite likely to trigger episodes of violence. Again, this follows the principle that more powerful and quick-acting drugs increase the probability for aggression.

Other Substances

Opiates are often associated with criminal behavior in order to procure the money to purchase drugs (Jaffee, 1985). However, anger is among the emotions least associated with heroin use by the users themselves (Seecoff, 1986). *Hallucinogens* are only occasionally linked with violence, which may take the form of delusional self-violence (Siegel, 1980). *Anabolic steroids* are a much more serious threat, with long-term use associated with addiction (Kashkin & Kleber, 1989; Tennant, Black, & Voy, 1988), "bodybuilder's psychosis" (Pope & Katz, 1987), paranoia (Tricker, O'Neill, & Cook, 1989), and aggression (Daigle, 1990; Hallagan, Hallagan, & Snyder, 1989; Kleinman, 1990). However, recent research suggests that aggression associated with anabolic steroid use may be largely confined to those already predisposed toward aggression (Slade et al., 1991). Nevertheless, extreme caution should be taken, as the possibility that anabolic steroid use might cause, exacerbate, or prolong aggression cannot be ruled out. *Cannabis* (marijuana) may be associated with anger or aggression. Stoner (1988), using Spielberger's State-Trait Anger Expression Inventory, found that increased marijuana use was associated with anger and that "persons who frequently used marijuana exhibited more aggressive behavior when motivated by angry feelings than did nonusers and occasional users, and with increased marijuana use, individuals expressed anger toward other persons or the environment more frequently." Others attempt to control their anger and aggression with marijuana, arguing that they are more "mellow" when intoxicated. Although often thought to be virtually harmless, marijuana is hardly a "safe" drug to take, especially if a person has any prior history of paranoia, since chronic marijuana use can increase these symptoms. Additionally, many individuals combine marijuana with other substances, a practice that produces unpredictable and possibly anger- or aggression-stimulating responses.

ASSOCIATED PHYSICAL AND PSYCHIATRIC DIAGNOSES

It is important for the therapist to consider the possibility that an individual may have a distinct physical or psychiatric problem that partially explains some of his or her anger or aggression. This complicates an already complicated picture. We must be able to make a differential diagnosis that includes the effects from a patient's use of alcohol and drugs; his or her anger problems, which may be independent from these effects; and the possible presence of anger-invoking mental and physical disorders.

The conditions listed below are some of those frequently encountered in a chemical dependency treatment setting.

Traumatic Brain Injury

Chemical dependency counselors frequently encounter patients with a past or recent history of brain injuries from vehicular accidents, falls, beatings, or suicide attempts. These injuries can cause permanent damage to the frontal lobes and the deeper structures of the brain, producing frontal lobe syndrome, which is often associated with the inability to control one's anger.

Individuals with a history of such accidents may not be able to drink at all (or much less than before) lest they become terribly angry and violent. Counselors need to warn them, and their families, that they must curtail their drinking or drug use to help avoid uncontrollable anger. It is helpful to explain to these persons, in the presence of family members (there may be memory problems), that a single beer (or dose) now may have the effect produced by a six-pack prior to the trauma. Furthermore, the results of drinking or using drugs may now be far less predictable than before.

Intermittent Explosive Disorder

There seems to be disagreement among physicians and psychiatrists about this diagnosis. Some doctors give this label to anyone who periodically becomes excessively violent. Others are more selective, considering it to be a form of brain malfunctioning similar to epilepsy. We recommend this more conservative approach. The following symptoms need to be present to justify the diagnosis of intermittent explosive disorder: (1) the presence of discrete and limited episodes of assaultive and destructive episodes; (2) an absence of generalized anger or aggression between episodes (Reid & Balis, 1986); (3) following an episode the individual appears stunned and remorseful about the behavior (Bolton & Bolton, 1987); (4) the period of violence is minimally provoked, poorly focused, carried out in a state of clouded consciousness, and may be followed by partial amnesia about the violent incident itself (Conn & Lion, 1984).

Attention Deficit Disorder and
Attention Deficit Disorder, Residual

Children with attention deficit disorder often have difficulty restraining aggressive impulses. So, too, might the approximately 25% of these children who retain some ADD symptoms as adults. This condition, diagnosed as "attention deficit disorder, residual," is characterized by restlessness, emotional lability, impulsivity, and "hot temper" (Wender et al., 1985). It has been associated with adult alcoholism (Wender, Reimherr, & Wood, 1981) and drug abuse (Gittleman et al., 1985). The presence of attention deficit disorder in children or adults, especially when combined with hyperactivity, increases the likelihood of aggression.

Premenstrual Syndrome

Irritability and violence have long been associated with premenstrual syndrome. In addition, women report greater desire to drink during the premenstrual phase (Bender, 1987), tend to utilize drugs to alleviate premenstrual symptoms (Bender, 1987), and absorb alcohol more quickly into the blood stream at this time (Halliday et al., 1986). Markoff (1984) further reports that women being treated for alcoholism tend to deny PMS symptoms because the combination of these two disorders seems overwhelming to them.

Personality Disorders

Two personality disorders are seen more commonly than others in a chemical dependency treatment center. These are antisocial personality disorder and borderline personality disorder.

Antisocial personality disorder is associated with Cloninger's Type II alcoholism (1987). These individuals, almost always men, have a long history of aggression and other antisocial activities, beginning early in life and usually predating the use of mood-altering substances. They will normally continue to have problems in these areas even after discontinuing alcohol and/or drugs, although abstinence may lessen the severity and frequency of these episodes. Counselors treating these persons should be alert to the possibility of instrumental violence — that is, intentionally planned aggression designed by the individual to intimidate and control others—as opposed to behavior that centers around real emotional distress.

Individuals with borderline personality disorder often appear to have a "bottomless pit" of anger. This anger is triggered by fears of rejection and abandonment. It often takes the form of "splitting," in which the person decides that someone who had been "all good" is now "all bad," a "thing" worthy of destruction. Borderline patients also have the reputation of splitting treatment teams, so that staff members become hostile toward one another. Alcohol and drug abuse are common among borderline individuals. Researchers in one study (Vaglum & Vaglum, 1985), for example, estimated that as many as 30% of female alcoholics may meet the criteria for borderline disorder.

Major Depressive Disorder and Bipolar Disorder

Many depressed persons turn to alcohol or drugs for temporary relief of their symptoms (sometimes, in extreme situations, even a blackout is preferable to the despair of depression). Unfortunately, such use of mood-altering substances probably increases the probability of suicide attempts and decreases and diminishes the ability and motivation to take antidepressant medications. Also, continuing depressive symptomatology after treatment is a major predictor of relapse (Pickens et al., 1985).

Individuals with bipolar disorder suffer all the usual signs of depression during one phase and then swing into another phase characterized by impulsivity, restlessness, and an elevated mood that easily can turn into irritability and argumentativeness, belligerence, and outright assaultiveness (Conn & Lion, 1984). Random and impulsive drug use frequently occurs during this phase.

Post-Traumatic Stress Disorder

Although neither substance abuse nor chronic anger or aggression is part of the diagnostic criteria for PTSD, both have been cited as commonly occurring within this population (Daley, Moss, & Campbell, 1987; Keane et al., 1985). Keane notes that both anger and substance abuse may be "reinforced by their ability to reduce aversive feelings." He recommends a thorough screening of PTSD clients in both areas. It is certainly our experience that many chemically dependent individuals perceive a close linkage between their use of mood-altering substances and the violence they observed and/or participated in in their pasts. They may have less understanding of how their current episodes of anger or aggression correlate with their drug or alcohol consumption, if only because of their preoccupation with the past. Another problem is that of justification: PTSD survivors might rationalize their current anger and aggression as perfectly understandable given what they have endured. Chemical dependency counselors will have to guard against joining them in this pattern of responsibility avoidance.

CHRONICALLY ANGRY ALCOHOLICS AND ADULT CHILDREN OF ALCOHOLICS

Certain people seem to carry more anger than others as part of their basic personality structure. These individuals have developed a pattern of thinking and being that is rooted in chronic hostility, suspiciousness, and cynicism.

Several writers have tried to describe the characteristics of habitually angry persons. They have discovered that there may be several types of angry persons. For instance, some angry individuals strike out against the world while others turn their anger inward. Many chronically angry persons know they are angry; others repress knowledge of their anger and honestly deny it. In general, researchers have generally described three types of chronic anger: *undercontrolled,* in which an individual readily translates his or her anger into aggression against others; *overcontrolled,* where anger is experienced emotionally but not turned into aggression; and *repressed (or suppressed),* in which the individual is completely or mostly unaware of that anger (Hecker & Lunde, 1985).

Charles Spielberger and his associates (Spielberger, 1988; Spielberger, Krasner, & Solomon, 1988) have made several useful contributions to the understanding of chronic anger. First, they have described an immediate anger state, which consists of subjective feelings of irritation, annoyance, fury, and rage accompanied by physical agitation. They contrast this with what they call "trait anger," defined as a characteristic tendency to respond to the world with anger. Persons high in trait anger "frequently experience angry feelings and often feel they are treated unfairly by others" (Spielberger, 1988, p. 5). They go on to note that some individuals high in trait anger are particularly sensitive to criticism and perceived insults, while others are quick-tempered, impulsive and readily express their anger with little provocation. Spielberger notes that persons with high trait anger may turn their anger inward or outward or both. They may try desperately to control their anger or they may prefer to express it freely. He notes that the 25% of the population who score highest on the Spielberger State-Trait Anger Expression Inventory are likely to experience and/or express angry feelings so much that they encounter difficulties in their lives. His research indicates that many chronically angry individuals develop serious health problems, in particular an increased risk of heart attack.

Patricia Potter-Efron conducted a research study that utilized Spielberger's State-Trait Anger Expression Inventory (STAXI), a self-reporting instrument that has been widely used and normed against a variety of populations. In this study, the STAXI was completed by male alcoholics currently in inpatient treatment, male and female alcoholics currently in outpatient treatment, and females being treated currently in outpatient settings for "adult child of alcoholics" symptoms (Potter-Efron, P., & R. Potter-Efron, 1991).

The anger norms for each of these groups were well above the scores for the normal population. In general, it appears that a far higher number of persons with alcohol problems (their own or family members) suffer from chronic anger.

More specifically, the highest anger scores were reported by male alcoholics being treated in inpatient settings. Indeed, over 70% of these persons ranked in the upper quarter (Spielberger's cutoff for likely problems with anger) on national anger norms, with over 50% in the top tenth (indicative of even more extreme problems with anger).

Compared with outpatient males, inpatients scored particularly high on the Trait Anger T scale, a measure of quick temperedness, and Anger In, which reports the tendency to be angry at oneself. However, both inpatients and outpatients were above national norms on Anger In and Anger Out, another indicator that angry people often direct their anger both at others and themselves.

Both inpatient and outpatient males were low on Anger Control, the measure of how much individuals attempt to contain their anger.

In summary, inpatient males as a group appear to have more intense experiences of anger than the general population, expressed both internally and externally, and relatively poor ability to control anger expression. They are likely to have hot temper, impulsive anger, and trouble with immediate situations. Outpatient alcoholics appear to be less quick tempered and to be less intensely angry than inpatients, but they still have significant problems with anger that they make little effort to control.

Inpatient females also scored high on many measures of anger. They scored well above national norms for impulsive anger (Trait Anger T) and sensitivity to criticism (Trait Anger R). They also direct their anger evenly inwardly and outwardly against others. Over half (53.5%) of these respondents scored at or above the 75th percentile on national norms and one-third (33.3%) were in the upper tenth. Unfortunately, there are no national norms available to compare their scores on Anger Control with other women.

Outpatient females seem to be a slightly less angry group, although the differences are not as striking as with males. These females appear to have less sensitivity to criticism (T Anger R, with scores at the national average), and less inwardly directed anger (Anger In, but these scores were still well above national norms with 47% at the 75th percentile or higher). Since their Anger Out scores are quite high, these respondents appear to direct more of their anger toward others than themselves.

The STAXI was also administered to a limited number (n = 21) of women currently in outpatient treatment as adult children of alcoholics. Their scores were virtually identical to those of females being treated in outpatient settings for alcoholism, with the exception of a lack of extreme anger (90th percentile or higher) in the areas of State Anger and Anger Out. They, too, scored well above national norms on many measures of anger.

It seems reasonable to assume, from this data, that any treatment group focusing upon the problems of alcoholism may be composed of a disproportionately large number of chronically angry individuals. We believe this statement is probably accurate for those consuming other mood-altering substances as well; however, this study did not test for substances other than alcohol. We also believe, from clinical observation, that mere abstinence from alcohol does not assure "recovery" from anger concerns.

Walfish (1990) used the STAXI with 809 adult clients in residential treatment facilities, finding that individuals with a history of drug abuse score higher than nonclients on trait anger. Interestingly, Walfish found no differences among clients based on drug of choice (alcohol, cannabis, cocaine, opioids).

One question these studies raise is whether or not there are consistent gender differences in anger experience or expression. In general, the answer appears to be negative. Tavris (1989) concluded that "the studies failing to support the prevalent belief of sex differences in anger pile up like autumn leaves," citing as differences only a tendency for men to display anger more openly in public and to hold in more anger than women, while women tend to cry more when angry (Choti et al., 1987). Various other studies do describe gender differences, however. For example, Thomas (1989) found that women are more likely than men to express anger via physical symptoms; Smith et al. wrote (1989) that women viewed angry behavior as less appropriate than did men; Stoner and Spencer (1986) report that women score higher than men on trait anger; and Snell, Miller, and Belk (1988) noted that women are more likely to express anger to friends. Clinically, we have not seen any clear differences between genders with regard to the identification of problems with specific kinds of anger.

Few racial differences have been noted in the United States with regard to anger. One exception is the finding that blacks have more suppressed anger than whites (Gentry, 1983; Johnson, 1989), which might be explained by the lower social status of many blacks and the concurrent need to bury one's anger. In addition, blacks have higher blood pressure (especially among those who harbor grudges and hold in anger [Johnson & Broman, 1987]) and intensity of state anger reactions (Johnson, 1989). One similarity is that anger predicts health problems with blacks (Broman & Johnson, 1988), as it does with the population at large.

SOCIAL, CULTURAL, AND FAMILIAL INFLUENCES

We will not attempt a definitive exploration of macrosocial influences on anger, aggression, and chemical abuse here. However, it is important to note that social and cultural expectations greatly influence whether, how much, how often, and the manner in which substance use relates to the appearance of anger and/or aggression in any population. For example, many Native Americans have grown up in a culture that proscribes the direct expression of anger. On the other hand, membership in some gangs and subcultures almost automatically compels its members to engage in acts of violence, often while intoxicated.

American society as a whole is often faulted for allowing people to use intoxication as an excuse for violence. Responsibility for antisocial behavior is attributed to the influence of the drug rather than to the person who ingests it. The user gains a "time-out" from normal expectations (MacAndrew & Edgerton, 1969): "It wasn't my fault. I was drunk." Those writing from a family violence perspective deplore this use of intoxication as an excuse for violence (Coleman & Strauss, 1983; Gelles, 1972). Family violence counselors, with some justification, argue that chemical dependency counselors have failed to insist that their clients accept full responsibility for their drunken or "stoned" behavior.

This "time-out" pattern is part of a complex interaction within American society between power, aggression, and addiction. While Finkelhor (1983) mentions that aggression often travels from the most powerful toward the least powerful members of a family, Elkin (1984) describes the tremendously disruptive power of a drinker both within the family and in other social situations. He hypothesizes that "people get drunk in order to become powerful in interpersonal situations" (p. 20). These relationships can become normalized, so that families, organizations, and friendship groups begin to function as " alcoholic families" (Steinglass et al., 1987) or "addictive organizations." The important point is that chronic anger/aggression or alcoholism/addiction may add to an individual's power over and control of others. When both are present, the angry addict may gain an even greater advantage over his or her sober and less angry associates.

The general concept that alcohol automatically acts as a disinhibitor of control and thus as a facilitator of aggression, deeply engrained in American society, has been challenged by several anthropologists (Coid, 1986; Heath, 1983), who argue that this connection is cultural, not physiological. These individuals cite many cultures in which drinking is not linked with aggression at all or in which the targets of aggression are very selective. These writers, as well as many observers of American culture, emphasize the need to consider drinkers' sets of beliefs about how drinking affects them, the immediate setting they drink within, and the entire range of social controls that govern the relationship between drinking or drug use and aggression.

Some families seem to train each other to be violent (Patterson, 1985). They do so by ignoring non-angry communications and attending primarily to anger, by emphasizing the importance of power and control, and by not teaching socially appropriate social skills. Details of this pattern are discussed in Chapter 10.

It is important to recognize that chemically dependent families often share certain characteristics with families in which aggression occurs, such as an acceptance of loss of control as a way of coping with the world and the existence of rigid role expectations (Potter-Efron & Potter-Efron, 1985), as well as role reversal (Jesse, 1989), role confusion (Bavolek & Henderson, 1990), denial and minimization (Levy & Brekke, 1990) and distorted communication patterns (Levy & Brekke, 1990). This implies that members of these families may tend toward both chemical abuse and violence and that treatment of both problems is needed. Furthermore, stress increases proportionately to the number of stressors within a family. Linkage of chemical dependency, family violence and family disruption creates a situation of multiple stressors that increases the risk to children (Johnson & Montgomery, 1990) and adults for continuing mental health problems.

EXERCISES

2-1 Differential Sources of Anger

To distinguish whether a substance or another condition is of
major importance in generating anger in an individual it may be
helpful to have him/her keep a small notebook listing all the
times he/she feels angry, whether there was a situational trigger
for that anger, how he/she behaved, and what the response was
on the part of others. For example, if the notebook indicates that
a marijuana user is generally *not* so angry when using as he is
otherwise, the clinician might consider whether there is a mental
health problem, such as depression, that the user has been attempting to medicate. How anger is described in the notebook
may help the counselor to determine whether family therapist or
psychiatric evaluation for a mood or personality disorder would
be more appropriate.

2-2 Connecting Anger and Substance Use

Identifying the particular ways in which anger and a mood-
altering chemical interact in the life experience of a particular
client, as well as how that interaction may affect the experience
of the client's family, is more complicated than identifying
whether the client is actively intoxicated or not. The counselor/
therapist may want to use a chart similar to the one following
to help the client determine the specific connections between
substance use and angry feelings/episodes.

Where the counselor has already identified a particular connection that she wishes to bring to the client's attention, the
chart can be used heuristically. It can be used to reconstruct
past behavior and to help a client examine historical connections
between anger and substance abuse. Further, it can be used as a
"research" instrument; in that case, the particular client or family
member would be asked to chart the client's behavior in order to
discover whether an identifiable connection exists. Such a chart
should include a place to note the chemical or chemicals used,
the positioning of the chemical use in the life process, and expressed irritability and anger. An example follows.

On the chart below, indicate the name of the chemical(s) used, each date you had an anger outburst, and the stage of chemical use you were in—whether you used or intended to use that day.

Chemical(s) Used: _____

Stage of Chemical Use	Dates of Anger Outbursts			
Immediate Use				
Intoxication				
Immediate Withdrawal				
Next-Day Withdrawal				
Procurement				

Polydrug users with irregular outbursts of anger can be asked to complete such a chart for each drug used, for a mixture of drugs, or for each common combination of drugs used. Family members who are very aware of the alcohol or chemicals used and times of use can help to make these temporal connections between alcohol or drug use and angry behavior.

A similar chart may be helpful in working with a dual diagnosis client with clearly shifting states of consciousness. Many recovering alcoholics are leery of using medications appropriately; sometimes charting anger during manic or depressed phases, with or without medication, provides information that helps a client prevent relapse. For example:

Mental State:	Expressed Anger		
Manic	Intoxication	Withdrawal	Procurement
drug use			
alcohol use			
on meds			
off meds			

Depressed	Intoxication	Withdrawal	Procurement
drug use			
alcohol use			
on meds			
off meds			

Similar charting can be done for any dually diagnosed person who functions well enough to be aware that these changes do occur and do affect his life and relationships. It is of great help in encouraging some clients to deal with alcohol/drug issues more appropriately or to maintain more consistent use of medications. Acting out angrily can have convincing consequences. When the counselor can aid the client in clearly linking such acting out to alcohol and drug use, a motive for sobriety and/or appropriate user of medications—instead of less appropriate self-doctoring—may become more significant to the client.

With family input this format can also be used to chart past behavior. This helps to establish with the client that drug and alcohol use is damaging to others as well as self-destructive. Helping the chemically dependent/dual diagnosis person determine how his anger relates to his substance use is an important part of the process of helping him become aware of the need for abstinence. Even when a chemically dependent dually diagnosed client cannot or will not be abstinent from alcohol and other non-prescribed mind-altering chemicals, the information can be helpful in decreasing the frequency of institutionalization.

3

MODELS of NORMAL ANGER, ANGER AVOIDANCE, and CHRONIC ANGER

B efore considering what can go wrong with how people deal with their anger, it is valuable to examine a model of the normal anger process. We will present such a model in this chapter, one based on a combination of the theory and principles of gestalt therapy, assertiveness training, and cognitive-behavioral concepts. This normal anger process will be contrasted with two other conditions: anger avoidance, in which a person systematically attempts to ignore anger; and chronic anger, in which someone becomes overinvolved with anger. This approach is designed to help the therapist identify some possible areas of intervention for each client with anger issues.

A Model of Normal Anger

Gestalt therapists (Polster & Polster, 1973; Zinker, 1977) describe a naturally occurring sequence that consists of five major components: (1) an initial *awareness* of a sensation, emotion, or thought; (2) an *excitement* stage that serves to focus a person's attention upon the particular issue; (3) an *action* stage during which the excitement is transformed into behavior; (4) a *contact* stage that gives the person both internal and external feedback on those actions; and (5) a *withdrawal* stage, in which the person withdraws energy and interest from that concern and goes on to something else (a new awareness). This process is illustrated in Figure 1.

Here is a simple example of this process: (1) I become aware that I am slightly thirsty but choose at first to ignore it. (2) After a while, my thirst becomes too demanding to ignore. I stop whatever else I am doing and focus upon my bodily responses. (3) Then I take action by pouring a glass of water and drinking it. (4) Contact happens as I taste the water and feel the accompanying sensations. (5) Having slaked my thirst, I withdraw my interest from this issue and start to become aware of something new.

Anger would normally be handled in exactly the same manner. A woman might become aware that she is feeling some anger because her colleague at work failed to ask her before making a decision that significantly affects her. She then spends time thinking about the incident, perhaps becoming somewhat agitated (excitement phase). That leads to such actions as talking directly with her colleague or reporting the problem to her supervisor. Her contact comes in the form of feedback from her colleague as well as her own internal response to her behaviors. Finally, she is able to "let go" of the concern and get back to her other duties and interests.

Many individuals seem to follow this model when they become

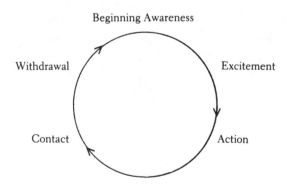

FIGURE 1:   Awareness Cycle

angry. These persons generally are comfortable with their anger. They tend to view anger as a necessary and normal part of life. They may not enjoy the physical and mental aspects of anger, but they do not avoid appropriate amounts of anger. In particular, *these persons use anger as a signal that something is wrong in their lives.* They utilize their initial awareness of their anger to go on a search to discover the nature of the problem and its solution. These individuals are usually able to express their anger in moderation. They don't run away from legitimate concerns because of fear of their anger. Nor do they hang on to that feeling when it has served its purpose. Instead, they have the ability to listen to their anger, act on it, and then withdraw.

Before addressing anger problems, some of the positive aspects of anger should be noted. This is important information in a society that seems to look with suspicion upon the experience and expression of anger.

- *The capacity to feel anger is natural; it is built into our bodies.* This normal capacity serves important survival functions on both physical and emotional levels, in helping individuals recognize and respond to their needs.

- *Anger is a signal that something is wrong.* It is crucial that we learn to attend to this signal rather than trying to ignore it. Suppressing these signals on a regular basis can lead to long-term harm. For example, the spouses of substance abusers who ignore their appropriate anger are less likely to be able to confront the problem effectively.

- *Anger warns others that something is wrong and to be careful.* It is a "relationship" cue that helps indicate the presence of tension and even danger. This use of anger can serve to maintain the functioning of the social network.

- *Awareness of anger increases our awareness of ourselves and others.* Anger is an emotion that signifies a separation or distance between persons. It stimulates an increased awareness of one's individual identity and the boundaries between people.

- *Anger many be needed to survive some dangerous situations.* A "fight" response can mobilize an individual's resolve, helping that person to battle social injustice, the ravages of debilitating illness, or threats to one's safety.

- *Anger may be the last emotion to resist numbness and despair.* This is often true with survivors of physical and sexual abuse and in deeply stressed families struggling with alcoholism, depression, or long-term illness. Such expression of anger prevents physical and emotional collapse, preserving a capacity for the eventual experience of other emotions when those can be more safely expressed.

- *The expression of anger can occasionally help a person to feel good, strong, or whole.* Anger can provide a sense of emotional "intactness," a sense of strength or well-being when stressed.

- *The expression of anger can be a gift of caring, involvement, and vulnerability, leading to greater intimacy in relationship.* Individuals may need to risk immediate, short-term conflict with others in order to build deeper, more intimate relationships. Anger avoiders who cannot tolerate any expression of anger may find the quality of their friendships and partnerships limited by their shirking of legitimate anger.

- *Dealing with one's anger can lead toward reconciliation.* Anger may be a signal that a relationship is currently unbalanced or out of focus. When this anger is acknowledged, it can be utilized to begin a search process designed to restore mutual harmony and comfort.

- *Anger may be part of a normal grieving process.* Elizabeth Kübler-Ross (1969) has long noted that normal grief often involves a period of anger, sometimes intense, in which the griever may be furious with the lost person, others, God, or self. This anger seems to provide energy that eventually helps mourners move through the awareness cycle and onward with their lives.

- *Anger can lead to and stimulate creative activity.* Anger

stimulates people to find new solutions for difficult problems, solutions that may be more effective than old ones.
This is part of anger's general function of raising the level
of energy available to an individual.

■ *Moral anger can be used to fight for justice and fairness.*
Moral indignation and outrage are terms that represent
the merger of anger with ethical concerns. This anger is
particularly volatile, energizing such processes as social
change and religious revolutions.

■ *Anger can gain people's attention, sometimes when nothing else does.* Anger has a shock value that may startle
others into attending to persons and situations they
would otherwise ignore or avoid.

ANGER AVOIDANCE

Anger avoidance is defined as *a pattern of thinking, acting, and
feeling in which individuals attempt to ignore, avoid, and suppress
their anger.*

Many people from chemically dependent families habitually
avoid anger. There are many reasons for the development of this
pattern. These will be discussed in the next chapter, along with
the effects of anger avoidance. Here, the focus is on how anger
avoidance can be placed into the awareness model. Please refer
to Figure 2 for an illustration of the defenses against anger awareness and expression.

Anger avoiders may be handicapped in dealing with their
anger at any or every phase of awareness. Initially, avoiders may
be *desensitized* to their anger. This means that they seldom notice
the physical and cognitive cues indicative of anger. For example,
clients in therapy may raise their voices, tap their feet quickly, or
frown while discussing a certain topic, all possible signs of anger,
and yet have no conscious awareness of such actions. They have
lost, or never developed, the ability to notice early signs of anger.
This protects them from these feelings of anger, but at the cost
of ignoring their own bodies and minds. Additionally, others may
be aware of their anger while they are not, a distinct handicap in
the communication process.

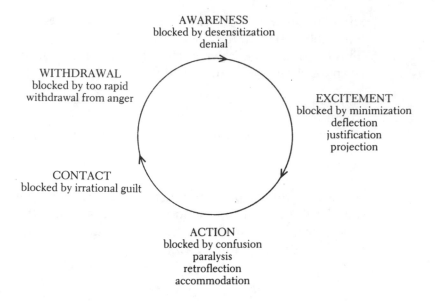

FIGURE 2:   Anger Avoidance Defenses Against Awareness

Denial is another way to block awareness of anger. The alcoholic who completely denies that he or she has a drinking problem, in the face of massive evidence to the contrary, may be the same person who "never gets angry, no matter what." Similarly, the family member who "never gets mad" at the drug abuser denies a reality that cannot be sensibly ignored. Needless to say, people who don't, can't, or won't see a problem never have to take action.

Sometimes individuals cannot completely evade their anger. However, avoiders can still refuse to pay full attention to it. There are several mechanisms available that keep individuals from getting excited about their anger and from clearly focusing upon it.

Minimization is one of these defenses against anger. "Oh, it's just a little problem, nothing to get all upset about," says the mother of an adolescent who has come home dead drunk once again. Then she adds another defense, *justification:* "Besides, he's just a boy trying to learn how to be a man. Every kid goes through that stage. He's no different from anyone else."

Deflection is another defense against awareness during the excitement phase. Deflectors try to turn their (and others') attention to something else. "No, I'm not mad, just a little disappointed and sad, that's all," or, "Well, I'm just too busy to think about this much right now. Yes dear, I guess you're right and I really should talk to our son, but I simply don't have the time." Deflection serves the purpose of preventing someone from taking action.

Projection is another defense against awareness that takes place at this stage. Here individuals are excited enough. However, that excitement is misdirected. The classic example of projection occurs when individuals give their own anger away to others. They then believe the other person is angry with or at them when in fact they are angry themselves. Projection allows excitement but prevents appropriate focusing of anger. Projectors don't take responsibility for their angry feelings. They can withdraw or react to the person they are projecting their anger upon, without having to accept their own angry feelings or aggressive impulses.

Persons who get through the first two phases of the awareness cycle have discovered that they are angry and that they need to pay attention to that anger. Now they are ready to do something—unless they have learned that one should not act on anger. If that is so, there are defenses that they can activate to prevent action.

Confusion is one such mechanism. Some individuals seem to become hopelessly confused just at the point of action: "Yes, I know I have to do something about my husband's drinking. But what? I think and think about it. I get so angry! But I never come up with a solution. So I don't do anything and it gets worse and worse." As long as this woman stays confused, she will not have to take effective action.

Paralysis is a similar state. Here the person knows exactly what to do but cannot do it: "We've gone over this a dozen times with our counselor. If she comes home high one more time I'm supposed to leave, go to an Al-Anon meeting, and detach. But it never works out that way. I just can't do that to her." Again, paralysis serves a protective function. It keeps this person from taking action that could significantly affect his life. Paralysis maintains the *status quo*.

A third defense against using anger to take action is *accommo-dation.* Accommodators give in to others instead of standing up to them. They often do this because they are even more scared than angry. The victim of battering, for instance, may be terribly angry at her attacker and still choose to accommodate him: "Sure, I get furious with him when he comes home drunk and belliger-ent. But he might kill me if I try to fight him. So I just give him what he wants and hope he passes out soon."

Gestalt therapists have offered the term *"retroflection"* to indi-cate the defense of turning against oneself action which is really intended for another. With anger, individuals might literally scratch themselves on their arms rather than "scratch his eyes out" or break out in a rash instead of taking rash action. Retroflec-tors have discovered or decided that the only safe outlet for their anger is to direct it at themselves. That way, they can be angry without risking harming others. Suicide is, perhaps, the ultimate retroflection.

Some anger avoiders do manage to take action. Even then, though, problems may appear. For one thing, they may become numbed. This *inability to feel* their anger means that they go through the motions without getting helpful internal feedback. Having finally confronted his wife and telling her to end her affair or lose the marriage, the newly recovering addict might say that now he is feeling nothing at all. He doesn't feel good or bad about his action; he isn't angry or not angry. He has gone numb in response to his effort to use his anger productively.

Irrational guilt is another problem that haunts anger avoiders at this phase of the awareness cycle. This guilt can be overwhelm-ing and inappropriate. The guilt is not over having harmed some-one with one's anger. It is about having been angry at all. Such guilt punishes anger avoiders even if their use of anger was en-tirely appropriate. The internal message is this: "Stop that right now. How dare you get angry! Don't you ever do that again."

Anger avoiders may continue to have problems with their anger during the withdrawal phase of awareness. They tend to *withdraw too rapidly* from their anger. An example is the spouse who kicks her partner out of the house until he agrees to sober up and get treatment—only to relent after his promise but before he does anything specific. Anger avoiders have difficulty holding onto their anger. Anger is such an unpleasant experience that they want to flee from it too quickly.

In summary, anger avoiders fail in many ways to experience and express their anger. This topic will be continued in Chapter 4.

CHRONIC ANGER PROBLEMS

Chronic anger is defined as a *pattern of thinking, acting, and feeling in which a person seeks, embraces, and/or prolongs anger experiences.* Later in this book, chronic anger problems are described in detail. Here our task is to explain how chronic anger patterns fit into the awareness cycle (see Figure 3).

Once again, analysis of the awareness cycle can begin at the stage of initial awareness. Chronically angry individuals certainly display little, if any, reluctance to be aware of their anger. These persons usually seem all too ready to find reasons to become irritated, irate, or enraged. They are frequently *oversensitive* to anger cues and pay selective attention to them. Chronically angry

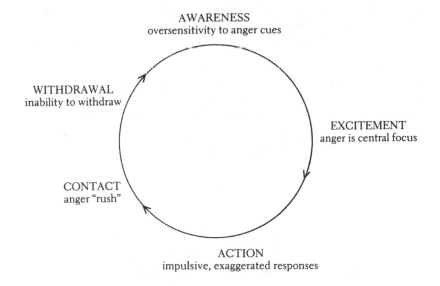

FIGURE 3: Chronic Anger Awareness Issues

individuals seem to welcome a minor stimulus, such as another driver cutting them off on the road, and use it to precipitate a burst of anger.

At the same time, these persons may be undersensitive to cues for other feelings. Thus, the chronically angry person tends to ignore "invitations" to joy, sadness, fear, etc., while concentrating on noticing anger opportunities. There is at least a hint of paranoid process thinking in this effort, although most chronically angry persons would not be classified as paranoid.

Excitement is the second stage of the awareness cycle. Once anger is activated, excitement builds rapidly, becoming the *central focus* of chronically angry individuals. Anger becomes compellingly interesting. The person can only think about what harm has been done, what must be done about it, and how angry he or she is. The mind becomes targeted on the thoroughly familiar sensations and thoughts that accompany chronic anger. A surge of adrenalin also serves to activate and concentrate the anger and to lessen these individuals' ability to think calmly and clearly about the situation. The more they focus on their anger, the angrier they get. It is difficult, for this reason, for chronically angry individuals to have a "little" anger. Their anger quickly becomes concentrated and intensified.

The third phase of the awareness cycle is action. This resolves the question of what chronically angry people do with all their excitement. The answer is that they are likely to spring into *impulsive and/or exaggerated action*. The anger "takes over" these individuals, who then explode into verbal or physical action. Many will report that they "lose control" at such times. The fine line between anger and aggression is easily crossed in these circumstances.

Chronically angry persons may attempt to justify this irresponsible action in several ways. Frequently a person will just state that "my anger made me do it," pleading that they really had no choice in the matter at all. Additionally, there may be a plea that "I had a right to do it, I was so mad at what they did to me." Moral indignation and outrage are used here to both fuel and justify the anger.

We've now reached the contact phase of the awareness cycle. The concern at this point is with the kind of internal and external feedback chronically angry people receive during and after an anger outburst.

If a rage response has been triggered, it is difficult at this time for the very angry person to get any feedback at all from the outside world. Studies of children indicate that their internal processes simply take over during a rage (Parens, 1987). Children cannot even be comforted at these times because they are so involved with their feelings. All that can be done is to keep them safe until they regain touch with the world. A similar process may occur whenever chronically angry adults fly into a rage. For a short time these persons cannot "listen to reason" because their ability to reason has vanished. This is one reason why the only effective tactic to use on these occasions is a time-out.

After action comes the contact phase of the awareness cycle. During this segment chronically angry individuals may experience an internal *"anger rush."* This is a surge of strong feelings that are interpreted and felt to be exciting and exhilarating: "I feel so alive when I'm angry. It breaks through my boredom. Frankly, sometimes I look for excuses to get mad just so I can get that feeling." Chemical dependency counselors may recognize these statements and note the addictive properties of strong anger, a theme that is addressed in Chapter 8.

Later, individuals may feel waves of regret and remorse. However, the immediate internal feedback of chronically angry persons in response to their anger may be quite positive.

The withdrawal stage presents problems for chronically angry people. Basically, they *cannot* or *will not* withdraw from their anger. This produces two major effects. First, these individuals tend to "brood" over past insults and slights. If these individuals were ovens, they would appear to have only two settings: "HIGH" and "SIMMER." Secondly, they tend to develop strong resentments as they dwell on these old problems. There is a tendency to refuse to settle accounts; to do so would mean giving up one's anger and that would force the chronically angry person to become aware of other things.

This characteristic brooding pattern means that chronically angry people never really completely let go of their anger. They cannot utilize the withdrawal phase of the awareness cycle to finish issues. Instead, they cling to their anger. One result is that they are then likely to watch for opportunities to activate that anger all over again. Thus, their failure to release their anger returns these individuals to the beginning of the anger awareness cycle predisposed to notice and accept additional anger cues.

EXERCISES

3-1 Teaching the Awareness Cycle

You may want to present and explain the awareness cycle (Figure 1) to clients before connecting it with the problem of expressing anger. Giving clients a homework assignment to help them explore the meaning of the cycle in their experience outside the counseling session encourages them to apply a new way of looking at awareness and feelings to the big and small events of everyday life. Since understanding *how* an event occurs provides a great deal of information about how to alter its occurrence, becoming aware enables clients to process experience in a way that clearly moves them toward appropriate expression and control of feelings. A therapy group can be given a 20–30-minute assignment, as described below, and still have time to process what they learned, and discover how others' cycles of awareness are similar or different from their own.

A good basic assignment is for each individual to leave the crowd, going off alone for 20–30 minutes just to explore his or her own cycle of awareness as it is currently occurring. Instruct participants to do the following:

> Take some time for yourself now, to explore how your own cycle of awareness is working today. Go and wander around alone, without being with another person. If others want to talk with you, tell them you are busy, but will get back to them in a little while. Then allow yourself to wander, and notice what calls itself to your attention. It may be a plant or other kind of object, a smell, a breeze, a sound, or a combination of these things. Notice whether you allow yourself to focus on it. Let yourself move toward or away from it, and take some action to explore it. This may mean touching a tree, holding an inner dialogue with a wall,

or crouching to see something better. Let yourself have some contact with the things that call themselves to your attention, and when you have had enough contact, say goodbye, and move on. Notice whether you go through one long cycle or several short ones.

The goal of teaching the awareness cycle is to increase self-observation and awareness. During discussion it will be apparent that focusing on something often leads to action, and action leads to a more intense contact. Some individuals will find they have trouble focusing while others will discover that they have difficulty withdrawing and coming back after once establishing contact. Ask several individuals to share, in order to demonstrate to the group the varying ways that individuals experience the world.

3-2 *Anger Cycle Diary*

The purpose of this exercise is to get clients to apply knowledge of the awareness cycle to anger experiences. Provide clients with several copies of the Anger Cycle Diary given below. Ask them to record several incidents of anger, encouraging them to notice how these experiences with anger are the same or different from the normal anger cycle.

When each client has completed several entries into the Anger Cycle Diary, have him or her evaluate how s/he is currently dealing with anger issues by completing the Anger Analysis Form. Since writing things down may imprint them more effectively on the memory, it may be useful to have the client do the analysis as homework, and then to discuss the results in individual or group sessions.

For some clients, whose cognitive or literacy skills are more limited, a discussion/interview using the questions on the Anger Analysis Form will be satisfactory. It is important to choose the method that most encourages clients to work, since they may already be dealing with frustration and/or low self-esteem related to their problems. The purpose of the Anger Analysis is not to emphasize clients' failures, but to increase their ability to observe themselves and to move them toward making a specific plan to change behavior in ways that they have come to see as significant, as well as necessary.

Anger Cycle Diary

Date: _____

Description of the Anger Incident: _____
_____
_____
_____

1. In this incident, I (a) noticed; (b) ignored; (c) looked for my angry feelings in the following way(s): _____
_____
_____

2. In this incident, I (a) focused on; (b) minimized; (c) emphasized my anger in the following way(s): _____
_____
_____

3. In this incident, I (a) took a reasonable action; (b) did not act; (c) acted impulsively on my angry feelings in the following way(s):
_____
_____

4. In this incident, I (a) shared my anger clearly and tactfully; (b) felt badly about sharing my anger; (c) had a strong rush of anger and liked expressing it, in the following way(s): _____
_____
_____

5. In this incident, I (a) let go of my anger as soon as the problem was resolved; (b) guiltily took back my anger as soon as I could; (c) hung on to my anger and resentment even after I expressed it.

6. Now that I have had time to think more about this incident, I can tell myself _____
_____
_____

7. The main thing that I will do to change how I deal with my anger in the future is _____
_____
_____
_____

Anger Analysis Worksheet

1. Place an "x" on the cycle of awareness pointing to where you need to learn a new way to deal with your angry feelings. Do this for each incident in your anger diary.

2. Now that you have looked at some everyday incidents of anger, describe the patterns that you see yourself repeating.

_____
_____
_____
_____

3. Where in the cycle do you do the best in being appropriate with your anger? _____
4. Where in the cycle do you have the most difficulty in being appropriate with your anger? _____
5. List the problems you see in your own words, and then list your goals. For example, if the problem is that when you are angry you act impulsively, a goal might be to think things over before acting on angry feelings.

Problem: Goal:
(a)   (a)
(b)   (b)
(c)   (c)

3-3 *Men, Women, and Anger*

This exercise can be conducted in a single-sex group, in one direction only. For a mixed-sex group, ask male members of the group to gather in the center and discuss the messages they got about anger: in their families of origin, from peers, at work, and at home. Then ask the female members of the group to gather in the center and discuss the messages they got about anger: in their families of origin, from peers, at work, and at home.

Have the two groups note the differences, and ask all members to decide how *any member* in group is allowed to express anger in group, without imposing sex-linked roles. Discussion may include looking at some of the common societal messages linking angry behavior to gender, such as "a woman who is angry is a bitch" and "an angry man has lost his head." Process each group incident of anger according to the new rules this exercise generates over the next several group meetings.

4

ANGER AVOIDANCE

TREATMENT

CONSIDERATIONS

The general issue of anger avoidance was introduced in Chapter 3. Now the goals are to understand this pattern in greater depth, to relate it more clearly to substance abuse problems, and to suggest relevant treatment approaches and strategies.

A certain amount of anger avoidance is both normal and useful. No one could afford to get angry all the time over every annoyance or intrusion. Even serious issues might better be ignored at times. For example, some adolescents go through a period of being ornery, challenging, or hostile, even though they are generally positive; the best explanation for their behavior seems to be the immense physical and mental changes that accompany this stage of growth. Many parents will choose not to be angry with much of this behavior on the theory that it is not a central part of their child's character and will go away on its own soon enough. Fortunately, they are often correct. These parents, by avoiding unnecessary conflict, minimize unproductive battles over power and control.

Anger avoidance becomes problematic, however, when individuals avoid conflict so frequently that they lose the element of choice. Consistent anger avoiders have learned that the expression or experience of anger is bad, dangerous, or immoral. They believe that: (1) they can only be good persons by suppressing or containing their anger; (2) to become angry is to risk badly hurting others; or (3) conflict is never safe and to stay safe themselves they must avoid contributing to conflict.

Chemical dependency counselors and other therapists need to help anger avoiders understand and deal with their anger in ways that also address relevant substance abuse concerns. The material presented below is designed for that purpose, providing both general information and more specific strategies and tactics.

SOURCES OF ANGER AVOIDANCE

American Anger Avoidance Beliefs

Anger has long been considered a suspect emotion in American society. Someone who gets too angry too often is regarded as a "loose cannon," dangerous and unpredictable. Such persons must be monitored and controlled carefully. Even when their anger is justified, angry people seem to make others uncomfortable. This society allows little room for "crusaders" or others who try to channel their anger into useful channels. Anger just isn't a "nice" emotion.

Carol Z. and Peter Stearns (1986) have studied the history of anger beliefs in American society over a 200-year time span. They report a steady trend away from anger since the end of the 18th century. They note that during this period, "the goal of restraining anger . . . forms an important part of the American character ideal." The Stearns describe how Americans have become a "distinctly more orderly people," who now seek to punish without anger and to reduce the appearance of spontaneous anger. They mention that Americans have far fewer outlets for anger than before. For example, it is no longer acceptable for someone to get angry either at work or home. The Stearns note that, while other feelings are encouraged, anger has been discouraged: "The modern impulse to tolerate wider emotional expression is highly selective; it carefully excludes anger."

Certainly this pattern does not apply equally to everyone in the culture. There are many "pockets of anger" in American society, particularly among disaffiliated groups and subcultures. Still,

CASE STUDY: Whatever You Do, Never Make Waves

Melinda Murray is a 50-year-old artist, a gentle woman who has never married. She is respected by many, adored by few. She labels herself codependent "because I let people take advantage of me too often. I so much want to be their friend that I never say no to anybody."

Melinda lives near her elderly aunt, a woman who practically raised her after Melinda's mother and father divorced. Sadly, Aunt Flora suffers the beginning stages of mental and physical deterioration, but she still lives alone. Lately, she has been more and more demanding of Melinda. Every time Melinda wants to say no to her, though, she becomes overwhelmed with guilt: "How can I be unkind to Aunt Flora when she took care of me? I feel awful just thinking about it."

One day we did a guided fantasy. Melinda was in the bathtub (as a child), playing with her toys and having a great time.

"So what do you want to do now?"

"Oh, I want to make waves with the water. I want to make waves and splashes."

"Well then, go ahead."

"No, I can't. Aunt Flora told me never, ever to make waves. She says that good girls never make waves."

We kept talking. Would Melinda even consider making a small wave? A little one that wouldn't splash water out of the tub? One look at her face gave the answer: Melinda had

the Stearns' position is essentially correct. Anger is not well-tolerated in American society. People are more often rewarded for containing their anger than for its expression.

Prohibition Against Women's Anger

Women as a group have long been told that anger is "not ladylike." Little girls' anger is more likely to be punished than

CASE STUDY: continued

turned white with fear. Melinda not only wasn't supposed to make waves. She wasn't supposed to even think about it.

Deeply embedded belief systems are slow to change. It took another six months of personal growth before Melinda told me, at the start of a session, that "Yesterday I made waves. And you know what. Everybody survived it. I guess it's OK to make waves once in a while." ■

little boys'. Later, they may feel fear-tinged guilt whenever they even notice their anger. If that isn't sufficient to prevent the appearance of anger, as adults women are accused of being hysterical, irrational, or bad when they notice or express their anger. Lerner (1985) notes that many women have difficulty utilizing their anger effectively because of the lack of support and training.

This prohibition of anger for women may be part of a larger picture of differential moral development. Carol Gilligan (1982) writes that many women believe that they are only good when they take care of others. Gilligan argues that taking care of others and disregarding oneself occurs as a stage of moral development. Many people go on to the next stage, in which they learn that it is possible to care for oneself as well as others. However, many women, and men, get stuck in caretaking.

Anger avoidance is one way to guard against harming others. Anger is seen as selfish behavior. The thought that anger may signify that a woman must pay attention to her own needs is either not considered or rejected. Anger avoiders often confuse acts of self-caring with acts of selfishness. Anger, because it is perceived as "selfish," is seen as evidence of moral inadequacy. To be angry is to risk harming others, so anger cannot be tolerated or encouraged.

The result is that many women and some men are overcome with irrational guilt whenever they sense the presence of their own anger. These individuals need permission to notice and accept their own feelings and to learn, in particular, to listen to their anger without condemning themselves as selfish or bad.

Above all, they need to learn to distinguish acts of self-caring from truly selfish behaviors.

In *Shame, Guilt, and Alcoholism* (Potter-Efron, 1989), the relationship between anger, guilt, and selflessness, particularly the distinction between irrational (neurotic) and rational guilt, is described in greater detail.

ANGER AVOIDANT FAMILIES

Some families are generally anger avoidant. This means that many or all of the members habitually attempt to minimize their expressions of anger. Children who grow up in these families will often take this tendency to evade anger with them into their adult relationships. Several characteristics of anger avoidant families are discussed below.

There Is at Least One Anger Avoidant Parent

This parent models an aversion to anger in his or her behavior. In addition, the children will usually be able to see that this parent is afraid of or disgusted by anger. They learn from this person that the expression of anger is bad, dangerous, or shameful.

There Is a Focus upon Maintaining Relationships at All Costs

The anger avoidant family attempts to keep itself intact by prohibiting the expression of anger. Anger is treated as a serious threat to the stability of the group, since it could lead to walkouts, divorce, and aggression. Because it could cause or increase division or separation, anger is simply too dangerous to allow. Frequently individuals in these families have witnessed uncontrolled anger, often in their alcoholic or addicted families of origin or past adult relationships. They have concluded that anger is always destructive. Some members might believe that they or others are too fragile to handle anger: Unless everyone stays calm, dad will have a heart attack, mom will get depressed, or one of the children will have an anxiety attack. Family members develop a myth that the power of their anger itself can create a catastrophe.

In treatment, anger avoidant families need to confront these myths about personal and family fragility and to discover that they are strong enough to experience and viably process anger as individuals and families.

Anger Is Repressed, Ignored, and Denied

Members of anger avoidant families use all the defenses mentioned in Chapter 3. They are particularly adept at not noticing the signs of their own or others' annoyance. These early anger indicators are missed because family members don't want to see them and train each other to ignore them. They turn blind eyes to such small cues as a slightly dirty look, momentary hesitations before someone agrees to do something, or a raised tone of voice. Anger avoidant families may need retraining in observing their own behavioral cues as well as those of others. How each expresses anger (a look, tears, silence, sighs, etc.) may be a very individual matter, since no agreed upon cues exist that can be acknowledged and recognized by all.

The Family Uses Accommodation and Appeasement to Avoid Conflict

Conflict is perceived as difficult and dangerous in anger avoidant families. Actual negotiation of differences can be threatening because people might become angry. Instead, the family develops ways to skirt tension. The first goal is simply to avoid anything controversial. But if that is impossible family members will turn to accommodation and appeasement. Accommodation means trying to maintain harmony by anticipating problems and giving people what they want without requiring them to ask for it. Appeasement is more an effort to maintain or restore peace by giving in to unreasonable wants and demands. Thus, the squalling infant gets fed "just to shut her up," the furious adolescent succeeds in ending curfew by pouting, and a spouse squashes any concerns about drinking with the threat to leave home. Family appeasement patterns often lead to the creation and maintenance of spoiled bullies.

Use of Manipulative Techniques

Anger avoiders have trouble asking directly for what they want. These requests might trigger somebody's anger; being turned down could initiate their own anger. Consequently, members of these families develop more subtle strategies, including "hinting" at needs, passive-aggression, and playing the role of martyr. In treatment, anger avoidant individuals and families need to be confronted gently with the specific patterns they use to manipulate and to express anger, and by which they get "hooked" into compliant behavior.

A "Stuff and Blow" Pattern of Relationships

Anger avoiders frequently fail to pay adequate attention to early cues of their annoyance or frustration, since they aren't supposed to get angry. They "stuff" their anger and hope it will go away. One result is that they may go into sudden rages when their submerged anger finally surfaces. The result, unfortunately, only endorses their fears. They really do lose control of themselves when thcy get mad, and they get mad over small things — a final straw — that invalidates their anger. Because of this, some anger avoiders end up being sent to counselors because of their apparent problems with aggression and hostility. These persons usually reside in anger avoidant families with others who are even more afraid of anger than they are. Treatment involves learning to identify early cues of anger and teaching family members to confront problems before they develop large backlogs of anger to ventilate.

Resentments Linger in Anger Avoidant Families

Anger that cannot be expressed often solidifies into resentments. The result is unresolved, barely stated feuds that simmer just under the surface of apparently peaceful families. These resentments may never be stated aloud. Rather, the family chooses to "just let things blow over" and "not talk about it." Unfortunately, resentments do not always diminish over time. They sometimes get worse when everyone has time to dwell on personal injuries. Substance abuse counselors know that the resentments built up over years of trying to ignore someone's chemical dependency seldom vanish just because that person goes through treatment and sobers up. In anger avoidant families treatment includes confronting the guilt affected family members may feel about even having angry feelings now that the substance abuser is sober and straight. Only after that can resentments really be processed thoroughly enough to be let go.

The Right to Be Angry May Be Reserved for Particular Individuals in the Family

Anger avoidant families occasionally exempt certain of its members from the prohibition against any display of anger. This may be because of traditional roles: "Well, that's the way men are. They're always getting mad about something." Or anger may be reserved for the most powerful person in the family, usually but not always a parent. That person acts as a dictator, intimidating others: "You better watch out when she really gets mad. You better give her what she wants or she'll stay mad for days"; "If you get out of line, you'll get in trouble." A third alternative is that someone is excused for his anger because he is viewed as sick, weak, or fragile: "Well, he blows up a lot when he drinks. But he can't help it. It's the disease that does it to him." Or, "She's just depressed—don't pay any attention to what she says." Of course, an angry person, when ignored, often becomes even more resentful and angry. Meanwhile, other family members are still expected to be models of reasonableness. In essence, these families have one set of rules for most family members and another set for the angry person.

In treatment, these families need to set rules and boundaries that apply to everybody. Family members may need to learn appropriate assertion techniques, and the angry family member needs to learn that intimidation does not produce affection, respect, or even the kind of long-term relationship with others that will meet his real needs.

ANGER AVOIDANCE AND
SUBSTANCE ABUSE CONCERNS

There is no single relationship between anger avoidance and substance abuse. Varied connections are possible, including several that are described below.

Alcohol or Drugs May Be Used to Help Contain Anger and Aggression

One function of mood-altering substances is to numb one's feelings. This can be very important for those who have made a commitment to anger avoidance. Whenever these feelings threaten to surface, anger avoiders may turn to these substances for relief. Sometimes this means having just a few "tokes" of marijuana to help calm down a bit. Other times it might mean drinking until passing out "because that's the only way I can get rid of my rage." Many people will drink or use drugs alone under these circumstances. Their goal is simply to sink into a stupor in which they don't have to feel anything at all.

Anger avoiders who use substances in this way most often avoid feelings in general. They seek a drug-induced state of euphoria, indifference, or emotional oblivion. Anger may be the most dangerous feeling for them, the one that most threatens their sense of place in the world order. That anger must be avoided, even at the cost of severe health and welfare problems. Oddly, anger avoidant substance abusers may trade off losing control over their consumption of alcohol or drugs in order not to lose control of their anger.

It is important to identify what it is that most frightens a person about his anger. Has the individual come to believe that it is dangerous to express anger because it will be punished, or harm others, or give him an identity that he does not want ("just like mom [or dad]"). Or he will simply feel very out of control, or it will lead to abandonment, etc.? Appropriate treatment includes finding or creating nonthreatening situations in which the client can retest these beliefs and learn how to express his anger appropriately.

The anger that is being avoided may indeed be powerful. Many clients experience difficult periods of anger and rage during or shortly after treatment. Some may suddenly have realized that they are the victims of childhood sexual abuse, current physical or emotional abuse, etc., and that they have used drugs to repress that pain. What they haven't known is that they—and others—can survive their anger. They may not need to use anything to keep from experiencing their anger if they can be helped to share that anger in a safe place. The provision of a safe place for anger expression is a primary therapeutic process with these individuals. So is treatment that can help them understand the process and effects of abuse, the nature of such defenses as projection, displacement, and repression, and the unique ways in which their own capacity to be angry and express anger have been affected.

Persons who use substances to avoid their anger certainly increase their risk of developing true chemical dependency over time. They may begin simply seeking to be less tense or irritable at a given time, but they gradually learn to depend upon these substances for relief from their anger. Identifying exactly how a person's anger is controlled by chemical use may help with intervention in the ritualistic aspects of anger repression through substance abuse.

Suicidality is another risk associated with anger avoiders who drink or use drugs to repress their anger. Those who attempt to drown anger with alcohol, for instance, may become morose and depressed during either the intoxication or withdrawal phases. Those who cannot allow themselves to direct that anger outward may turn it onto themselves. Even then, it isn't always accurate to say that they are consciously angry with themselves. More likely, these individuals might state that they thought they would do the world a favor by taking their lives. Any suicidal or self-hating statements from an anger avoider who is using a substance need to be taken seriously by counselors and treatment personnel. Further information will be provided in Chapter 11 on self-destructive anger.

Anger Avoiders May Use Alcohol or Drugs to Gain Temporary Permission to Get Angry

The disinhibiting effect of alcohol and other substances is well-known to the public, even expected at times. Disinhibition provides a "time-out" from normal social expectations. In particular, intoxication is widely used as an excuse for anger and aggression. People attribute their anger to the drug itself, displacing responsibility for their behavior onto the substance ("I should never have taken that first drink, but who would have known what it would lead to?" "I didn't know what I was doing—I was stoned out of my mind").

Even individuals who are generally quite passive use this excuse. Anger avoiders who do so usually display a "Dr. Jekyll and Mr. Hyde" pattern of behavior. They steer far from their anger while sober only to become predictably nasty when drinking or using drugs. Most frequently, the anger comes out as sarcasm or crude verbal attacks. Occasionally, it emerges as physical aggression. Typically, their supposedly drunken behavior is more an embarrassment than a threat to their families.

"Dr. Jekyll and Mr. Hyde" represents a subset of a larger behavior pattern. We call this behavior "stuff and blow" because many anger avoiders alternate long periods of apparent calmness, during which their anger builds ("stuff"), with short but powerful anger outbursts ("blow"). Even if no mood-altering substances are consumed, these anger avoiders often attempt to disown the "blow" phase, claiming that they aren't really angry persons and that they cannot understand what happened to set them off. Obviously, though, this misattribution of responsibility is much easier when blame can be affixed to an outside source such as alcohol.

Anger avoiders are frequently overloaded with guilt. They attempt to be "selfless" in life and so cannot afford the luxury of anger. They may, however, occasionally decide to reward their selflessness by drinking or using drugs: "After all I've been through today, taking care of everybody else, I deserve a couple of drinks." Drinking to get through the day provides another justification for their anger. They are "just letting off steam" after a hard day repressing their anger. Drinking and anger may be seen here as legitimized selfishness, which balances periods of selflessness.

Both Anger Avoidance and Substance Abuse May Be Part of a General Denial System

Denial is a rather primitive defense against painful awareness. Some individuals may utilize it only in one or two major areas of life. For others, denial is a pervasive defense. They get through life essentially by denying unpleasant reality.

Unfortunately, breaking through denial in one life area is no guarantee that the system as a whole will be affected. For instance, we treated one man who was clearly (to us) both an alcoholic and a very angry spouse abuser. He was able to face his drinking problem after standard alcoholism outpatient treatment. However, it took another year before he could accept or even admit his violence. In effect, this man had developed a *dual denial* system, which in turn was part of a more universal world view in which he denied his problems. Such dual denial systems are common and must be recognized by counselors as a significant impediment to general recovery.

Because this is so, the denial system as a whole—not just denial of the effects of alcohol or drugs—must be addressed in treatment. A substance abuser who uses alcohol or another substance to repress his anger will be in increased danger of relapse without a good understanding of how this works in his life, and what other options he has to deal with his anger. If a client is anger avoidant, and if that anger avoidance is linked in any way with substance abuse, anger work will be needed. Affected family members as well as the identified patient may need to address this issue.

Anger Avoiders May Use Substances as a Form of Passive-Aggression

"I just can't help it. I'm sorry. Please don't be mad with me." Thus speak anger avoidant substance abusers to their families, employers, etc. In turn, if these people are also anger avoiders, responses may include understanding, forgiveness, comforting, helpfulness, but certainly not appropriate anger.

Anger avoiders tend to feel misunderstood and injured if responded to with anger. They may argue (gently and sadly) that they certainly didn't intend to harm anyone with their behavior. That's the last thing in the world they wanted. Certainly others should recognize their innocence, even if this has happened before. Why are all these people so angry? They must be hard hearted. In fact, this whole scene may be so painful that they "need" to get high again to feel better.

Passive-aggression occurs when someone acts out against others without recognizing and/or acknowledging the presence of anger. Other identifiable behavior, such as forgetfulness and procrastination, usually masks the underlying behavior. Drinking and drug use also may be a form of passive-aggression used by anger avoiders to hurt others indirectly. In essence, the anger avoider can once again misattribute problems to the drug. It is not essential that the problematic behavior be obviously aggressive. Getting too stoned to pick up the children or too drunk to get to work on time may be just as effective as screaming invectives at your spouse or workmates. In fact, being able to use and/or abuse a substance to get back at a controlling partner is one way in which a passive-aggressive anger avoider can use relapse to punish others.

Some Individuals Become Anger Avoiders After Achieving Abstinence

Certain persons, mostly those who were very aggressive during their drinking or using careers, are horrified with themselves after they sober up. They are very guilty, which leads them to vow never to hurt others again. The only way they can assure themselves that they will not harm others (and as penance for their past wrongs) is to renounce all signs of their anger: "I was a monster before. I beat my wife and kids. Now I refuse to get angry at all. I can't stand the thought of becoming that monster again."

This "all or none" approach can create problems for the recovering person. Fearing any display of anger, these anger avoiders tend to become "doormats," unable to assert themselves appropriately. This rigid pattern of thinking and acting increases the risk of relapse to substance use as tension mounts—a relapse to bury the shame and guilt of another violent incident. While this form of anger avoidance is an attempt to find a healthier way to live, it does not promote a self-nurturing lifestyle. These individuals need to gain acceptance of themselves in past and present and to learn self-accepting ways to deal with their anger and aggressive impulses.

Family Anger Avoidance Prevents Effective Confrontation of Substance Abusers

In general, families that cannot utilize appropriate amounts of anger will be ineffective in confronting substance abusers. Several examples of this pattern were mentioned in Chapter 3. Family members may fear angering the user or hurting his feelings. They may deny problems in order to avoid anger or they may be too "polite" to deal with such messy issues. Whatever the specific reasons, anger avoidant families usually evade alcohol and drug problems as long as possible. Rules governing members of anger avoidant families may included "don't think," "don't question," "don't get mad," "don't see," "don't get angry," "don't talk about it," and "don't act."

In contrast, the substance abusers in anger avoidant families may have permission to be angry and aggressive. If so, these persons will use rage to intimidate others. They say, in effect: "I will get very angry if you challenge my using. Someone could get hurt. Better back off!" Family members have learned that these signals mean trouble. Gradually the angry substance abuser coerces the rest of the family to ignore his behavior—or else. This possibility should be kept in mind in treatment settings. Families that appear inept and anger avoidant may be so primarily because of fear.

Treatment Suggestions

Anger avoidance is a pervasive pattern that constrains behavior, thoughts, and feelings. The sheer breadth of this pattern makes it difficult to address, much less "cure," with a short-term treatment focus. This is particularly true when the primary concern is alcohol or drug abuse because so much time and effort must be devoted to that task. Still, some useful efforts can be made within the context of inpatient treatment, during extended outpatient programs, during aftercare, in programs for codependency or for adult children from dysfunctional family, and in related couples or family therapy. The suggestions offered below are useful with a wide range of clients.

The Therapist Can Probe for Anger Avoidance During a Standard Assessment Process

How their new clients handle feelings concerns most intake interviewers. Simple questions, such as, "What do you do when you get angry?" can be asked routinely as probes to help identify both anger avoidant and chronically angry individuals. Certain phrases are especially revealing of anger avoidance: "Oh, I just never get angry"; "Gee, I've never thought about that"; "I don't like getting mad. It makes me feel awful." Nonverbal cues may reveal a person's discomfort with anger, such as a very quiet voice or a timid appearance. Personality tests, such as the MMPI, may identify those individuals who are relatively extreme on either pole of anger expression. There are also more specific tools, including the State-Trait Anger Expression Inventory (Spielberger, 1988), which can be utilized if anger problems are suspected at intake.

Anger avoiders may easily slip through intake undetected, especially if the focus is upon substance use. It is more difficult to detect the relative absence of something, especially if one is looking for evidence of excess. Eventually, however, anger avoiders will expose that pattern through their attitudes and actions. Whenever it is noticed, it is valuable to address anger avoidance.

Present/Explain Anger Avoidance to Clients as Normal, Understandable, and Modifiable Behavior

Anger avoiders commonly believe that their behavior is proper, morally correct, civilized, necessary, and positive. Unless others have already called the problems of anger avoidance to their attention, initially they may anticipate praise for this behavior from the counselor.

The therapist who "attacks" this pattern too quickly may be seen as "one of them," someone who promotes unacceptable or dangerous aggression. It is crucial for therapists to convey understanding and appreciation of their clients' anger avoidance behaviors. Remember that anger avoidance may have developed as a necessary defense with survival value in a threatening and uncertain world.

Once the counselor has established rapport by identifying with and understanding the anger avoidant client's behaviors, he can proceed to suggest some of the negative consequences of anger avoidance, both generally and specifically with regard to current concerns. It is even more therapeutic when anger avoiders can identify these consequences. When given permission and support, they usually can do so fairly quickly.

Change should be presented as an *option*, not an expectation. People have the right to avoid anger, even when that means ignoring their own best interests. However, individuals gain freedom by understanding that this is a choice they make, rather than something obligatory. Most anger avoiders change this pattern slowly. Counselors need to be patient.

Link Anger Avoidance with Alcohol and Drug Abuse Concerns

The goal is for substance abusers to see clearly the links between anger avoidance and substance abuse. Ideally, recovering persons go through a "eureka" experience: "Hey, I just figured this out. I get drunk a lot of times when I'm afraid to tell _____ how mad I am." Then the counselor can backtrack, helping the client identify behaviorally (by thought, feeling and action) exactly what the beginning signs of that anger are. Counselor and client together can design useful ways to intervene in the process, eliminating the person's felt need to become intoxicated in order to avoid anger.

It's likely that many anger avoiders initially will need help making these connections. Group therapy is valuable here. In a group some clients may be avoiding anger, while others may be chronically angry. The therapist should move people toward appropriate expression of anger, encouraging group participants to be the active proponents for actual behavioral change. Learning how to become aware of and use anger to take effective action can be presented as a relapse prevention tool. It is important in group therapy not to focus entirely on chronically angry individuals, even though these persons have the most obvious anger problems. Be sure to identify and engage those group members who would rather not even think about their anger.

Link Anger Avoidance and Family Responses to Substance Abuse

Family members may have an enlightening experience as they discover how much of their "enabling" behavior has resulted from anger avoidance. For instance, we once treated a family in which the wife had two primary beliefs: (a) The family's good community reputation is extremely important; (b) any hint of conflict will ruin that reputation. Of course, her husband's drinking, if it became known, would damage the family image. But so would any public signs of divisiveness. Consequently, she made great efforts to disallow any show of distress or anger among family members. Her children had standing orders to smile and be happy, to keep quiet about their father's actions, to "forgive and forget," and most of all, to *never ever* get mad.

This family illustrates the power of one person to impose anger avoidance rules on the entire household. Sometimes the rule maker may not even live in the home: "I try to do what my mother said—she always told me that only dogs get mad, never people." Therapists need to identify and quietly challenge anger avoidance rules and the authority of the rule makers if the family is to make any effective systemic changes.

We have noted the pattern when the chemically dependent individual is angry and every other family member nice; frequently, however, the pattern is reversed. That's when the user and partner play the game of "drunk and bitch" (although this sounds sexist). This term connotes the combination of frustration, endless nagging, and impotent fury that can characterize the spouse of an alcoholic or drug abuser—this spouse may be of either gender. In this game, the more the drunk drinks, the more the bitch bitches, and vice-versa. Other possibilities include one or more children acting out the family anger by taking on the role of "bad" person, drawing attention away from the alcoholic, or the total exclusion of anger in the completely anger avoidant family.

It's useful to be specific. Get the family to respond *exactly* to such questions as, "What did you do when she came home loaded again last week?" and even, "What did you do with your anger, if you had any, when she came home loaded again last week?" If only one family member professes any anger, check to see if that individual is the depository of the family outrage. If nobody got angry, find out if that is the normal routine and let yourself wonder out loud how that happens ("I wonder where your anger goes when nobody ever gets mad?"). If many persons or everyone in the family professes anger, then assess for chronic anger problems.

Relate Anger Avoidance Behaviors to Defenses Against Awareness and Action

These defenses were presented in Chapter 3. Drawing the basic awareness circle (Figure 1, p. 32) is useful with clients. Describe it and then write in and describe some of the more common defenses against anger noted in Figure 2 (p. 36). Ask clients to identify their defenses as you put them on the circle. This procedure can be done during individual, couples, family, and group sessions, often with major benefits for treatment planning.

Treatment planning is easier once a person's particular anger avoidance defenses are identified. In general, the strategies are as follows:

- People who cannot be aware of their anger need to learn that anger is possible for them, what it looks and feels like, and that anger has positive value.
- Minimization, justification, etc., are all defenses designed to dampen the power of one's anger response. However, when that response is too muted, action be-

comes impossible. One reason individuals use these defenses is that they are frightened of the power of their anger. Many of those who cannot focus on their anger (excitement phase) need to learn the difference between excitement and anxiety, so that they don't run from sensations that accompany anger.

- Blocks against action, such as confusion and paralysis, are easy to understand and hard to change. Here one focus can be on what dangers someone might face if he or she were to try to do something. These dangers should be taken seriously by the therapist even if they seem unlikely to happen. It is sometimes helpful to those who are blocked in action to have permission from the therapist to *stay* stuck, but to notice how they feel while they are paralyzed. Permission to go nowhere may result in an increased ability on the part of the client eventually to take appropriate action. Remember that it's very possible to underestimate the risk of a situation when it is being discussed in the safe haven of a therapy session.

- Contact problems are usually those in which individuals get too little positive feedback for their anger from themselves or others. This vacuum needs to be anticipated, predicted, and prepared for during therapy. The counselor can say something like this: "Now, you're finally ready to take action, right? OK, but remember not to expect anybody in your family to appreciate what you're up to. They won't understand your doing something with your anger because you've never done that before. And by the way, don't be too surprised if you feel really guilty afterwards." Peer support for positive action is very helpful at this stage.

- Those who give up too quickly on their anger need understanding of how hard it is for them to stay angry. They may repeatedly back off just before their anger results in effective change, which can be a source of great frustration to the counselor. It is vital that the counselor not become angry or annoyed with anger avoiders at these times, since this will only add to their shame. Rather, clients need to be understood and to hear that the helper knows how difficult it is for them to take action (displease the family by going into treatment, leave the nonrecovering substance abuser, confront irresponsibility, etc.). No matter what decisions they make at the moment, clients need to feel that they are acceptable and that the counselor is looking for long-term rather than immediate change. Given this reassurance, some persons can then take the very action they have just been given permission to avoid.

Encourage Anger Avoiders to Learn Specific Techniques with Which to Communicate Their Anger

People who spend their time avoiding anger aren't likely to possess very many useful skills in expressing it. Just as individuals afraid of heights won't usually collect a set of mountain hiking gear, anger avoiders are generally unequipped to address their anger concerns. They need a new set of tools and a safe place to learn how to use them.

Necessary tools for anger avoiders include such things as fair fighting rules, assertiveness training, and relaxation training (to help with the anxiety that often accompanies their anger). A list of fair fighting rules will be presented in Chapter 10. Assertiveness and relaxation training techniques are readily available to most counselors (Alberti & Emmons, 1986).

Individuals can use therapy sessions to mentally and/or physically rehearse use of these tools. Role-playing is a good idea. What seems most important is that anger avoiders think and feel about their own anticipated standard reactions so that they can plan some new ones. One thing that seems to help is to acknowledge that they will surely be afraid of actually using their anger, fearing its power, but that everybody will survive it. (Of course, this statement cannot be made if there is contravening evidence, such as a history of dangerously violent episodes.) It is also important to encourage growth through a sequence of successive approximations. People who have been whispering all their lives cannot be expected just to stand up and shout.

Help Anger Avoiders Learn to Tolerate the Anger of Others

Anger avoiders generally shudder in the presence of anybody's anger, not just their own. This means that clients will need to learn to endure being both the targets of and witnesses to anger. These are two different situations.

Some persons who have great problems with anger have witnessed extreme forms of aggression. For example, as a child, a female client had seen her sister's husband beat her sister repeatedly and severely. Now she felt tremendous survivor guilt ("I should have been able to stop it"), as well as a dread of anger. This kind of experience may be fairly common in chemically dependent households.

People who have been the targets of aggression may come to live in terror of offending others. Here the underlying panic must be encountered therapeutically before any change will occur. Somehow they must learn that they are safe enough now (if they are) to accept the expression of anger. Of course, nothing can be expected if someone remains in physical danger. Survival always takes precedence.

Anger avoiders may project their fear of anger onto others. They believe that others will go crazy if they get angry, that others will automatically hurt someone with their anger, or that others' anger with them means they will be abandoned, or even that an angry person will likely commit suicide (perhaps just like her mother or father did). Therapists can bring these projective identifications to the surface. Then the anger avoidant person can begin to realize that a specific individual who is angry with him or her at the moment may only be angry, not dangerous.

Counselors need to be aware of their own tendencies toward anger avoidance. If not, they may be too nice, perhaps failing to confront difficult situations and avoiding treating anger in their sessions. This topic is covered in Chapter 12.

EXERCISES

4-1 *Loose Cannon Fears*

Have group members discuss the "loose cannons" in their families of origin—those family members who acted out their anger most noisily or were most aggressive to others. Have group members complete the sentence, "If I am angry, I'll be just like _____," and examine some of the fallacies associated with these statements. Discuss the errors inherent in such fallacies, pointing out that:

a) Similar does not equal same.
b) Same feelings don't necessarily lead to same behaviors.
c) Kinship does not equal identity.
d) A happy/sad/angry person may behave very differently from another happy/sad/angry person.
e) Just because a person has once behaved like someone else does not mean this person will always behave like that other person.

4-2 *Can I Be Good, Safe, and Angry?*

Present the following statements to the group:

1. I can only be a good person by suppressing or containing my anger.

2. To become angry is to risk hurting others.

3. Conflict is never safe. Being angry creates conflict; therefore, to be safe, I must never be angry.

Have group participants take 10 minutes to list any ways in which they learned these beliefs from other people's words, behaviors, or nonverbal messages. Then have them pair off, or ask for volunteers to be discussants. Ask one member of each pair to argue in support of the belief, and one to argue against it. After participants have had adequate time to present disagreeing viewpoints, begin processing by pointing out that such discussions are examples of conflicts. Ask group members to notice how they feel, if they have felt anger, how they have appropriately or inappropriately controlled their anger, and what actual behaviors occurred or would have had to occur for them to feel hurt by each other.

Help the group to differentiate between anger (a feeling) and aggression (angry behaviors). Ask participants to revised, realistically for themselves, the three statements originally presented.

Following this exercise, the group can discuss the messages they were given by the events in the examples they wrote, and suggest alternative ways of expressing anger without being aggressive or hurtful.

4-3 *Anger Avoidance Role Plays*

Role play an anger avoidant family trying to deal with an angry person. Ask for volunteers to play parents and children, and one person in any position to role play being angry. Instruct the other family members to avoid conflict as much as possible. Role play eating a meal or watching television together. Give as few instructions as possible when generating this role play. Participants will fill in the gaps automatically by playing themselves and family members they know well.

Follow the role play with a discussion of feelings about the anger exhibited in the role play. Have participants focus on the consequences to self and others of avoiding any conflict around an angry person.

Explore this same kind of role play again, this time with the angry person managing his anger rationally and quietly. Allow other role players to respond as they feel.

Another variant is to have an anger avoidant family collude to avoid a significant problem, such as a member's abuse of alcohol or drugs.

Combining the two situations, have an anger avoidant family avoid an angry alcohol or drug abuser.

4-4 *"Yes/No" Fight*

Have group members (or couple) line up in two facing lines. Tell them they are about to have a fight, but one in which only two words are allowed: "yes" and "no." One group is given the word "yes," the other "no." Participants are encouraged to experiment fighting with their word in many different tones of voice, using different gestures. All talk at once. No physical contact allowed. After about three minutes, each side switches to the opposite word. Process what happens.

This is a good exercise to defuse fear of conflict, since all participate at once in a generally humorous encounter. Lack of content makes it very difficult to "injure" another and leads participants toward an understanding of their own habits and patterns. Typically, anger avoiders have trouble saying "no," while chronically angry persons have difficulty saying "yes."

5

ASSESSMENT of CHRONIC ANGER PROBLEMS

Many substance abusers or persons who are from chemically dependent families develop chronic anger problems, as was described in Chapter 3. Here we want to elaborate on this pattern by describing four traps that ensnare chronically angry individuals. These are problems with behavior, cognition, affect, and spirituality/meaning. We will also describe an instrument that is useful for the assessment of chronic anger patterns. Finally, we will describe an Anger Inventory that helps therapists identify certain specific patterns of anger avoidance and excessive anger particular to each client.

FOUR TRAPS IN CHRONIC ANGER

Chronic anger problems differ widely among individuals. Particular clients may have any one or more of these specific issues:

- They may be impulsive and/or explosive with their anger.
- They may be somewhat paranoid in their thinking, which makes them vulnerable to angry defensive "counterattacks" against those whom they believe want to hurt them.

- They may develop long-term resentments and be unable to forgive.

- They may deliberately fly into rages to intimidate and control others.

- They may become furious when their shameful self-concept or a sense of inadequacy is exposed, either accidentally or purposefully, by others.

- They may too regularly experience bouts of outrage and moral indignation.

- They may turn most of their anger against themselves through acts such as self-mutilation and self-sabotage.

- They may be tormented by irrational amounts of envy and jealousy.

- They may develop an addictive relationship with their anger, in which they come to depend upon their anger for stimulation.

Therapists must be alert to these specific processes while assessing chronic anger. Each individual will have a unique blend of these various forms of anger. Indeed, some chronically angry persons would hardly recognize the problem in others. As one of our patients said: "I don't know why Sue and I are in this group together. I get in trouble everyday with my anger because I can't control it. All Sue does is complain about what happened to her when she grew up." Therapy must reflect each client's particular needs.

We have found it useful to classify chronic anger issues into four general areas. These reflect the major human activities of acting, thinking, feeling and seeking meaning in life.

Acting

One trap that ensnares habitually angry individuals is that of *habitually angry behavior,* which involves overlearned, automatic activity. Many persons with angry habit patterns began developing them in early childhood. With reinforcement over time, these behaviors became firmly established. In adulthood, these behaviors are maintained with a minimum of effort. Acting in ways that encourage both their own anger and the anger of others becomes the *modus operandi* of the habitually angry person. In fact, it may seem that almost everything chronically angry individuals do is an invitation for trouble. Certainly the man who greets his partner with: "Well, there you are. What stupid thing did you do today?" almost guarantees that his immediate future will be filled with anger. Unfortunately, many angry people are unaware of the extent of their belligerence. The greeting above would seem perfectly normal to them.

Angry habits obey the same principles as any other habit: They meet some of a person's needs; they are reinforced externally by the reactions (attention, obedience, etc.) of others, although the reinforcement schedule may become less and less frequent over time; and they relieve a person's anxiety by providing a safe and predictable outlet. Angry habits consist of regular and predictable sequences of actions. These actions are accompanied by equally predictable thoughts and feelings.

It is vital to ascertain the exact form and sequence of these behaviors, thus promoting the development of specific interventions designed to interrupt and redirect them.

Thinking

The second trap that chronically angry persons encounter involves *negative thought patterns*. Chronically angry individuals often have a negative bias in their thinking, viewing innocent remarks or incidents as personal threats or insults. They tend to see the world through "anger-colored" glasses. We have found that these individuals usually have beliefs that strongly support their continuing hostility. Typical thoughts include: "The world is a bad and dangerous place"; "everybody is out to get me"; "all men (or women) are wicked and only interested in one thing"; "everybody wants something." These beliefs seem to justify their venomous attacks against others. In addition, many chronically angry individuals seem to live by the principle of "I never met an invitation to get mad I didn't like." Every perceived slight or insult, no matter how apparently insignificant, becomes an opportunity for an angry response. These individuals are loyal to the concept of fighting every battle that can be fought—and getting angry each time.

Therapeutic intervention here centers around the concept of choice. First, though, these thought patterns must be identified, most frequently through questioning the thoughts that angry persons use to justify their behaviors. Only then will it be possible to begin challenging those thoughts by helping clients alter their world view. This approach is described in greater detail in Chapter 9.

Feeling

Emotional extremism is another trap for chronically angry clients. Not only do these individuals get angry all the time, but they easily become enraged. They overreact to their anger, responding far out of proportion to the actual trigger event. They may ventilate their anger in bursts of rage, only for it to return almost immediately, perhaps even hotter than before. They may stew for days over a trivial insult, fuming out loud or silently for hours at a time.

These individuals have great difficulty moderating their anger. Some of them have developed compulsive anger patterns that look amazingly like addictions: Their tolerance for anger has become so high that they no longer even recognize small amounts of it; they need *lots* of anger to feel normal; anger has become the most important thing in their lives; they derive more pleasure (or stimulation, which may or may not be defined as pleasurable) from anger than from anything else, and their lives have become unmanageable because of it.

A typical complaint here is that "I just lose control of my anger. It takes over." These persons are not referring just to their behaviors. Rather, they are indicating that their feelings are overpowering them. The adrenalin rush that they experience when they get angry pushes them into a state where their normal cognitive controls are overwhelmed. Rage rules their bodies. On such occasions it is vital that clients learn to take a time-out before they say or do something dangerous or damaging.

Seeking Meaning in Life

Finally, chronically angry persons may easily become *"mean-spirited."* Chronic anger can affect the very meaning of life. Gradually, chronically angry persons become habitually cynical, critical, and bitter. They lose track of positive aspects of life because there is little room for joy or love in the universe of the perpetually angry person. Deep, unending anger seems eventually to damage the spirit as much as it affects someone's thoughts and behaviors.

Chronically angry individuals often become defensive and vigilant. Spiritually wounded, they may have lost hope of ever finding contentment. To protect themselves from the pain of this disappointment, they may utilize their anger to erect walls between themselves and others. Over the years, they may attempt to break through these walls. However, they are unlikely to succeed until they have dealt with their pessimism, distrust, outrage, and despair.

An inability to forgive is common at the spiritual level of chronic anger. Rather than forgive, many chronically angry individuals cling to their resentments. Unable to forgive, they cannot let go. Unable to let go, they cannot find peace. Intervention around the theme of resentment and forgiveness is described in Chapter 9.

During the assessment process, it is important to seek information in all these areas. Most persons with anger problems will experience at least a few problems with each of these four issues. However, the primary therapeutic focus of attention may differ with each client. For example, a man who comes to treatment or therapy with an inability to forgive his drug-dependent mother is very different from a woman who is convinced that men cannot be trusted and that she should be angry with them whenever possible. Proper and thorough assessment will greatly improve the therapist's ability to plan appropriate therapeutic goals and tactics.

AN ANGER ASSESSMENT INTAKE FORMAT

Table 3 lists questions designed to assess individuals with probable chronic anger problems. These questions may be utilized with clients specifically identified (by themselves, the referral agent, or the counselor) as having anger problems. Generally this assessment is completed during the second client session, after having completed a standard mental health intake. For clients whose primary focus is alcohol or drug treatment, this assessment can be deferred until later and/or incorporated into therapy sessions in a less formal way.

Question 1 asks clients to describe their anger and violence in their own words. This helps the therapist learn several things, including whether or not the client believes there really is a problem. Since many clients with anger issues are referred to counseling against their will, it may be useful to ask them which of their behaviors others have expressed concern about. It is important to attend to the clarity or vagueness of the client's description, here and throughout the intake. In general, the more vague the clients' reports, the less they have thought about their anger or the more they may be reluctant to describe it in detail.

Question 2 concerns the latest anger episode, which frequently is the springboard that propels clients into counseling (or to their alcohol/drug counselor to discuss their anger problems). The goal is to get a clear picture of exactly how, when, where, and why (from the client's perspective) this event occurred. Please note that we don't assume that violence accompanies anger. These connections have to be ascertained empirically. Also, it is important to determine alcohol and drug use specific to the incident. Finally, the client is asked about the representativeness of this most recent episode. If it is not typical, then it is vital to ascertain both the reasons for its distinctiveness and the more typical pattern.

Question 3 asks about the worst episode of anger or violence. This question helps establish the overall risk factors for clients and family safety. Frequently the worst episode was also the last. If so, you can also use this question to gather information about how the client's anger has progressed, by focusing upon gradual or sudden changes in the situation. Otherwise, this question

TABLE 3
Anger/Violence Intake

1. Patient's concerns in own words.

2. Most recent incident—describe in detail.

    When?

    With whom?

    What happened?

      How started?

      Main angry actions?

      Main angry words and thoughts?

      Main physical sensations?

      How ended?

    Any use of alcohol or drugs by anyone involved?

    Any use of physical violence, use of force, threats?

    Effects on client/others?

      Immediate?

      Continuing?

    How typical is this incident? If not, explain.

3. Worst incident.

    When?

    With whom?

    What happened?

      How started?

      Main angry actions?

      Main angry words and thoughts?

(continued)

TABLE 3
Continued

Main physical sensations?

How ended?

Any use of alcohol or drugs by anyone involved?

Any physical violence, use of force, threats?

Effects on client/others?

Immediate?

Continuing?

4. Frequency of problems. How often have you had trouble with your anger:

This month?

Last six months?

Previous adult?

Adolescent?

Child?

5. With whom do you get angry?   What about?

__ Partner/boyfriend/girlfriend _____

__ Parents/step-parents   _____

__ Your children (step-children) _____

__ Other relatives   _____

__ Employer/fellow workers   _____

__ Teachers   _____

__ Friends   _____

__ Others (whom?)   _____

(continued)

TABLE 3
Continued

6. Family of origin. Describe what the following people do/did with their anger, especially when you were growing up:

   Your father/stepfather:

   Your mother/stepmother:

   Your brothers and sisters:

   Other significant persons (grandparents, teachers, etc.):

   Is there any family history of bad temper, assaults, homicides or suicides?

   In general, what did you learn about anger from your family?

7. Any current problems with or history of: Describe:

   __ Brain injury   _____

   __ Stroke   _____

   __ Epilepsy/seizures   _____

   __ Attention deficit disorder   _____

   __ Premenstrual Syndrome   _____

   __ Depression   _____

   __ Post-traumatic stress disorder   _____

   __ Other serious illness   _____

8. Any medications currently being taken?

9. Legal history relating to anger/aggression. Be specific.

   Current:

   Past:

(continued)

TABLE 3
Continued

---

10. Use of alcohol/drugs frequently associated with anger/aggression.

substance	current or recent use?	past use?	frequency
Alcohol			
Amphetamines (includes "ice")			
PCP			
Steroids			
Barbiturates			
Cocaine (includes "crack")			
other(s)			

11. Connections between your use of alcohol/drugs and anger/aggression.
    __ Anger/aggression gets worse when using
    __ I only get in trouble with my anger/aggression while using
    __ I'm less angry/aggressive when I drink or use drugs
    __ Others tell me there is a connection but I have trouble believing it
    __ There seems to be no connection at all
    __ Other alcohol/drug connections with anger/aggression (explain)

12. How have you attempted to control your anger?
    __ I never have
    __ Talk to myself   What messages? _____
    __ Leave the scene   How long? _____ What do you do? _____
    __ Try to relax   How? _____
    __ Talk with people   Whom? _____
    __ Go to a self help group such as A.A.
    __ Other?   What? _____

13. Is there anything else you can tell me that might help me understand your anger and
    how it affects you and others? _____

---

helps the counselor gather historical information about the client's past problems with anger and aggression. It is not unusual, especially with clients who have achieved abstinence from alcohol or drugs, to hear that they used to be far more aggressive than they are now but that they are still very angry a lot of the time.

Question 4 asks about the recent and past frequency of anger episodes. In general, the most difficult clients to work with will be those who report they had the reputation of being temperamental children and "hot-headed" adolescents. Their anger is more likely to be characterological in nature, as well as the product of countless behavioral repetitions.

Question 5 — "With whom do you get angry?" — attempts to distinguish between persons who get mad at just about everybody and those whose anger is more selective. Again, therapy will usually be easiest with those with the narrowest band of anger. For instance, the woman who describes herself as generally easygoing but rageful in response to her husband's cocaine addiction or affair will need help in this one particular area. Treating the woman who uses her husband's behavior as just one of many "reasons" to get mad will be more difficult to treat. Incidentally, discovering that clients are only angry with certain persons and under specific conditions helps combat their frequent claim that they cannot control their anger at all. "How can that be," the therapist might ask, "when you are showing me that you actually do and can control your anger most of the time (or with everybody else)?" It is also useful in some circumstances to ascertain whether a client can control anger with one gender but not the other, or with persons larger than himself but not smaller, etc., and to confront this difference as evidence of the client's ability to control anger.

Question 6 addresses the client's family-of-origin practices and beliefs about anger. Sometimes clients report that nobody in their families had any anger problems. That leads to an interesting probe: "How, then, do you think you learned to get this angry?" More frequently, at least one person in the family of origin modeled out-of-control anger. Occasionally, the entire family was steeped in anger. Then this question becomes relevant: "If you were to give up your anger, what would your family think?" Since certain clients minimize their family history of anger or aggression, it is necessary to inquire directly about any record of assaultiveness, homicidality, or suicidality.

Question 7 asks about medical and psychological conditions associated with anger and aggression. This material is reviewed in Chapter 2.

Question 8 concerns current use of medications. Any unusual anger pattern that occurs concurrently with medication use may be a side effect of that medication. Staff medical personnel should be consulted in this area.

Question 9 focuses upon clients' legal history as it relates to their anger and aggression. Never assume that clients will give you this information unless you ask for it directly. Even when specifically court-ordered to get treatment for anger, the client may not volunteer this information.

Questions 10 and 11 concern clients' present/past use of intoxicants and their awareness of the connections between their use of alcohol/drugs and their anger/aggression. It is crucial to probe for alcohol/drug involvement, even with clients not identified as having that problem. Individuals coming into therapy for anger can very well have overt or covert substance abuse issues, which may be identified during this interview. Recovering alcoholics or drug users should be asked about how their past use of these substances affected their anger.

Question 12 asks how clients have tried to control their anger. The response "I never have" is as ominous as that of the probable alcoholic who never has tried to limit or control his drinking. However, clients have often tried various tactics to limit their anger. It is valuable to find out what has worked best. Sometimes all a client needs is a reminder about what has worked before to begin to take positive action.

Finally, question 13 offers clients the opportunity to add information and to be the final expert on their own anger. "Well, I guess you might want to know that I'm the victim of incest"; "My grandfather killed his wife"; "I never had these problems in my first marriage": such responses can indeed help the therapist. This question also addresses the likelihood that clients have not been entirely truthful during the session. They are now responsible for any material left out of the interview because the counselor happened not to ask exactly the right question.

This anger intake instrument is just one part of a complete evaluation. It complements a standard mental health or alcohol/drug assessment. In turn, it might be complemented by asking clients to take appropriate personality or cognitive performance tests, anger inventories such as Spielberger's State-Trait Anger Expression Inventory (Spielberger, 1988), or substance abuse assessments.

THE ANGER INVENTORY

In addition to the general anger assessment tool noted above, we have developed another instrument to identify specific patterns of anger used by clients. This instrument, the Anger Inventory, is presented in Table 4.

Each pair of questions addresses one typical pattern of angry behavior. A score of 7–8 points or higher on each pair indicates

TABLE 4

Anger Inventory

Here are 20 statements that people often make about their anger. Read each one of them and then circle a number from 1 to 5.
  1 – This statement does not apply to me at all.
  2 – This statement is true once in a while.
  3 – This statement is somewhat true for me.
  4 – This statement is frequently true.
  5 – This statement applies to me a great deal.

1. I try never to get angry.	1	2	3	4	5
2. I am very uncomfortable whenever anyone else gets angry.	1	2	3	4	5
3. When I get angry at somebody, I may say something about it but not directly to them.	1	2	3	4	5
4. People often tell me I'm mad when I don't see any signs of anger.	1	2	3	4	5
5. I get so mad sometimes I just explode.	1	2	3	4	5
6. I blow up a lot when I get angry.	1	2	3	4	5
7. I get mad so I can get what I want.	1	2	3	4	5
8. I try to scare others with my anger.	1	2	3	4	5
9. I hang onto my anger for a long time.	1	2	3	4	5
10. I have a hard time forgiving people.	1	2	3	4	5
11. I often feel outraged about what people try to do to me or others.	1	2	3	4	5
12. I become very angry when I defend my beliefs.	1	2	3	4	5
13. I get very angry when someone insults me.	1	2	3	4	5
14. I become angry when I feel "bad" about myself or inadequate.	1	2	3	4	5
15. I get angry with people who are more successful than I am.	1	2	3	4	5
16. I am a jealous person.	1	2	3	4	5
17. I like the strong feelings that come with my anger.	1	2	3	4	5
18. Sometimes I get mad just for the excitement.	1	2	3	4	5
19. I just can't break the habit of anger.	1	2	3	4	5
20. I seem to get angry all the time.	1	2	3	4	5

possible problems in any particular area. The patterns are as follows:

- (Questions 1 and 2): Anger avoidance.
- (Questions 3 and 4): Passive-aggression.
- (Questions 5 and 6): Explosive anger.
- (Questions 7 and 8): Instrumental anger.
- (Questions 9 and 10): Resentment.
- (Questions 11 and 12): Moral anger.
- (Questions 13 and 14): Shame-based anger.
- (Questions 15 and 16): Envy and jealousy.
- (Questions 17 and 18): Excitatory anger.
- (Questions 19 and 20): Habitual anger.

This inventory is easy to administer and interesting to clients. The results help clients identify specific styles of angry thinking and behaving. While some individuals "specialize" in one or two types of anger, others score high on several sets of questions, indicating a more generalized anger pattern. Also, therapeutic goals and strategies can be developed with greater exactitude with this information, helping in treatment planning. Please note, however, that many clients understate the amount of their anger early in therapy. This instrument simply provides a starting point for a discussion about clients' anger styles.

The first four questions together tap the general theme of anger avoidance, which has been described in previous chapters. However, we make a distinction between those who attempt to avoid their anger entirely and those who use passive-aggressive tactics to express their anger without full recognition of their feelings. With clients, incidentally, it may be useful to label passive-aggression as "sneaky anger," an easier term with which to identify. Many individuals score high in both of these areas, although the connection is not automatic. Anger avoidance concerns have been discussed in Chapters 3 and 4.

Questions 5 and 6 concern the theme of explosive anger. Individuals high in explosive anger will need particular help with learning to take time-outs and to anticipate and de-energize potential anger provocations. This material is covered in Chapter 9.

Questions 7 and 8 identify anger that is used intentionally to manipulate or control others. Only a few individuals initially identify with this instrumental use of anger, since it is not acceptable in our society to admit that one intentionally attempts to intimidate others. As noted in Chapter 2, clients with the diagnosis of antisocial personality disorder are likely to utilize anger in this manner, although anyone might under specific conditions. We describe instrumental anger as "intentional anger" to clients. Treatment for this kind of anger may focus upon the ultimate negative consequences of manipulating others with anger and/ or the development of values that conflict with the use of instrumental anger.

Resentment is the theme of questions 9 and 10. Metaphorically, resentment can be viewed as "hardened" anger, initial displeasure that has solidified into long-term dislike of another. The existence of resentment is often associated with individuals who have had to endure continuing difficulties, such as living with someone who is chemically dependent. The tendency to build and store resentments is described more fully in Chapter 9, along with relevant therapeutic strategies.

Moral anger is measured with items 11 and 12. This type of anger may be a positive force (see Chapter 6), propelling individuals to fight for their perceptions of justice and fairness. It can also be dangerous, since moral anger allows people to excuse anger and aggression as morally justified. Moral anger is particularly problematic for those with relatively rigid, "black and white" patterns of cognition. These persons will need training in empathic identification with others whose values differ from theirs if they are to become less habitually morally angry.

Rage (questions 13 and 14) is one commonly utilized defense against shame (Potter-Efron, R., 1989). This rage tells others to stay away, since contact threatens that individual's core identity. Shame-prone individuals may project their anger onto others, typically responding to others with contempt in an effort to humiliate them as they experience their own deep humiliation. Clients whose anger is primarily shame-based will need much help in building their self-esteem. Their anger and violence will typically recede as their self-concept improves.

Envy and jealousy (questions 15 and 16) are complex mixtures of thoughts and feelings that typically contain strong elements of anger. Envious persons resent the success of others, taking it as a repudiation of their own good qualities (Ulanov, 1983). Jealousy more involves efforts to guard and protect that which is perceived to belong to someone (Pittman, 1989), including both material possessions and interpersonal relationships. The presence of irrational jealousy can be a predictor of violence (White & Mullen, 1989).

Jealousy is especially resistant to intervention; very jealous individuals become obsessed with their need to control the object of their jealousy and cannot attend to anything else. Initial therapy with highly jealous individuals must focus on behavioral interdiction of the client's most inappropriate actions (following a partner, threatening others, etc.). An exercise useful with envy and jealousy is presented at the conclusion of this chapter.

Questions 17 and 18 concern excitatory anger. Here individuals seek out the powerful stimulation of rage, gaining feelings of excitement. We often present this category, especially with individuals who are recovering alcoholics or drug abusers, as "addictive anger," since anger-seekers often behave in ways similar to recovering persons who "like to live on the edge." Therapy here centers upon helping clients live a life of moderation in general and with their anger. See Chapters 6 and 8 for more detailed discussions of this type of anger.

Finally, individuals who score relatively high on the last two questions are those whose anger has become habitual, a central theme in their lives. Many clients who specifically seek help for their anger problems will have developed a definite proneness toward anger, so that much of their daily lives revolves around anger incidents. These persons need a long-term treatment plan that can help them dislodge these deeply rooted habits of thinking, feeling, and behaving. The habit of anger is described in Chapter 7.

EXERCISES

5-1 Anger, Jealousy, and Envy

Present the following acronyms to the group (or individual) and discuss how these feelings and perceptions create and intensify one's experience of anger. Then help the group (or individual) make a list of good alternative actions to acting jealous or envious.

J = JUDGMENTAL
E = EAGLE-EYED
A = ANGRY
L = LONELY
O = OVERSENSITIVE
U = UNFORGIVING
S = SCARED
Y = YEARNING

E = ENTITLED
N = NEGATIVE
V = VENGEFUL
Y = YEN

6

THE FUNCTIONS of

CHRONIC ANGER

Chronic anger creates both emotional and interpersonal difficulties for affected individuals. Despite strong discouragement from others, many persons develop this pattern of living and seem to cling to it.

Why do people stay chronically angry when the cost is so great? Few chronically angry persons report that they feel very good about themselves or their behavior. They frequently suffer from physical and emotional isolation. They have trouble feeling other emotions, even such positive ones as joy and love. They sometimes sense that they are caught in traps of their own making. Why don't they just let go of their anger and get on with their lives?

There is no single answer to this question. Chronic anger is a complex issue. Each individual develops his or her anger in a unique manner that depends upon genetic predisposition, family of origin, and adult experiences. People get stuck in their anger for many reasons, over many years.

However, clients use their anger for certain purposes that are regularly observed in therapy. Sometimes they know clearly that they use anger for one or more of these goals. At other times they have little understanding of why, how, or what they are doing; nevertheless, their anger tends to be utilized in predictable doing; nevertheless, their anger tends to be utilized in predictable circumstances to achieve predictable ends. We offer here a list of these major functions of anger:

- Signaling that something is seriously wrong.

- Attempting a solution for problems in living.

- Engaging in a long-term habit that becomes its own reason for being.

- Attempting to gain power over others.

- Attempting to gain status over others.

- Keeping others physically and/or emotionally distant.

- Holding relationships together through intense interaction.

- Defending against shame and threats to one's self-concept.

- Defending against other feelings, such as sadness, hurt, weakness, and vulnerability.

- Claiming a position of righteous superiority.

- Being a mood-altering experience.

TYPICAL FUNCTIONS

A Signal that Something Is Seriously Wrong

Even chronically angry individuals may have legitimate complaints and concerns. In an effort to help clients tone down and control their anger, counselors may easily forget this. They begin to consider every anger episode as irrational, which in the long run may lessen their credibility.

We have mentioned previously that anger is an emotion that conveys a specific message to the person who feel it: "There is something wrong here that needs attention." This message signals the person to examine the situation and prepare for action. Anger helps individuals focus attention upon their problems.

However, *anger itself does not reveal the exact source or nature of the problem*. Someone's anger may result from something going wrong inside the individual (hunger, fatigue, anxiety, depression, etc.) or from relationship concerns. Counselors can help their clients learn not to rush to conclusions about what is wrong. Frequently, the immediate target of one's anger turns out to be a mere substitute for the real source, for instance, when someone's unexpressed frustration at work occasions an explosion at the first item out of place at home.

Chronically angry individuals have to guard against their oversensitivity to anger cues. They often hear danger signals ringing when nothing is really wrong. They need to learn this message: "I'm getting angry right now. But I better not jump to conclusions. This could be a false alarm."

Therapists can help chronically angry individuals slow down their reactions to anger. This guards against impulsive aggression. Clients need to ask themselves such questions as: "Who am I really upset with?" "Is there anything going on inside me I need to look at?" "What can I do that will help me instead of making things worse?"

An Attempted Solution for Problems in Living

Anger is a good signal of trouble. Unfortunately, it is a poor solution. Nevertheless, many chronically angry individuals try to resolve their issues through anger. This seldom works, since anger is only a feeling, not a specific guide to action.

We have seen people in A.A. and therapy groups who have learned (or mislearned) that the expression of anger itself makes you feel better and helps resolve problems. So they ventilate that anger, saying things like: "I don't see why you're upset with me. They told me in treatment to tell people what I'm feeling. I was really mad so I yelled at you. That's exactly what I'm supposed to do. It's your problem, not mine." The predictable end result of this thinking and behavior is that these recovering persons (or family members) compound their difficulties instead of alleviating them.

Chronically angry individuals try to solve real problems with emotional solutions. But to yell at or hit someone "because I was angry" makes no more sense than to quit a job "because I was tired" or to marry "because he makes me feel good." Certainly people need to use their feelings to help plan actions. However, feelings alone do not provide effective guidelines for appropriate action.

Chronically angry persons may believe that anger solves problems better than anything else. There is some immediate truth to this, especially if they have succeeded in intimidating others with their anger. Many individuals who use anger to handle their problems will usually discover that they get worse, however. Anger simply does not work effectively when it is the only tool in someone's toolbox. To repeat: anger is a good signal but a poor solution to our problems.

A Long-Term Habit

One danger of functional analysis is being seduced by the idea that everything must have a current purpose. We believe that most people with chronic anger problems do gain some value from their angry behavior in the present. However, it may also be useful to view their anger as a vestige from the past—an old habit pattern that may have had value then but is mostly an impediment now. This approach is particularly valuable with persons in recovery programs who want to make a real break from their past. Therapists can help these clients view their excessive anger as an outdated remnant from an old lifestyle. Recognizing that they are dealing with old habits and defenses, many recovering individuals are able to begin to give them up without a severe threat to their sense of self.

A habit is something that has been learned so well that little or no conscious thought is necessary to do it. Just as most persons don't need to think about how to tie their shoes, chronically angry individuals may automatically respond to their worlds with anger. Anger is normal. The sun rises; winter comes; these persons get angry.

Persons with an anger habit do gain efficiency because they do not have to take the time to think about their actions. For example, a woman who always reacts to new situations with suspicion, distrust, cynicism, and defiance does not waste energy assessing new situations. She simply flows naturally into her usual pattern of thoughts, actions, and feelings. Of course, this person loses the ability to be flexible. She may eventually suffer badly by responding to the world from a rigid framework. Still, at the moment of immediate tension, her habitual anger helps her know exactly what to do.

Many chronically angry individuals have developed an anger habit and may cling to it fiercely, spending hours every day getting and staying mad. Anger feels normal, familiar, and part of the daily routine. It simply does not seem possible to go through life not feeling angry on a regular basis.

Habitually angry persons need to become more aware of their anger instead of allowing it to continue dominating their lives. Making choices about their anger can help them begin to replace automatic responses with new feelings and behaviors.

An Attempt to Gain Power over Others

Very few people like to confront a visibly angry person, whether that individual is a family member, business associate, or total stranger. Many chronically angry persons are quite aware of this fact. They utilize it to gain power over others through their supposedly irrational outbursts. Some will openly admit that the only way they know to gain and keep control is through periodic blowups. The basic message they send to the people around them should be familiar to most substance abuse counselors: "I want what I want and I want it now!" Since they frequently get what they want by getting mad, chronically angry individuals may have little incentive to change. Why bother to sit down and talk calmly when standing and yelling have been so effective?

Anger that is used to control others is labeled "instrumental anger," in contrast to "expressive anger," which represents a person's emotional state. The goal of instrumental anger is to gain something by intimidating others. This kind of anger often works its way down the power chain in families — the strongest or angriest person physically or verbally attacks the next strongest, who then attacks the next, etc. (Finkelhor, 1983).

Chronically angry individuals who are chemically dependent can use their addictions to gain or keep power (Elkins, 1984): "Better do what he says, kids. You know how mad he gets when he's been drinking." Alcohol and drugs add elements of unpredictability and irrationality to already difficult situations. Their desire to maintain control may be a hidden reason some chemically dependent individuals are reluctant to quit using.

Individuals who use anger for power often do suffer major consequences for their actions, especially in the family. Holding a shotgun on a group of persons and ordering them to love you doesn't work very well. Although these "hostages" may say or do things that appear loving, they will resent doing so and will probably stop whenever the gun is pointed in a different direction. One can buy power through intimidation but not affection or respect.

Clients seldom admit the extent to which they use instrumental anger. They would prefer others, including their therapists, to believe that their anger is simply an expression of emotion and not a deliberate attempt to intimidate. The first hint that instrumental anger is a concern may occur when they mention that they feel stronger or more in control when they get mad. This use of anger is also difficult to relinquish, especially since many chronically angry persons are relatively unskilled in the use of more sophisticated negotiation and communication techniques. Chronic anger, for many, has become a substitute for appropriate social skills and the hard work necessary to establish substantial, negotiated, strong relationships.

An Attempt to Gain Status

An adolescent, normally a quiet young man, recently found himself suspended from riding a school bus after a brief but active argument with the driver. He reported that his prestige at school had risen considerably among his peers. Defiance has its rewards, especially among teenagers and other culturally disenfranchised groups.

Status, like power, may not be the original intent of an anger explosion. It can become a secondary gain, however. Persons who gather respect or admiration in this manner are more likely to return to argumentative or apparently hostile behavior in the future. They have discovered that their anger is appreciated, adding to their sense of self.

Chronic anger may develop as an individual accepts the role of "hothead" or rebel to gain prestige, notice, or esteem. Individuals can become trapped in this role, feeling that to retain their status they must find reasons to become and stay angry. They may fail to realize that the world is passing them by and that what once gave them honor now produces ridicule. "Here comes Joey," people may say, "You just have to see him when he blows his top. He's always upset about something."

Again, it is difficult to give up a behavior that has been so well rewarded. For example, one alcoholic male we treated would go to a bar, drink several beers in rapid succession, and then begin challenging all around him to a fight. He was a wonderful battler and could easily beat up several antagonists, partly because he would go into true blind rages on these occasions. Everyone at the bar feared him. He treasured this reputation, even more so after he developed arthritis and could no longer work as a truck driver. When he gave up drinking, one thing with which he needed help was grieving the loss of his status.

A Way to Maintain Physical and/or Emotional Distance

"Keep away" is a powerful message that angry individuals deliver to others. Anger drives people out of one's life, perhaps forever. This may not be the exact intent of chronically angry persons, however. Sometimes they only desire a few moments of privacy. They try to say, "Leave me alone for now. Come back later." But when they say this by being angry very often or very loudly, others may hear, "Get lost forever. I hate you."

Many persons become distinctly uncomfortable when they have an opportunity for closeness or intimacy. Afraid to love, they regularly push others away or shove them aside. Explosive anger is ideal for this purpose, but so is persistent grumbling and unfriendliness. Others literally allow angry people extra room, standing farther away from them while avoiding any topics that might trigger their fury.

Chronic anger provides a buffer zone against tender feelings. Irate individuals avoid the feelings of vulnerability that accompany intimacy. Anger protects these individuals against their fear that they will be injured if they allow themselves to be close to anyone. They use their wrath to keep others at a safe distance. They justify this behavior with arguments that nobody can be trusted, that people are just out to use them, or that they have been hurt too often before to try again. Whatever their rationalizations, they succeed in maintaining their isolation by threatening anyone who attempts to befriend them.

For some chronically angry individuals, this anger may partially cover a particularly strong fear that closeness threatens their very identity. These persons fear being engulfed by others through the process of intimacy. They push people away to avoid feeling overwhelmed. Chronic anger used this way helps individuals maintain their sense of personal existence by erecting a barricade between them and the world.

A Means to Hold Relationships Together
Through Intense Interaction

Oddly enough, anger can sometimes act as the "glue" that holds relationships together. Persons in these couples and families have become "conflict-habituated" (Cuber & Haroff, 1974). These individuals fight all the time. They argue as soon as they greet each other in the morning and when they say good night. The "partnership" seems to be held together by the anger and running battles that both express and contain tension.

These relationships look like disaster zones because of the ongoing civil war. Still, outside observers will note that such pairs or units share an intense degree of passion. There is a curious combination here of high energy, magnetic attraction, and aggression. This "I can't live with you and I can't live without you" relationship has often been portrayed on stage or television ("The Taming of the Shrew," "The Honeymooners"), presumably because the average individual is fascinated by the paradoxical dynamics of such unions. Unfortunately, while these fantasy relationships may end happily, with all tension resolved at the end of each episode, real-life couples and families that are conflict-habituated suffer serious problems and mutual pain. In fact, the members of such families are usually miserable because they can connect with each other only through anger. Furthermore, children raised in these units learn that what appears to be intimacy is possible only through conflict. In one angry family, we observed that pinching someone hard was the only way to say, "I love you." This pattern, of course, always led to fights.

Some conflict-habituated relationships would simply collapse without these endless arguments. Couples who spend most of their time fighting might not know what to do if they were not attacking one another. The battling itself apparently holds these relationships together, with participants substituting angry passion for true intimacy.

Chemical dependency counselors are undoubtedly familiar with clients who regularly seek moments of physical or emotional intensity. Indeed, Craig Nakken (1988), in his writings on addictive personalities, describes persons who regularly confuse feelings of intensity with those of intimacy. Moderation of any kind is difficult for these persons. Passion itself is valued. Intense anger then becomes a way of demonstrating true love, and a calm relationship is experienced as boring and loveless. In these relationships love is defined as anguish and ecstasy. These couples and families might well appear chaotic, immature, and dangerous to the therapist. However, it is important not to underestimate the strength of the bonds that hold these persons together. Anger can sometimes cement people as efficiently as love.

A Defense Against Shame and Threats to Self-Concept

Shame is a deep feeling of defectiveness at the core of a person's self-concept. Shamed individuals feel deficient, inferior, worthless and useless. They fear and expect abandonment because they think of themselves as not worth keeping. Many shamed persons have experienced powerful abandonments and mistreatments as children, perhaps connected with someone's chemical dependency. As a result, they may have internalized ideas that they are not good or not good enough, not competent, and not autonomous. They may even doubt their right to exist.

Shame is difficult to endure. We have written elsewhere (Potter-Efron & Potter-Efron, 1989b) about six major defenses people use to avoid their shame: denial, withdrawal, arrogance, exhibitionism, perfectionism, and rage. We will concentrate on the latter in this section.

Rage is most likely to occur as a response to a perceived attack against the core of one's identity. People feel humiliated when they think others have deliberately attempted to shame them, for instance, by pointing out their mistakes in public or by calling them names such as "dummy," "tramp," or "ugly." These insults attack the person's sense of self. They imply that there is something wrong with him or her that cannot be alleviated. In an effort to defend against such attacks on the self, some individuals will respond with tremendous explosions of narcissistic rage—a desire to annihilate the antagonist who threatens one's very being. This rage both defends against inner shame and transforms self-hatred into hostility toward the persons who injured them.

Many chronically angry individuals carry with them unrelenting memories of past humiliations. Since they have not released these memories, they are vulnerable to becoming rageful against individuals who remind them in any way of their past. They "stew" over past insults and injuries, playing them over and over in their heads. As Ernest Wolf (1988) writes, "The painful memory lingers on, and so does the slowly boiling resentment. At some point, weeks, months, or even years after the insult, the smoldering animosity is likely to break out into open hostility, perhaps a hot fury, perhaps a coldly calculating destructiveness" directed against the original person or a substitute target.

Those who use rage to defend against shame can be dangerous. many batterers, for example, display this pattern of behavior. They see others, including those they love, as regularly attempting to humiliate them, even while outside observers would observe no such indicators. Then they attack, thinking that they have the right to do so since they were injured first. These rageful assaults can even become fatal, since the battle, in the mind of the shamed and humiliated attacker, is over survival of the self.

Deeply shamed persons also use their anger to protect themselves against an initial exposure of the self. They become irate in order to push others away so that no one will see who they really are. They believe they are damaged and defective human beings. Therefore, they don't want others to get to know them, lest they be rejected and abandoned again. Anger acts as a barrier that protects a weakened self from dangerous exposure.

A Defense Against Other Feelings

Anger is easy to hide behind. It can mask other feelings, such as fear, sadness, and love. Angry individuals may or may not consciously realize that they are cutting off their feelings. Their main concern may be either not to feel these alternative emotions or not to expose them to others. Either way, they turn to anger because they are more comfortable with it than with other feelings.

A colleague of ours is fond of the phrase: "Anger never travels alone." Although this statement is an exaggeration, it is useful to offer to some chronically angry individuals as a cue for them to look under their anger for hidden feelings.

Substance abusers and their families tend to get locked into rigid habits of reciprocal interactions. Responding only with anger is one of these patterns. For example, a son of a prescription-addicted mother automatically becomes angry with her no matter what she says or does. This behavior might continue even after she achieves abstinence, unrecognized as a defense against "soft" feelings that expose that child's vulnerability.

Gaining greater flexibility of behavioral and emotional response is often a goal with chemically dependent persons and their families. This can be promoted by helping such individuals attend to the underlying feelings that have been overshadowed by anger.

A Claim to a Position of Righteous Superiority

Many individuals attempt to take the moral high ground when they get angry. In fact, this position in life is so attractive that certain persons regularly search for reasons to assume it. Their anger allows them to feel righteously indignant and morally superior.

CASE STUDY: A Man Who Turns Shame into Rage

Hank is a worker at a local assembly plant. He remarried recently for the third time. His last two wives left because of his constant verbal abusiveness. Hank has done a little better with that problem since he quit drinking. Now when he starts getting angry, he often heads to the nearest A.A. meeting. Plus, he reads the Big Book a lot, in particular the segments on letting go of anger and not storing resentments. Nevertheless, his anger is a constant problem for him. He's in therapy now because Betty, his new wife, has told him to learn to quit his bellyaching or get out.

Hank seems guarded in therapy. Yes, he talks about his anger, but mostly to blame Betty and others for making him angry. Working with Hank is like trying to put together a jigsaw puzzle with half the pieces missing. Progress is slow and uncertain.

Finally, the truth came out. In a burst of words, he tells about the sexual abuse he had suffered as a child at the hands of his older cousins. Every weekend he stayed at their house because both parents worked. He had been raped several times by his cousins, who had threatened to kill Hank if he ever told. The incidents took place over a three-year period. Each occurrence left him feeling more helpless and rageful. His impotent fury grew each time. It also generalized until he reacted to almost any request with rage. How dare anyone try to tell him what to do! He would never be humiliated again.

Some chronically angry people take the stance that they have every right to be angry because the world is full of injustices. They are overloaded with righteousness, believing they are entitled to scorn those with different values and lifestyles—persons they view as moral inferiors. They tend to hold others in contempt.

Morally outraged individuals develop the philosophy that they must fight for what is good or fair. They constantly sense and

Now the healing process could really begin. Hank could direct his anger at its real source, the cousins who attacked him. He could begin to separate that humiliation from normal demands on his time and energy. His self-concept could begin to heal as he worked through his sexual shame and the low self-worth that had become part of his being.

The next step was for him to share this material with his wife. He did so, with much reluctance at first. When she accepted it (she, too, had been a victim of sexual abuse) and didn't reject Hank, he felt tremendous relief. Eventually he even told a few of his A.A. friends about what had happened to him as a child. Then he took his daily anger to a closed meeting and finally connected it out loud with his past.

Hank still becomes needlessly angry almost every day. But the incidents are fewer than before, far less severe, and end much more quickly. Now he can often connect his anger with the sexual abuse ("Sometimes they'd make me lie in bed and wait for them to come for me. Maybe that's why I get so mad when I have to wait for Betty"). At other times he just recognizes the shameful feeling underneath his rage and knows where it developed. Betty helps him sort stuff out, and if that doesn't work he might give his therapist a call. At last he is gaining freedom from his traumatic childhood. ■

challenge injustice. They can make excellent advocates, unless and until they get carried away with their roles. They are often feared not only by their opponents but by those with similar viewpoints but less passion, since their anger is not well controlled. Others may sense that these individuals are fighting not only for a cause but also to demonstrate their moral superiority.

Morally outraged individuals often display a curious vacillation between idealism and cynicism. They may become quite bitter when the world fails to change. Then they retain their anger but no longer seek positive uses for it. Instead, they criticize new ideas, laugh with disgust at people who dare hope for change, and turn their contempt against the world. They may come to despise their own "naive" idealism, replacing it with pessimism and gloom.

Most substance abuse counselors have probably encountered individuals whose anger takes the forms of righteous superiority, contempt for others, and/or deep pessimism and doubt. This pattern is not uncommon among the substance abusers themselves, embittered family members, and "burned out" helpers who have become frustrated with their clients' slow progress or overwhelmed with the immensity of pain in the universe.

A Mood-Altering Experience

Craig Nakken (1988), in his book on the addictive personality, defines addiction as "a pathological love and trust relationship with an object or event." Objects include items like food, drugs, and alcohol. Events include activities such as spending, overworking, compulsive sexuality, and, we suggest, chronic anger.

Anger is a great energizer, a way to get "high" with excitement, to feel suddenly alive instead of dull or apathetic. We believe that many chronically angry individuals use their anger this way so that they can achieve moments of intensity in otherwise flat and listless lives. These persons seek out arguments and physical fights because their rage is thrilling and enlivening. They get a "peak experience" from their fury, a kind of euphoria not unlike sexual stimulation. (Indeed, a few very angry clients have told us they prefer the feelings of rage to orgasm.) Anger excites these individuals so much that they do not want to give it up.

Most persons prefer both their anger and their alcohol in moderation, becoming uncomfortable with the out-of-control experience that accompanies either form of excess. However, addicted individuals actually seek out these excessive states. They may

intellectually understand the value of restraint, but they also realize that moderation cannot provide the excitement they want
and perhaps think they need. They may not have other ways to
feel good. In addition, they may sense the danger of emptiness,
boredom, and depression that could appear if they were to give
up their addictive behaviors.

Many chronically angry individuals can be helped through
exposure to the concepts of addiction and abstinence commonly described in traditional chemical dependency treatment programs. For example, it is possible to demonstrate to certain persons a steady progression of their angry behavior over time,
as well as consistently increasing consequences as a result of
those actions. Certainly, many persons experience feelings of
both powerlessness and unmanageability because of their inability to contain their anger. And for some the concept of increased
tolerance for anger can be demonstrated, in that these persons
and their families have built up an incredible endurance for
anger (explosive rages can even become "normal" in these families).

This framework is particularly useful for those clients who are
currently in treatment or who have been working an abstinence
program as part of their recovery. It only takes a slight shift of
focus to help these individuals reframe their anger as another
addiction problem, something they can manage because they
have already been given effective and appropriate tools. Activities like going to self-help groups, daily meditations, and talking
with a sponsor can all be utilized to help these persons deal with
their chronic anger.

The concept of abstinence here needs to be adjusted for each
angry person, much as it is done in 12-step-oriented eating disorders programs. In general, we suggest to clients that abstinence
refers to a goal of freedom from anger "binges" and other out-of-
control experiences. We do not promote a total negation of anger
but rather a decision not to indulge in excessively angry outbursts.

Not every angry client will be helped by treating anger as an
addiction. However, it is important to ask all clients what pleasure they get from their rages. Some persons will deny any positive features of their anger. Others will do so at first, only to

return to this question later. Some will immediately begin to tell the therapist about how much they enjoy their anger.

EXERCISES

6-1 *Functions of Anger*

Provide clients with a list of the functions of anger, and space to write, as on the following worksheet. Ask them to list examples of how they have used anger in these ways, and to circle the three ways in which they most commonly use anger. Then discuss the benefits of anger as a signal, as well as the costs of the other uses of anger.

FUNCTIONS OF ANGER WORKSHEET

Here are common ways people use anger. From your own life, write examples of as many of these ways as you can.

Then circle the three ways in which you most commonly use anger.

- Use anger as a signal that something is seriously wrong.
- Use anger as an attempted solution for problems in living.
- Use anger as a long-term habit that becomes its own reason for being.
- Use anger as an attempt to gain power over others.
- Use anger as an attempt to gain status.
- Use anger as a way to keep others physically or emotionally distant.
- Use anger as a means to hold relationships together with intensity as the glue.
- Use anger as a defense against shame and threats to the self-concept.
- Use anger as a defense against feeling other feelings.
- Use anger as a claim to a position of righteous superiority.
- Use anger as a mood-altering experience.

6-2 Anger Habits

Ask individuals to notice what small "angry habits" they use, such as snapping, tapping a foot, sighing, swearing, etc. Then instruct group members to use their "angry habits" in the group for the next 15 minutes.

Follow this with a discussion of what people have observed about themselves and each other, and how they are feeling. Do a physical "shake-out" to get rid of the angry energy, and a group hug to allow people to "de-role" out of their angry habits.

6-3 Deliberate Anger

Some angry people get "mad" intentionally, to get what they want. Pretending to be angry to get something, they intimidate others into complying and/or providing what they want. Here anger *looks* angry but is often just a pretense—a kind of fakery.

Ask clients who use anger to manipulate (as an "instrument" or "tool" to handle people) to keep a list of the times when they deal with situations by making themselves deliberately angry. Ask them to include:

- The day of the event
- Persons who were with them
- What they wanted
- What they did
- Short-term results, including both benefits and losses
- Long-term results, including both benefits and losses
- Whether they actually worked themselves into a rage
- Any feelings other than anger

Now ask the clients to answer the following questions:

1. What did you want so badly?
2. What were you afraid of?
3. How were you feeling about yourself?
4. Whom were you trying to impress?
5. What were you hiding?
6. How do you feel about the consequences, both short-term and long-term?

7. How would you act with others if you chose not to manipulate them this way?

6-4 *Instrumental Use of Anger*

Use one of the following examples to stimulate clients to examine the long-term consequences of instrumental anger, that is, anger that is primarily designed to manipulate another person's behavior.

(a) Barbara dislikes cooking dinner. Often when she doesn't want to cook she goes into the kitchen and slams doors, bangs pots and pans, sighs and swears so that her anger is obvious to everyone. In order to avoid a bad evening, Joe offers to take the family out to dinner. In the short term, Barbara gets what she wants. But what negative consequences might there be, both short- and long-term, from her use of anger in this way? How will she feel about Joe when she manipulates him? How will he feel about her? What will happen to the food budget? How will the kids feel, and what will they learn? How will the children learn to use their anger with Barbara, Joe, and others?

(b) Buck and Sally both work, and the kids get home from school before they do. Buck likes the house orderly, but instead of teaching the kids how to make it that way, he gets angry at Sally for "letting the kids get away with making a mess." In order to avoid Buck's griping, Sally explodes at the kids each night when she walks in the door, even when it is clear that they have tried to do better. What does Buck gain and lose by his manipulative griping at Sally? What does Sally gain and lose by automatically blaming the kids for everything? What do the children learn? Do they gain or lose respect for Buck, Sally, and themselves? Does Buck's and Sally's anger really help them or hurt them or both?

(c) Harry has a fit every time Sue wants to go somewhere without him. When it gets to be too much for her and she threatens to leave the relationship, he tells her he will "get even" with her by doing something to hurt her, her family, or her friends. She stays. Harry gets what he wants with his anger. But what does he lose? If this is the way he keeps a relationship, how will he feel about himself in the long run? How will Sue feel about him? About herself? What are Harry's alternatives to getting what he wants through the use of angry threats?

Next, have clients offer some examples from their own lives. Begin with one in which the client manipulated others with instrumental anger. Then go to one in which he or she felt manipulated by another's anger. End with an incident where the client must take personal responsibility for being manipulative with anger, and clearly discuss the gains and losses incurred.

6-5 Shame and Rage*

Following are examples of common, everyday occurrences in which an experience of shame or anticipated shame triggers an angry response. Notice which ones are similar to times in your life when you have found yourself angry, frustrated, or even rageful.

(a) I am in a store and my child is making noise. I see another person looking at me, and I imagine that they are judging the way I handle my child. So I get angry at my child, and take my embarrassment out on him.

(b) A friend jokes publicly that I am, have, or am doing something that is different. I feel exposed and assume that she's trying to humiliate me. I either get very angry with her, think about ways to get back at her, or use my anger to be sarcastic and mean, trying to expose her in turn. Maybe this turns into a game of shame "hot potato" that looks good-natured at first, but blows up into a fight eventually, with the person who feels the most exposed getting most angry.

(c) I forgot to register a check I wrote, and I know that my partner is going to discover that, thanks to me, our checking account is overdrawn again. I feel embarrassed, and start thinking in advance about all the things my partner does wrong. When my partner does discover and confront me about my mistake, I blow up about all of his mistakes, thus not having to face my embarrassment about my own mistake.

(d) I am feeling sensitive about my work today, while I am writing. You come up behind my shoulder and immediately point

*Also see exercise 8-5.

out a typing error I've made. I feel exposed and tell you to mind your own business or do it yourself. Since you were trying to help, you feel confused by my anger.

Now make a list of similar situations you've encountered in the past few weeks. In each situation, notice how you felt exposed. How did your anger help to (a) avoid feelings of shame; (b) shift the focus to someone else; or (c) give you a renewed sense of power (feeling exposed tends to leave us feeling powerless as well as vulnerable).

1.

2.

3.

4.

5.

6-6 The Right to Feel

Ask group or family participants each to identify a situation in which they recently found themselves angry, whether anger was "logical" in this situation or not. Have them go over the situation mentally, remembering what occurred and how they were feeling. Ask them to briefly share their situation with the group and then to complete the sentence, "If I were not angry, I'd be feeling _____." For instance, anger sometimes accompanies and hides feelings of (a) sadness; (b) shame/inadequacy; (c) guilt; (d) disappointment; (e) hurt; (f) weakness or vulnerability; and (g) loneliness. Conduct a group discussion about the right to feel all the feelings that have come up without having to cover them up.

6-7 *Righteous Indignation*

Righteous indignation is one form of chronic anger. Right-eously indignant persons who are angry all the time can be asked to use a "mantra" or repeated motto for a period of a few days or a week to help stimulate their awareness of how they judge others and what may be underneath the need to find others morally unworthy. Suggested mantras or mottoes include:

- "I am not God."
- "Anger breaks bridges between us."
- "Anger expects; love accepts."
- "I'm OK; You're OK."
- "Different doesn't mean bad."
- "Don't cut what you can untie."
- "I need to get off my soapbox."

Discuss the results of using a mantra or motto in terms of: (a) what the client has become aware of; (b) how its use may have altered the client's behavior.

7

WORKING WITH
CHRONICALLY ANGRY
CLIENTS: GENERAL
GUIDELINES

This chapter presents a number of guidelines for therapists working with chronically angry clients. We have already mentioned a few of these, such as linking the client's anger to family-of-origin behaviors and beliefs. Other strategies—for example, discouraging excessive ventilation of anger—have at least been implied. Still others, including minimizing the risk of aggression through nonthreatening interventions, are new. Together, these principles serve as guidelines for work with all angry clients, but especially those who are chronically angry. The next chapter, then, will focus upon principles for working with chronically angry substance abusers.

General guidelines for working with chronically angry clients include:

- Respect the client's anger and right to be angry.

- Assess the risk for physical aggression against self or others.

- Minimize the risk of aggression through nonthreatening interventions.

- Do not encourage excessive ventilation of anger.

- Encourage clients to turn anger into appropriate action.

- Listen for other emotions connected with anger displays.

- Assess the behavioral, cognitive, affective, and spiritual components of clients' anger and plan treatment accordingly.

- Investigate clients' gains from their angry behavior.

- Relate anger patterns to clients' family-of-origin behavior and beliefs.

- Link anger patterns to current family (or other systems) patterns.

- Check for a history of physical, sexual, and emotional abuse.

- Check for the client being a perpetrator of abuse.

- Model your own ability to handle anger appropriately.

GUIDELINES

Respect the Client's Anger and Right to Be Angry

Anger is a messy emotion. Some therapists don't like to see it at all. Others tolerate it for a while, then become impatient with their clients who won't or don't work through it. Others readily encourage the expression of anger, as long as the client is not angry with them.

We need to respect the client's anger and right to be angry. This means that counselors should never assume that someone's anger is simply irrational. Doing so constitutes a failure of empathy, since this feeling seldom seems totally unreasonable to those who are angry. Our first task is to discover the meaning of the anger to the client, not to judge its appearance. We must be able fully to "hear" our clients' anger.

One implication is that calming down the angry client may

not always be the helper's task. Indeed, there may be situations when we want to encourage a client's anger. This is particularly true with anger avoidant individuals, but it may even be necessary with chronically angry individuals on rare occasions.

Clients may become upset and angry with their therapists. Again, this is not always problematic. It may be beneficial, a sign that a client trusts you enough to share these painful feelings. Helpers must learn to tolerate a certain amount of anger directed at them without panicking or counterattacking. This does not mean allowing oneself to become a target of abuse. But it is inappropriate to consider as dangerous or unacceptable every episode of client anger toward their therapists.

Nor can we explain all anger toward therapists as client projection and transference. Sometimes client anger may reflect a breach in the relationship. For instance, the counselor may have broken a promise to the client, been distracted by a phone call, or said something thoughtless. If so, we need to deal directly with the content of that anger.

On the other hand, it is not necessary to encourage every episode of anger. Nor should therapists assume that there is always a just cause for their clients' anger. What we are talking about here is an attitude of respect, balanced by an ear for reality. One way to phrase this is: Assume the legitimacy of a client's anger while listening carefully for underlying feelings and/or contradictions in content.

Assess the Risk for Physical Aggression Against Self or Others

Most angry clients are just that—*angry*. Only a small percentage of these individuals turn those feelings into physical aggression. Even those who do so are unlikely to be violent frequently, although they may often threaten aggression.

Nevertheless, it is necessary to assess the risk for violence with every angry client, both during initial encounters with these clients and on an ongoing basis. The possible damage is simply too great to ignore.

The most direct way to gain this information is to ask for it. Typical questions include: "Are you thinking about hurting _____?" "Have you been threatening to hurt anyone?" "I

see how angry you are today. Have you been able to control it?"
With continuing clients, one might ask, "We've talked about the
need for you to stay away from violence (aggression, hitting, etc.),
but I hear you're having trouble today. Have you broken your
promise? Are you thinking about it?"

Be aware that some chronically aggressive individuals are mas-
ters at only answering or responding to exactly what is asked.
Thus, inquiring if a person has hurt someone may get a negative
response because: "Well, you asked if I hurt her. No, I didn't.
She was able to get up and walk around right away and there
weren't any bruises." Here it is useful to frame your questions
using the client's words. Instead of asking if this client hurt someone, it might have been more useful to find out if he had "stuck
up" for himself, "disciplined" his children, or "pushed her around
a little," if those are phrases this particular client utilizes. Other
tactics involve asking broad questions or a wide series of questions covering a range of aggressive behaviors: hitting, slapping,
shoving, spanking, pinching, threatening, restraining, etc.

Remember to ask angry clients if they have any intention of
harming themselves, especially if there is any history of self-
mutilation, suicidal ideation, or suicide attempts. Sometimes clients' desire to harm themselves is linked to having harmed another person, especially if the person they have damaged is
someone close, with whom they are symbiotically entangled.

A person's history is the best predictor of violence. While no
one (often including the client) can predict exactly when or
where someone will become aggressive, the probability increases
whenever environmental situations similar to past episodes occur. For example, a woman with a history of child abuse may
report that "My stress level is up again. I just got laid off so I'm
home with the kids more." The last time this stress elevation
occurred she quickly became rageful at her children. This recur-
rence should be taken as a danger signal.

The use or return to use of alcohol or mood-altering chemicals
may also be a predictor of aggression, particularly for those who
have been treated for those concerns. And it is important to
remember that individuals with no history of violence may become very aggressive when exposed to both life stress and a new
or especially activating drug.

Counselors are charged with protecting the physical safety of clients, their families and the general public. We will not attempt to address this issue in detail here, since we are not legal experts. However, virtually every state has mandatory reporting laws regarding child abuse and the duty to report danger to others. The standard demand to honor our clients' privacy is normally waived in these two situations, as well as when suicide is threatened.

Minimize the Risk of Aggression Through Nonthreatening Interventions

Clients sometimes become irate with their therapists during individual sessions as well as with family and peers during couples, family, and group therapy. They may raise their voices, begin to make exaggerated gestures, pace around, and make increasingly emotional statements. They may directly threaten the counselor.

This is no time for "macho" tests—especially if you're our size. Rather, the goals are to help these individuals regain their composure and to reestablish the counseling setting as a sanctuary where violence is not permitted.

The first step is to make sure that you are speaking calmly and moving slowly. Remember that many individuals become angry when they are afraid. Therefore, anything the counselor can do to lessen clients' fear will usually also help with their anger. Your calmness will give everyone, including yourself, a "no panic" message. Your quiet authority may be needed. In some cases counselors may choose to give out "bursts" of extremely relaxed and nondefensive body language, such as opening one's arms, leaning back easily, relaxing face and eye muscles. These behaviors can have a profoundly calming effect on anxious, tense, and angry clients. These muscular and postural changes tell clients that the situation does not have to be threatening to either party. On some occasions giving this message nonverbally may have a stronger effect than a verbal message to "relax," which the angry client may feel obligated to oppose.

Secondly, encourage all those involved to sit down and lower their voices. Certain angry individuals may need to be told to push their chairs farther away from each other. Some clients may need to hear that specific behaviors are unacceptable in this setting and to be told clearly that the session will have to be ended if aggressive actions are not stopped immediately. Sometimes participants, including children and adolescents, must be informed or reminded about time-out policies and, if necessary, time-outs must be implemented. These policies should be stated from the start of counseling, not suddenly imposed when someone has begun to act inappropriately.

Thirdly, attempt to ally with everyone in the name of safety. The idea is to get the angry person(s) to *choose* calmness rather than making them do so. Statements such as "Remember, Sue, you told me you didn't want this session to end in a screaming match" can be helpful. In fact, each anger episode that occurs in therapy can ultimately be converted into an opportunity for all concerned to endorse non-aggression and learn new communication skills.

There are individuals who will simply not abide by these rules. For them, counseling sessions are just another place to demonstrate their anger and aggression. Therapy is not helpful with these persons and should be forsworn in favor of legal or community alternatives.

Do Not Encourage Excessive Ventilation of Anger

We have previously discussed the work of Carol Tavris (1989). Her main point is that ventilation of one's anger simply "rehearses" that anger. Rather than making individuals less angry, ventilation tactics may ultimately increase their overall level of anger.

Counselors in the chemical dependency field are trained to help their clients recover by encouraging them to express their feelings. The concept is that recovering persons who don't share their feelings will eventually drink as a way to manage those feelings. While there is certainly much truth in this model, it is a somewhat simplistic interpretation of recovery. It could also be argued that some persons relapse because they indulge in feelings excessively, not because they inhibit them. This certainly is the case with many chronically angry individuals.

Most chronically angry persons should not be encouraged to ventilate their anger. They already know how to do that. Instead, they need to learn how to contain their anger while experiencing and expressing other emotions. They need anger management and anger reduction skills.

An exception to this may be those chronically angry persons who deny their anger, become passive-aggressive, or develop long-term resentments that never get expressed. These individuals will need to learn how to recognize and share their angry feelings. Even here, though, the therapist must proceed cautiously. Blowing up at others should never be encouraged for its own sake or in the name of general mental health.

Encourage Clients to Turn Anger into Appropriate Action

Most chronically angry persons fail to realize how ineffective most of their anger is. Perhaps they mistakenly believe they are getting results because their bodies respond so intensely to their anger. Or they may feel powerful as they see others reacting to their anger with fear. What they don't recognize is that their gains are usually short-lived. Their angry behavior often does not produce any real changes in their situations. With help, they can understand that angry action is often useless or inefficient.

It can be helpful to teach the concepts of "useful" and "useless" anger to chronically angry clients. Useful anger signals real problems and leads to effective actions that result in long-term benefit to clients and their families. Useless anger occurs when individuals become irate over imaginary or trivial problems and when their anger is not directed into effective action that produces long-term benefits. As stated before, anger itself is a good signal but a poor solution for most problems. One goal with all angry clients is to help them productively use their angry energy. This often means converting aggressive behavior into assertive communication but may also include anger reduction strategies.

This process often occurs in several stages. First, clients report their explosions at others to their counselors. Second, with the active assistance of the therapist, they begin to catalogue the negative consequences of their actions. Third, they are taught some basic ways to stop their most damaging behaviors, such as by taking time-outs and challenging negative thinking (several tactics are discussed in Chapter 10). Ceasing old behaviors simply creates a social vacuum, however. Clients must then be helped to substitute new behaviors for the old, such as giving others praise instead of criticism. In doing so, they often discover that others are more cooperative when they are less hostile, which improves the likelihood of their continuing the new behavior.

These new actions are still problem-oriented. However, the definition of the problem may change, with a greater emphasis upon individuals' taking responsibility for their own thoughts, feelings, and actions rather than blaming others. They also begin to recognize that they often make themselves angry, in contrast to their old position of assuming that others are at fault.

Listen for Other Emotions Connected with Anger Displays

Chronically angry individuals may be oversensitive to their own anger cues and undersensitive to all or many other feelings. Therapists working with these persons need to wonder aloud about what other feelings might be hidden under the anger.

Fear is the most commonly hidden emotion. This is especially true for jealous clients, who camouflage massive amounts of insecurity with layers of possessive anger. Many males have been trained to convert fear reactions into anger because fear is seen as unmasculine. But for both genders fear may underlie or accompany anger displays and should always be considered.

Sadness is another common fellow traveler with anger. For example, a woman may feel sad, disappointed, and hurt about her partner's failure to remember her birthday. Instead of sharing these feelings, which would increase her vulnerability, she goes into a tirade about his lack of caring. Grief commonly includes a portion of anger — grief at a loss or a contemplated loss.

Anger can partially obscure deep feelings of shame and guilt, as we discussed in Chapter 6.

Certain chronically angry individuals substitute anger displays for joy and happiness. Once again the issue is avoiding vulnerability.

Therapists must be careful not to insist that their chronically angry clients explore their other feelings. After all, their anger is a defense against just this awareness. But we do need to invite these individuals to notice their entire range of feelings. Usually all that is needed is this simple question: "If you weren't so angry right now, what else would you be feeling?" Initially many clients will deny having other feelings. Gradually, however, they will start to answer this question and then to begin asking it of themselves.

Appropriate self-disclosure can be useful in helping angry clients confront their other feelings. A statement such as "When I was in a similar situation, I felt angry, but I also felt . . . " may help chronically angry individuals become more sensitive to a wider range of emotions. Thoughtful disclosures on the part of the therapist may enable chronically angry persons to examine their own internal processes less defensively.

Assess the Behavioral, Cognitive, Affective and Spiritual Components of the Client's Anger and Plan Treatment Accordingly

Chronically angry individuals differ in the patterns and manifestations of their anger. We have found it useful to distinguish four major life areas that may be affected. Each life area calls for differently focused treatment strategies. While most chronically angry clients have issues in each area, the relative significance of each area differs with every person.

The key word in assessing the behavioral component here is "habit." Angry behavior is seen as a product of overlearning. Certain individuals have practiced their anger for so long, on so many different occasions, that such behavior has become unthinking and automatic. Chronic anger is a deeply entrenched pattern of predictable behaviors. These behaviors are observable, familiar, and highly resistant to alteration. They occur in predictable chains that lead toward verbal or physical explosions if they cannot be intercepted. These behaviors are most easily altered at the beginning of the chain, before they gain momentum. It is necessary not only to stop old behavior but also to substitute newer and less damaging actions.

A behavioral focus usually involves attempting to locate how the client's angry actions have been or are currently being perpetuated. This may be a simple process, as when the client tells the counselor that she likes getting what she wants and the best way is by getting mad. However, the reward mechanism may be far more subtle or erratic, such as when parents of a angry child occasionally and unpredictably "give in" to that child's unreasonable demands, parental behavior that strongly reinforces the anger and makes it hard to extinguish.

Sometimes the rewards are mostly in the distant past. Habits that were formed years before, such as distrusting whatever others say or criticizing for the sake of criticizing, are maintained in the present even in the face of strong and immediate discouragement. Such behavior has become automatic and, if left unchallenged, can continue indefinitely.

With chronically angry clients who have developed these automatic, habitual patterns, the goal of treatment becomes behavioral retraining. The key point is that clients must learn to *do* things differently than before, since "old behavior leads to old results." New behaviors include such simple actions as sitting down and staying quiet rather than standing and yelling. Many are detailed in our "Fair Fighting" list provided in Chapter 10.

Behavioral change is usually a gradual process, with at least occasional setbacks. Clients will seldom be able to completely eradicate their angry overreactions to life's emergencies. However, they can usually learn to cut off many anger episodes, to replace anger-provoking and -maintaining behaviors with neutral ones, and to minimize the damage they do with their anger and aggression.

Counselors have a central role in this change process. Because counselors have not gotten caught up in their clients' anger routines, they can offer new behaviors and help them practice these behaviors in a safe setting. Since their clients initially are trapped in previously unquestioned behavioral routines, they may have to offer structured ideas to their clients on how to change. When focusing on behavior, counselors need to help clients develop a personalized repertoire of alternatives to angry behavior. In addition, they need to be able to help their clients creatively discover new solutions to old problems.

The goal, at the behavioral level, is to help chronically angry clients substitute new, less angry and aggressive actions for their previously automatic behaviors.

The key word in the cognitive realm is "choice." Many chronically angry individuals have developed such rigid styles of thinking that they automatically interpret others' words and deeds as hostile. They then respond defensively, never challenging their own distorted thinking process. Cognitive therapy consists largely in identifying the client's assumptions about the world and providing the client with an opportunity to challenge and alter them.

Many chronically angry persons believe that the world is full of people who spend their time thinking of ways to make them miserable. They view themselves as relatively helpless victims of the aggression and ill will of others. They feel continually vulnerable to attacks, which they are certain will come from the dangerous, thoughtless, or revengeful people who surround them.

This way of thinking has been labeled "paranoid process" thinking (Meissner, 1986). Meissner notes that individuals with this tendency see the world as "filled with sinister meanings and malevolent intentions." He suggests four characteristics of persons who have paranoid process thinking that are relevant here: (1) They blame others for their unhappiness; (2) they are continually suspicious of the motivations of others, remaining doubtful and guarded; (3) they feel superior to others (grandiose), always ready to criticize and find fault, while refusing to accept even constructive criticism; (4) they often believe that others are thinking about and plotting against them when there is no evidence that this is the case.

Many chronically angry persons are at least a little paranoid, although most would not meet psychiatric criteria for true paranoid disorders. One of the ways they stay angry is by convincing themselves that the world is bad and that they are innocent victims. They simply do not trust others and so have to stay on guard against a threatening environment. This belief system is often so firmly entrenched as to be virtually impermeable, much to the dismay of family members and others who try to help these persons feel better. They find that chronically angry individuals remain suspicious despite massive amounts of love and caring. The fact that chronically angry individuals often project their own hostile responses onto others fuels this "steady state" level of distrust.

Chronically angry persons also tend to make other cognitive assumptions that contribute to their problem. One of these is the belief that they simply are angry ("I'm just an angry person and I always will be"). Another is that they are helpless when faced with anger ("My anger takes over. I can't do a thing to stop it"). Averill (1982) labels this pervasive belief the "passion" model of anger. Anger is viewed as a strong passion that controls an individual when it strikes, along the lines of instant love, or a lightning bolt that strikes powerfully and irresistibly. Since people cannot stop this from happening, there is no hope to control it. Another problematic belief is that others are responsible for one's anger ("It's her fault. She deserves my anger"). Blaming patterns like this are a good way to support perpetual anger. Finally, many chronically angry persons believe that anger and aggression are good solutions ("Getting mad makes you feel better"; "A good spanking never hurt any kid"). They justify their chronic anger, turning it into a positive attribute.

Cognitive therapy with chronically angry individuals focuses upon helping clients discover their cognitive model, which includes their general assumptions about the world as well as their specific interpretations of immediate situations. The goal is for them eventually to dispute outdated or unrealistic beliefs that add to their anger. Counselors should note, however, that simply trying to argue clients out of these beliefs seldom works. For instance, the therapist who insists that nobody is out to get his client may well hear something like this: "But the world *is* a bad place. It's full of evil people." The client may then offer up example after example to prove this point: a spouse whom he must watch carefully so she doesn't talk with other men, an employer who passes him by at promotion time, relatives who gossip about him, so-called friends who inevitably turn into enemies because of the mean or uncaring things they do. As Meissner suggests, a better counseling strategy is to take a relatively neutral stand, empathizing with the client while simultaneously offering alternative explanations of life's events. The process is a gradual one, in which the first step is to appreciate the client's world view, then to bring it into doubt, and only then to help the client dispute it.

We will discuss two useful cognitive tactics in Chapter 9. These are converting disasters into disappointments and learning how to choose which anger invitations to accept.

When assessing the affective component, the key word is "moderation." As mentioned before, strong anger is a mood-altering experience that some individuals seem to seek. Anger acts as a physical stimulant, allowing a person to feel more alive and energetic. (Readers are referred to Chapter 6 for a more detailed discussion of this phenomenon.)

Therapeutic intervention at this level is complex. Counselors must validate their client's right to some anger while discouraging wholesale ventilation of that feeling. "Anger binges" must be eliminated to assure the safety of clients and their families. Anger management themes must be balanced carefully with the need for general anger reduction. Clients may also need to grieve the loss of the exhilaration that accompanies strong anger. This exhilaration may not be immediately replaceable, at least until the client develops a true capacity for intimacy.

Material on the use of an "anger thermometer" to help clients understand the difference between normal and extreme anger is discussed in the exercises at the end of this chapter.

Finally, let us consider the spiritual component. Chronic anger has negative effects upon a person's sense of place in the world. It encourages some people to become "mean-spirited." Gradually, they become filled with despair, bitterness, cynicism, and hate. Their anger, which they are unable to release, hardens into powerfully encrusted resentment. Anger begets rage, resentment begets hatred, and the chronically angry individual loses hope that life is or could ever be good. Many chronically angry persons feel deeply isolated, estranged from others and alienated from any sense of their own inner goodness.

"Forgiveness" is a central concept in the area of spiritual anger.

Forgiving others (and oneself) is a way to release long stored resentments (Potter-Efron & Potter-Efron, 1991). It allows people to get on with their lives. However, therapists cannot force anyone to forgive. Sometimes a person is simply too hostile to consider it. For example, a client was recently referred to us for "anger work" by another counselor. This client made it clear that he had no intention of forgiving his ex-wife: "Forgive her? Never! I'm going to make her pay first. I want to take the kids from her. I want my revenge." This individual is more than willing to be filled with rage. He is obsessed with the desire for revenge, a common occurrence with very angry persons who blame others for their pain. Hatred of others has worked its way into the very core of this person's being.

The therapist's best ally at the spiritual level is a client's emotional and spiritual exhaustion. At some point chronically angry individuals may decide that they just cannot continue living a life of unmitigated anger and resentment. Just like the alcoholic or drug addict, they get "sick and tired of being sick and tired." Therapists who are attuned to this pattern can help their clients reach this stage by calling their attention to the signs of their growing impatience and discomfort with their anger. Comments such as "You say you will never forgive your parents for what they did to you and yet you seem to be tired of carrying around all this hatred" and "What effects has all this anger had on you emotionally and spiritually?" can be quite useful in this regard. Other useful tactics include pointing out how much energy it takes to sustain this level of anger and focusing upon the loneliness that such estrangement creates in the client.

Investigate Clients' Gains from Their Angry Behavior

Chapter 6 describes possible gains from chronic anger. The challenge here is to gather and utilize this information.

It may be useful to take an entire outpatient session on this material relatively early in treatment, using it as a bridge between assessment and therapy. It is helpful to have a sheet prepared with the various functions of anger listed vertically on it, along with plenty of space to write, as described in the exercise on Functions of Anger at the end of Chapter 6. Each anger function can then be described to the client (and immediate family, if appropriate). They should be presented in a "Some people use their anger this way. Is this at all like you?" format. Clients can then be asked to rank order their responses to determine which functions are most relevant to them. Clients should also be asked if they use their anger for any purposes other than those presented on the list.

Clients frequently become quite interested in this material. Few of them have thought about their anger in terms of its function and so they gain important insights about their behavior, as well as incentive to change, while doing the exercise. For instance, a woman who realizes that she becomes angry primarily in order to keep others emotionally distant may become powerfully motivated to address her underlying fear of intimacy as part of her treatment. Therapists and clients can enter into a dialogue about how clients can get their wants and needs met in a more direct manner. For example, individuals who employ their anger as a defense against shame can be helped to recognize their shame, to tell people directly about it, and to begin getting therapeutic help with their shame issues, so that they no longer have to avoid or cover their shame by being rageful at others.

The topic of "gain" itself may also be profitable to discuss. It is important to help clients realize that they will probably not succeed in changing their behavior until they are honest with themselves about what they get from their actions. Some clients resist this, insisting that they gain nothing but pain and remorse from their anger. If so, it may be useful to discuss specific anger episodes they have described that seem relevant, with the focus upon identifying other possible benefits of their anger. However, there is no value in arguing with clients, even with those who cannot identify the functions of their anger. It is especially wise not to argue with clients who use their anger to resist therapist authority or others' definitions of the situation. The therapist can instead agree with the client, for the time being, that the only results of his anger are negative, and use that "fact" as a motivator for change.

Relate Anger Patterns to Clients'
Family-of-Origin Behavior and Beliefs

Gathering information about the client's family of origin is part of the assessment process described in Chapter 5 (question 6). During treatment, the goal is to help the client break family-of-origin connections that anchor anger.

The simplest connections are those in which a client emulates the behavior of the same-sexed parent: "My father was angry all the time and I'm just like him." Crossover identification is also possible: "My mother was a weakling and my dad was tough. So I decided to be like him." Therapy consists of helping these clients remember the negative consequences of that parent's anger and gently challenging loyalty bonds that prevent clients from choosing their own lifestyle. It is possible that maintenance of anger can be a loyalty issue, a way of clinging to a parent's perspective or even a parent's presence when an angry parent has died prior to any reconciliation.

Some individuals report that they always wanted to be the opposite of their parents, but "Even though I swore I would never be like my mother, I guess I am." Often this is modified as follows: "I don't hit anybody like she did, but maybe my yelling and screaming are just as bad." Often these people feel very guilty about their anger and aggression. However, they have not found effective alternatives to the behaviors they saw modeled when they were children. Therapy starts at a behavioral level but usually moves rapidly into powerful family-of-origin issues that bind individuals into behavior patterns they themselves despise.

Family of origin may or may not be a topic of concern with any client. Therapists do need to guard against distractions, especially if the client is both angry and aggressive: Family-of-origin concerns cannot take the place of an interest in the client's current functioning, but they can be used to cast light on that individual's present activities and the behavioral changes needed.

Link Anger Patterns to Current Family
(and Other Systems) Patterns

Angry persons often live in angry families. For instance, a drug addict may be irritable and irrational, especially when she is intoxicated. Meanwhile, her partner may have become hostile and resentful over the years, only partly because of her. He might even use her addiction as an excuse to indulge in bouts of morally superior righteous indignation. Meanwhile, some of the children in this family may have taken advantage of the chaos to become unmanageable, reacting to parental authority with rage. Even the baby may have already begun to respond with anger to the world. In short, some families center their emotional lives around anger.

Beyond the family, people may find themselves working in situations that generate hostility, perhaps with chronically angry colleagues or employers. Such systems certainly encourage anger among their participants. It is important to screen all angry clients for these extrafamilial sources of stress and anger.

Of course, we don't want to provide clients with "it's all their fault" excuses for their anger. Each person must take responsibility for his or her own thoughts and actions. However, it may be unrealistic to focus our energy entirely upon an individual, as if that person were solely accountable for all the family anger.

The family as a whole may be invested in a particular individual's anger. For example, family members may encourage one member's anger because they sense that the alternative for that person is deep depression, or because it gives the rest of the family a sense of togetherness, as they close ranks in response to him. Anger may give a family energy or keep it from being destroyed by its secrets.

Angry clients need regular help containing their anger and aggression. When they do so, some of these individuals then discover for themselves just how angry others in their families are. They may begin to realize that their partner may have a separate and discrete anger problem. Furthermore, they recognize that the family's problems will not end until *everybody* in the family does something about the pervasive anger. This can be a significant turning point in therapy, especially if the client uses this information to make a stronger personal commitment to anger reduction or management—for instance, by deciding to change his behavior not only to improve his own life but also to help the entire family. However, therapists do need to guard against their clients' messianic zeal. It is helpful for clients to

want to encourage their families growth but dangerous if they
invest too much of their time and energy in it. Again, the first
consideration is changing one's own actions, thoughts, and feelings. Therapists must remind themselves and their clients not to
become distracted by focusing too much attention on the anger
of other family members.

Some clients are reluctant to change until somebody or everybody else quits being so mad. These people argue, with some
validity, that they will be trampled if they act nicely while others
are still rampaging. Certainly this could happen, in particular
when they first alter their behavior. Still, usually someone has to
go first in these situations. Waiting until everyone else is equally
ready to quit being so angry may take forever. It is better to
encourage these individuals to adjust their behavior for the personal gains they will receive, with the hope that others will eventually notice and change as well. A useful analogy is that of
throwing a rock (their being less angry) into a pond: The ripples
from the rock's splash eventually touch everything on the pond.

Couples therapy with angry individuals seems to work best
when both partners identify themselves as having problems with
anger, since both partners are then motivated to learn anger
management tactics. Family therapy is another opportunity for
anger therapy. It, too, has the best prospect of success when the
family understands that it has an anger problem as a whole unit.
However, when only one person seems to have an anger problem,
individual therapy may be preferable.

Counselors should remember that couples or family counseling may place certain individuals at risk for being physically or
emotionally attacked. For this reason, we must be cautious in
scheduling couples or family work. Getting specific no-violence
and no-retaliation promises from each participant can help increase the safety of all concerned. However, such promises are
easier to make than keep. It is advisable privately to ask each
member of a couple or family if he or she has any reason to fear
participation in collective therapy. Even a moment's hesitation
may be reason to reconsider this move. Occasional individual
sessions in the midst of couples or family therapy may also provide a haven for clients to disclose what they have been too afraid
to reveal in larger sessions. If any evidence does emerge that a

client's participation in couples or family therapy puts her or him in danger, these sessions should be suspended.

Check for a History of Physical, Sexual and Emotional Abuse; Check for the Client Being a Perpetrator of Abuse

Many chronically angry persons have been the victims of physical, sexual, and/or emotional abuse. This information may surface during the initial assessment process or during the course of treatment. Abuse may have been perpetrated during the client's youth or may be occurring presently. Chronically angry clients may also be current recipients of abuse.

A history of abuse contributes to chronic anger problems in many ways. First, survivors of these attacks against the self may become embittered, blaming others for their inability to protect them. Second, a survivor's model of how to act and how to get what he wants in the world may reflect the aggression that worked in his family of origin. Third, others in a family may have been angry as well, teaching the survivor that chronic anger is normal. Fourth, a survivor may have learned to use rage as a defense against a shame-based self-concept, regularly attacking others around him when he feels inadequate.

We have just discussed the tendency of entire families to become angry. Similarly, physical and sexual abusiveness can occur among any or all members of certain families. At any given time an individual may be survivor, current victim, and/or perpetrator of abuse. Victims can easily become victimizers (Nielsen, 1990). One example would be a male incest survivor of an assault by an uncle who is currently being molested by an older brother and who molests some of the children he babysits. Another example is a woman who was beaten by her mother, is being currently verbally and emotionally abused by her boyfriend, and who hits her children.

It is important to assess the possibility that chronically angry clients are perpetrators of abuse. Very hostile individuals may rationalize such behavior as giving others only what they deserve, or they may see their abusive behavior as a weapon to be used in the perpetual battle between themselves and the world.

However, we want to caution counselors not to assume that physical or sexual abuse is inevitable with chronically angry clients. Anger does not always lead to aggression.

Emotional abuse is another concern relevant to anger and the perpetuation of abuse. A reasonable definition of the rather vague concept of emotional abuse is any behavior, physical or verbal, that is significantly disrespectful of the rights and needs of others. Chronically angry persons often specialize in attacking others' sense of self, inflicting damaging psychological wounds, and deeply shaming others. All this may seem perfectly routine to chronically angry individuals, simply an extension of their own sense of self. Never having been treated respectfully themselves, they inflict emotional abuse upon others as a matter of course.

Current physical and sexual abuse perpetration must be addressed as a first priority in treatment. Such activities must be reported to protect the safety of the client's family. Clients can be informed that ensuring the security of their family is a necessary aspect of treatment, something that is even more compelling than their personal issues (or their chemical dependency treatment). A frequently helpful approach to use with past victims of abuse who are now perpetrators is to tell them that you intend to protect their families in a way they themselves needed but did not receive as children. In any case, safety issues must take precedence over therapy, even if that means that the client withdraws from treatment.

Respectful communication should be stressed with those individuals whose chronic anger leads to emotional abuse. Many will need much help in this area. In particular, individuals who have not had any previous positive modeling will need to be given help in establishing appropriate standards and techniques for interacting respectfully with others.

Model Your Own Ability to Handle Anger Appropriately

Working with very angry persons can be challenging. Faced with another's irrational anger, it is easy to respond with alarm. The result can be inappropriate counselor displays of fear, anger, and aggression.

We will treat this subject in more detail in Chapter 12. For now, we want to emphasize the need for helpers to model anger control, anger reduction, and moderation in the communication of anger with their clients.

Angry clients invite counselors to explode with their own anger, especially if they directly attack the helper's competence or personality. In addition, it can be quite frustrating to listen repeatedly to the complaints of some chronically angry clients. For example, clients who consistently misunderstand the efforts of their families may astound and annoy therapists who have empathy with those others. Therapists need to resist these temptations to become angry. Giving in to them is seldom good therapy and should not be justified. Besides, most angry people have themselves often been treated angrily, and they have very effective defenses against counselor anger. Combining directness and patience is more useful for the therapist in working with angry clients.

Angry clients are best helped by calm and considerate counselors who clearly model an ability to control their anger without accepting abuse. Since most clients are not particularly hostile during therapy sessions, some of this modeling may have to come through therapist self-disclosure. Although these disclosures should be limited in quantity, it may be useful to tell clients a few stories about the anger invitations the counselor has received and what the counselor has done with them. As with any self-disclosure, the most effective sharing is that which is clearly relevant to the client (she could see herself in a similar situation), in which the therapist makes use of tools or tactics within the capacity (current or projected) of the client. Then, through the process of identification, clients learn that they can handle their anger in a more productive manner.

EXERCISES

7-1 *Freedom from Anger*

Encouraging clients to identify the other feelings they mask or lose in their anger is often a primary step toward real change in treatment. The following exercise is useful in this regard.

Instruct clients: "Fill in the following sentence, each time with a new answer. Try not to censor yourself. Write whatever comes to mind. If this is too difficult for you to do, fill in the sentence by observing what others do when they are not angry, and record these things. How would it feel to be free in these ways?"

If I were free of my anger, I might . . .

1. _____

2. _____

3. _____

4. _____

5. _____

6. _____

7. _____

8. _____

9. _____

10. _____

7-2 Internal Sources of Anger

Chronically angry persons often blame others for their discomfort. In order to stop blaming, they must become more aware of the conditions *inside* their skin instead of staying exclusively externally focused. The following checklist can be used by clients to help them become more aware of how internal conditions can contribute to their anger with others. Ask the client to complete one of these checklists for each anger episode.

INTERNAL CONDITIONS CHECKLIST

Did I sleep poorly prior to this anger episode?   Yes No
   Comments:

Did I have uncomfortable physical aches and pains   Yes No
prior to this episode?
   Comments:

Was I feeling insecure or inadequate in any way   Yes No
prior to this anger episode?
   Comments:

Was I using or withdrawing from mood-altering   Yes No
substances (including alcohol) prior to this anger
episode?
   Comments:

Was I feeling hungry, anxious, lonely, or tired prior   Yes No
to this anger episode?
   Comments:

Was I already feeling depressed, tense, or over-   Yes No
whelmed prior to this anger episode?
   Comments:

Was I feeling envious or jealous prior to this anger   Yes No
episode?
   Comments:

Was anything else going on inside me that might   Yes   No
have affected my thoughts or feelings prior to this
anger episode?
  Comments:

Ask clients to bring checklists to their appointments, and use them actively to help clients understand how their internal states affect their relationships with others.

7-3 *Aggression Management*

Ask each group member to make a list of the aggressive behaviors s/he needs to stop. Use the following simple format:

Physical aggression I need to stop:

Threats of aggression I need to stop:

Verbal violence I need to stop:

Have the group divide into smaller groups of two or three. In these smaller groups, have individuals help each other work out a PLAN for stopping the aggression, starting with physical aggression. Use the following format:

MY PLAN

Instead of   I will

When people have completed this task, bring the group together as a whole once again. Ask each group member to share his plan with the rest of the group. Establish a group time for regular reporting and problem-solving related to these plans during the next several weeks.

7-4 Loud and Soft Anger

Many chronically angry persons think they have to express their anger aggressively and loudly, with mean looks and biting words. They feel that if they haven't yelled at someone or called names, they haven't really "gotten their anger out." Some have grown up in angry families where only the noisiest anger demands attention.

During individual or group sessions, have the angry individual practice expressing anger to an empty chair representing someone with whom he or she is angry. Work one specific situation at a time. Point out that often the most effective expression of anger is quiet and definite (be prepared to give examples). Have the client experiment with ways of expressing anger that are more reserved than usual, but which are clear and definite.

Encourage clients to notice how they feel about themselves during this process, as well as how well they think they are getting their point across. Give your own feedback and ask for group or family feedback as well. In some cases, it may be possible to establish that less noisy anger expression *increases* the person's self-respect and credibility.

7-5 Calming Mantras

A mantra is a short sentence that can be the focal point of meditation, a compulsively repeated accomplishment to a day's activities, or a comforting reminder when needed. Chronically angry persons can benefit from a calming mantra assigned to them to use for a day, a week, or a month. Some will benefit from trying a new mantra each week, eventually finding the phrases that best comfort and control their angry feelings. Some suggested mantras for angry clients include:

- I will stay calm in this situation.
- Live and let live.
- Nobody's out to get me.
- Easy does it.
- No big deal.
- Nobody can make me mad.
- I'm beautiful.
- I'll look for the good instead of the bad.
- I can go with the flow.

7-6 *Accepting Differences*

Ask two partners who are disagreeing at a mild or moderate level to switch roles, and notice how they feel in the other's position. Ask them to argue that position the very best they can for their partner. Discuss the results with them, and introduce the concept of "being on each other's side" as a valid relationship concept. Have them role play "doing dishes efficiently" versus "having fun doing dishes" (or mowing the lawn, vacuuming, etc.). Encourage them to explore and approve of the differences in habits and values between them.

7-7 *The Anger Thermometer*

ENRAGED

MAD

ANNOYED

Draw a thermometer on the blackboard similar to the diagram shown. Label the bottom with a word indicating slight anger, and the top with a word indicating great anger, such as "annoyed" and "enraged." Ask clients to help fill in the thermometer by suggesting other words related to anger and indicating where they should be placed on the thermometer. The person suggesting each word is responsible for determining its relative position along the thermometer.

The following is only a partial list of words we've seen used on thermometers: annoyed, irritated, angry, mad, pissed off, rageful, furious, livid, seeing red, displeased, sullen, sulky, vexed, hateful, violent, out of it, explosive, upset, uptight, offended. Use any suggestions from the group, accepting them without judgment.

When as many words as possible have been filled in, begin at the base of the thermometer and ask for examples of situations that might cause someone to feel angry at each of the different levels, moving up the thermometer. A great deal of fun generally ensues, as both anger avoiders and chronically angry clients learn a more complete anger vocabulary. At the same time, participants become aware that what they mean when they say they are "pissed off" may be *very* different from what recipients of this message understand. Thus, this exercise expands the feeling vocabulary of clients and underscores the need for clearer communication.

7-8 *Managing Projection*

Since the purpose of projection is to not own up to one's own feelings, getting a client to recognize how he projects works best as an "inside out" activity.

(a) Begin by asking clients to identify and write down three positive qualities in others. Then ask them to own up to how they personally possess these qualities, either by discussing them with you or, preferably, by talking directly to the person they see as possessing these positive qualities. The instructions are first to share the positives seen in the other person, and then to acknowledge how they share these positive qualities.

(b) Then ask clients to identify and write down three negative qualities in others. This time clients are asked to own up to the negative qualities themselves, without confronting the other person (unless both are participants in a long-term therapy group where such confrontation is desirable and monitored by the therapists).

(c) Next clients are asked to spend time noticing what irritates them in others and identifying honestly whether they have these qualities also. Ask them to see others as teachers who can help them see themselves better for a time. Often clients will develop additional insight and increase their tolerance of others. They may become less perfectionistic as well.

8

WORKING in a CHEMICAL DEPENDENCY TREATMENT SETTING

The guidelines offered in Chapter 7 are generally applicable with all chronically angry clients. More specific suggestions in this chapter are intended for clients who are being seen currently for substance abuse concerns. They are also intended for clients who identify themselves as recovering alcoholics or drug addicts, regardless of whether they are currently in treatment for that condition.

Guidelines for working with chronically angry individuals within a chemical dependency framework include:

- Investigate the relationship between the client's ingestion of mood-altering substances and the appearance/severity of anger and aggression.

- Consider the possibility that mood-altering substances may have been used to contain anger.

- Challenge the belief that mood-altering chemicals are the cause of the client's inappropriate anger.

- Never offer chemical dependency treatment as a panacea for anger. Clients will need to work through problems related to anger during and after treatment.

- Promote chemical dependency treatment as a place to learn tools that can help clients understand and manage their anger.

- Invite clients to work through chronic anger issues as part of a general recovery program.

- Selectively employ the anger addiction model as a conceptual link between chemical dependency and anger management themes.

- Link relapse prevention with ongoing awareness and resolution of anger themes.

- Relate the client's anger to codependency and dysfunctional family-of-origin themes where relevant.

- Refer the client to an anger management specialist if significant anger issues remain after treatment for chemical dependency or codependency.

GUIDELINES

Investigate the Relationship Between the Client's Ingestion of Mood-Altering Substances and the Appearance/Severity of Anger and Aggression

As previously discussed, there are many possible connections between anger/aggression and substance use and abuse. Remember that anger and aggression may be associated with either the intoxication or withdrawal stages of alcohol or drug ingestion. In addition, certain substances, such as amphetamines, can produce or exacerbate paranoid thought processes. Alcohol and drug use may trigger irritability and the disinhibition of intrinsic anger. While no drug can be assumed to be "safe" for all persons, neither can any be labeled as invariably associated with anger or aggression. Each situation must be assessed empirically.

The simplest way to gather information about connections between substance abuse and anger or aggression is, of course, to ask the client. However, counselors need to recognize that they may very well be dealing with a *dual denial system*. Chemically dependent individuals may minimize both their use of mood-altering substances and their anger and aggression. Breaking through denial in one area does not necessarily lead to change in the other. Clients who finally recognize the severity of their alcohol or drug use do not automatically begin to face reality in other areas of their lives.

For example, the family of an older man complained that he was a long-term alcoholic and a former batterer who still was very abusive verbally to his wife and grown children. At the completion of outpatient treatment, he could admit (still somewhat reluctantly) that he had a drinking problem. However, he still adamantly refused to acknowledge his family's concerns about his anger. Six months later, faced with his wife's serious threat to leave, he was finally ready to face his anger and to deal with long buried issues from his family of origin that contributed to it (his father was both alcoholic and dangerously physically abusive).

Denial is a powerful defense against the truth. Each denial system may have to be encountered therapeutically and treated as a separate and distinct entity. With many clients there may be little generalization from one denial system to another.

Other clients can more easily make connections between their anger and substance consumption patterns. This is particularly true for "Dr. Jekyll and Mr. Hyde" types who become angry or aggressive only while under the influence. It is more difficult for individuals whose alcohol or drug use "sometimes" leads to excessive anger or aggression while perhaps helping them to feel "mellow" on other occasions. Counselors must be careful not to exaggerate the causal link between substance abuse and anger or aggression with these clients, insisting that substance abuse always leads to aggression, since doing so only lowers counselor credibility with those whose experience does not clearly match this simplification. Therapeutically, it is often sufficient to demonstrate that the client might get into trouble with anger when intoxicated. The analogy of playing Russian Roulette with one's anger may be useful here. Although these clients may not get angry every time they use alcohol or drugs, there is always the possibility they will, and when they do the results can be disastrous to them and their loved ones.

Consider the Possibility that Mood-Altering Substances May Have Been Used to Contain Anger

We have discussed this theme in connection with the topic of anger avoidance, noting that many anger avoiders utilize drugs in an effort to keep from recognizing or dealing effectively with their anger. Even chronically angry persons may sometimes attempt to get high for this purpose. Some individuals vacillate from one extreme to the other in expressing and avoiding their anger, much as a person with bipolar affective disorder switches between manic and depressive stages. At times these persons will drink or use drugs to disinhibit their anger, only to then use drugs to distract them from that anger. They may typically use one substance, such as alcohol, to promote their anger, and another, like marijuana, to dampen it.

Certain clients may go through chemical dependency treatment only to discover that they are becoming very angry during sobriety. This usually occurs with individuals who have used substances to contain their anger for many years. Now they are sober, with one less buffer between their feelings and their sense of self. They may be amazed to realize that they are actually capable of anger. Furthermore, they have few tools to deal with this anger productively, since they have avoided it before. They may very well be terrified, fearing that they will be consumed by their anger. Their families are unlikely to be pleased with this unexpected development. Therapists can best help by anticipating the emergence of anger, explaining it when it occurs, and helping clients accept their newfound anger without excessive ventilation or repression.

Some clients will make vows to avoid all forms of anger and violence as part of their recovery process. Such declarations must be handled with respect on the part of the therapist for the deep levels of shame and guilt of many recovering chemically dependent persons, who may see this commitment as a way to atone for past aggressive behavior. Unfortunately, such rigid promises may be unrealistic. They may even be dangerous to clients, who will then view their failure to stay totally serene as further evidence of their defectiveness and thus doubt their ability to succeed in any endeavor, including maintaining abstinence. Counselors may be able to help these persons realize that swinging like a pendulum from avoidance to explosion is not an effective long-term recovery plan.

Challenge the Belief that Mood-Altering Chemicals Are the Cause of the Client's Inappropriate Anger

"I was drunk" is never an entirely satisfactory explanation for anger or aggression. It is particularly unsatisfactory when it is stated by someone accused of battering, child abuse, or other forms of physical assault. All too frequently these arguments are made by people who wish to avoid taking responsibility for their actions. It is easier for them to make the substance itself the culpable party.

On the other hand, it is unrealistic to counter this proposal with an equally absurd claim that alcohol or drugs have nothing at all to do with anger and aggression, especially if the client is being treated for chemical dependency. Most frequently, these mood-altering substances are implicated somewhere. They distort judgment and allow some individuals to become disinhibited from normal constraints.

The key is to challenge simplistic solutions so that clients can eventually acknowledge both their substance abuse and their problems with anger. The goal is to discover how these two are linked with each client. See the exercises at the end of this chapter for aid in exploring this area.

It is often useful to investigate clients' assumptions about the connections between anger and substance use. For instance, one person might believe, "I was drunk. All drunks get angry. Therefore, I got angry." This explanation may fit the client's past experience and the beliefs of his family ("Oh, he always gets mad when he drinks. But all men do, don't they?"). Obviously, these beliefs constrict the client's choices. They can be challenged with new information provided in a non-accusatory manner. Some beliefs will have to be challenged repeatedly by both peers and counselors.

Never Offer Chemical Dependency Treatment as a Panacea for Anger

"Dry drunk" is a term that refers to those individuals who quit drinking or using drugs but fail to alter their thinking or lifestyle in any other way. The clear implication is that abstinence alone is not sufficient to achieve happiness or serenity.

Even working a 12-step program may not be enough to help chronically angry chemically dependent clients. Some programs do provide useful ideas on anger reduction and management. However, some persons, especially those with a separate diagnosis of major depressive disorder, may continue to be angry and irritable regardless of how often they attend Alcoholics Anonymous meetings.

Chemical dependency counselors must be wary of promising more than they can deliver. *Never promise clients that simply getting sober will remove their anger.* Until there is empirical evidence to the contrary, anger and chemical dependency should be regarded as independent variables.

Our clinical experience is that about half of the individuals who complete chemical dependency treatment immediately become far less angry and hostile. Anger is reduced to normal levels for some clients, while it is somewhat lessened in others. The head-clearing provided by abstinence may account for some of this change. And since for certain individuals the substances themselves were powerful stimulators of anger, their absence decreases irritation.

Chemically dependent clients with anger problems need to make a commitment to address these problems either during or after chemical dependency counseling. It is vital that therapists not collude, wittingly or unwittingly, with clients by "hoping" their anger will magically disappear with the achievement of abstinence.

Promote Chemical Dependency Treatment as
a Place to Learn Tools that Help Clients
Understand and Manage Their Anger

Many specific practices, tactics, and strategies commonly utilized in chemical dependency treatment programs are also valuable for those struggling with chronic anger issues. Clients with both problems can be assured that completing chemical dependency treatment will provide them with recovery tools that will also help them with their anger. This is one way to maintain the focus on alcohol and drug problems without completely losing track of related anger concerns.

Many chemical dependency programs, for example, ask their clients to complete a "feelings collage" early in treatment. This is an assignment in which clients collect or draw pictures that demonstrate selected feelings and then describe times when they felt such feelings. The goal is to help clients regain access to affects which have long been neglected. Many chemically dependent persons have lost contact with all or many of their emotions as their addictions have become primary. The feelings collage is usually presented in group therapy, which promotes mutual bonding as well as giving all members permission to feel.

Feelings collages are valuable to chronically angry persons. They provide the opportunity to rediscover feelings that may have been overshadowed by anger. Very angry or resentful individuals may also expose these tendencies in a caring peer environment. They may come to realize for the first time how limited life is when it is centered around one activity, substance consumption, and one feeling, anger.

Most chemical dependency treatment is group focused, with an emphasis upon peer communication. Socialization is encouraged as a way to combat the physical and emotional isolation common to addicted persons. This, too, is helpful to chronically angry individuals, especially those who tend to silently brood over their alleged injuries as they build resentments. Peer acceptance is also important for those clients who cover their shame with rage. These clients will often demonstrate this pattern with their peers, just as they do in other contexts. However, the result may be different from elsewhere, because peers in treatment, instead of letting themselves be pushed away, may help their angry cohorts deal with their shame issues. If so, these persons learn to trust others more and to use their rage less.

Some of the slogans of traditional 12-step chemical dependency programs are certainly applicable with chronic anger: "Let go," "One day at a time," and "First things first" may all help clients keep their minds on a positive channel. "Let go" applies to releasing old resentments. "One day at a time" helps those who work themselves into rages by imagining negative futures. "First things first" reminds people to focus on immediate issues while resolving problems.

Several of the A.A. steps can also be stressed to help those who identify themselves as chemically dependent with anger issues. For instance, the first step reads, "We admitted we were powerless over alcohol and our lives had become unmanageable." We have occasionally substituted the word "anger" for alcohol with clients who have already embraced this idea for their drinking or drug use. Clients can relate to the possibility that their angry behavior is similar in many ways to their other compulsive behaviors. The fourth and fifth steps, which ask participants to take a moral inventory and to present it to another human being and to God, help individuals recognize how their anger has enveloped and damaged them. The eighth and ninth steps, which encourage the person to take an inventory of all persons they have harmed and to make amends to those people, also has direct implications for those who have been harmfully angry or aggressive.

We realize that not all substance abuse programs are oriented to the 12-steps or Alcoholics Anonymous. Still, counselors need to be aware of this powerful resource and the many aspects of it which can benefit angry clients.

Invite Clients to Work Through Chronic Anger Issues as Part of a General Recovery Program

The emphasis here is upon providing clients with specific tools that can help them with abstinence (or control of their substance use if that is the program goal). However, the goal is really broader. It is to help certain individuals accept the goal of anger management as part of their total recovery program.

Within the context of A.A., it is often said that people sometimes get "sick and tired of being sick and tired." This phrase captures the despair of those who are caught in compulsive or addictive cycles of thoughts and behaviors. The chronically angry alcoholic or drug addict is really doubly captured—in chemical dependence and in chronic anger. Many such persons feel utterly helpless and hopeless about changing their lives because of this sense of despair.

Most chronically angry persons are as unhappy as they are angry. Until they find ways to release themselves from their rages, resentments, and uproars they cannot achieve any sense of serenity. They may indeed quit drinking or using drugs; however, this alone is insufficient to create peace of mind. Dealing with persistent or relentless anger must become a central theme in their recovery programs.

A minority of clients fits this category. Many chemically dependent individuals have no special problems with anger. Others have occasional problems under specific situations, such as moments of irrational jealousy. Still others might become predictably irate with particular individuals, such as their parents; they need help with these reactions. Anger is part of all of our vocabularies, and it will arise from time to time with almost every client during or after treatment.

Nevertheless, there is a significant proportion of drug and alcohol abusing clients who are chronically angry. These individuals need to be identified and helped to graft anger control or anger reduction themes into their overall life plan. Their chances for chemical dependency relapse decrease significantly when this is accomplished.

Counselors cannot force anyone to make a commitment to anger management, but they can offer invitations. Fortunately, many clients are exhausted from their lives of hostility and substance abuse. They may be greatly relieved to find people who recognize that they have been just as stuck with their anger as with their drugs and who are willing to assist them with both concerns.

Family work is invaluable. Other family members can often

detail how the client's anger has contributed to household problems and the relation of that anger to substance use. Clients can use family programs to discuss and perhaps release old grudges. The entire family can be encouraged to deal with anger in productive ways. Techniques to do this will be described in Chapter 10. The important goal is to help the family define its future not only as drug or alcohol free but also as free from aggression and useless chronic anger.

Selectively Employ the Anger Addiction Model as a Conceptual Link Between Chemical Dependency and Anger Management Themes

We introduced the concept of anger addiction in Chapters 5 and 6 when we described the mood-altering capacity of anger. To quickly review, some persons use anger to get "high." Such individuals feel very alive and energized when irate, more so than at any other time. Their anger excites, exhilarates, even intoxicates them. Frequent and stronger bouts of rage and fury are the logical consequence of this experience, as people gradually train themselves to tolerate and seek out this experience. Alcohol and drugs may be used to increase these anger sensations even further, as well as to seemingly release individuals from responsibility for their anger or aggression.

Eventually, the anger may gain control of persons who originally just wanted to have a little excitement in their lives. At this point, nothing but anger matters much anymore. The rest of life seems bland, dull, boring. Only strong anger, and then rage, and then perhaps blind rage, will provide these individuals with a sense of power and purpose. They have developed compulsive and unmanageable behavior patterns.

The reader may be wondering here about the distinction between addictions and compulsions. Unfortunately, no clear distinction exists as yet in the field of chemical dependency. Some writers reserve the term "addiction" for situations in which a clear physical (cellular) accommodation process can be observed or at least described. Others, such as Nakken (1988), describe addiction in a much broader framework ("a pathological love and trust relationship with an object or event"), which is virtually indistinguishable from compulsion. This process is described here as anger addiction simply because we believe clients, especially chemically dependent clients, can better identify with this term than with "anger compulsion."

The concept of anger addiction is offered primarily for those who are currently in abstinence-centered chemical dependency treatment programs or who have completed such programs in the past or who identify themselves as already belonging to an A.A.-type self-help group. As noted before, the concept of abstinence must be adjusted for each individual; however, in general it refers to a goal of freedom from anger binges and other out-of-control anger experiences. The experience and utilization of normal anger are promoted in the same sense in which normal eating behavior is encouraged among those who have eating disorders.

Those who gain from personally accepting the idea that they are anger addicted are those who can use the implications of that concept to move from being controlled by their anger to understanding and accepting their need for help in that arena. Chronically angry persons need to quit being victimized by their anger. Instead they need to regain a sense that their anger represents a small portion of who they are as complete individuals. As one of our clients said, "Once I thought that my life was like a bus and I was only a passenger on it. Anger was the driver. Now I'm the driver and anger has taken a seat back there with all my other feelings."

In training workshops with professional counselors who are also recovering from chemical dependency, many of these individuals recall times when they would label themselves as anger addicted. For most, such periods occurred while they were also in the midst of their chemical dependency. Sometimes they were hostile and cantankerous before they developed their substance abuse pattern. Infrequently, the anger periods followed abstinence (and may have predicted or precipitated a relapse). Some recognize that they are currently in such a phase in their lives. A few realize that they have been angry all their lives — before, during, and after abstinence and regardless of their professional training. Many of these therapists have found the concept of anger addiction useful in understanding both past and current aspects of their lives.

CASE STUDY: A Woman Addicted to Her Anger

"I need help with my rages," began Ellen, a 30-year-old Native American who identified herself in our first session as a recovering alcoholic/addict and sex addict. "When I get mad there's just no stopping me. I tell people not to cross me because I can either be their best friend or their worst nightmare." Indeed, Ellen was in danger of losing both her job and her boyfriend because of her anger. Within the last week she had gotten into an argument with one of her colleagues over an alleged insult, had a shouting match with a customer, and participated in a verbal and physical brawl with her partner. She had a long history of anger, one that predated her use of alcohol or drugs. She also had many justifications for her smoldering rage, including racial discrimination, abuse and neglect as a child, biochemical depression, and "most people are assholes."

Every area of Ellen's life was affected by her pervasive anger. Her relations with her family of origin were strained, she was on probation for two previous assaultive episodes, she was in danger of physically attacking her small child, money was a problem because of past fines and property damage, even her personality changed when she let herself become a "warrior."

But oh, the excitement! Ellen's eyes glistened with energy when she described her anger. It was then that she seemed most alive, least depressed. These rages were more than a

As a metaphor anger addiction may be useful to certain clients. Therapists can suggest that the clients' problems with anger seem much like those he or she has had with mood-altering chemicals, and can expand upon these similarities between anger and mood-altering chemicals by proffering a list of parallels, such as buildup of tolerance, loss of control, negative consequences, and inability to stop even when trying to do so. Clients may find themselves curious about this comparison and become active in the process by adding to the list of likenesses with, for example, such personal items as, "Yeah, and I said I would never be like

CASE STUDY: continued

habit, more than a pattern of distorted thoughts. Ellen's anger brought her to the edge of danger, like a mountain climber blindly reaching for a handhold. She might fall, she might suffer terrible consequences for her anger, but meanwhile she felt an indescribable exhilaration.

Therapy with Ellen was two-pronged. First, she needed an assessment for depression by a psychiatrist. She was immediately placed on an antidepressant which helped her with her underlying lack of energy and joylessness as well as "taking the edge off my anger."

The antidepressant alone, however, was not enough. Ellen still had to confront her mood-altering behavior, her need for intense excitement that was part of her rages. This she did by completing a "First Step" on anger, coming to understand that she had been "powerless over anger" and "my life has become unmanageable." Like all first steps, this one provided her with an opportunity to make a commitment to abstain from "anger binges," another name for senseless rages. Ellen could now approach her anger from the perspective of yet another addiction to be addressed as part of her general recovery program.

Ellen and I did a visualization in which she saw herself finally taking off her warrior's armor so that she could comfort her scared and lonely inner child. She's learning to know that child better now, to love and protect her without rage or violence. ∎

my father and here I am just as much a drunk and an angry bully." Counselors can then follow their clients through these comparisons, anticipating that they will eventually want to ask how they can quit being so swallowed up by their anger. This allows therapists to stress those components of the addiction model with which each individual client most identifies and to design treatment plans that emphasize these dimensions. For instance, the angry alcoholic who truly endorses the first step (which stresses powerlessness and unmanageability) might be encouraged to "do a first step" on anger. Others, whose emphasis might be more upon the need to attend support groups, can be encouraged to discuss their anger in these groups, so that they can learn how to let go of it.

The addiction model may be useful in dealing with the anger issues of others, as well as for the chemically dependent. It may be quite useful with affected family members and with some persons who have no past or present substance abuse issues. The concept of anger addiction may be offered as a possibly valid metaphor to any client with chronic anger concerns. However, clients who have already been exposed to and/or accepted an addiction model are clearly more likely to incorporate it into their perspective.

Link Relapse Prevention with Resolution and Continuing Awareness of Anger Themes

Anger has a significant advantage as an indicator of relapse potential: It is hard to ignore. For this reason, anger awareness can be valuable to professionals treating individuals attempting to maintain abstinence from alcohol or drug use.

Relapse is now construed by most theorists as a series of events, mostly internal, which gradually prepare people to return to using. For example, Gorski (1983) lists a set of 37 characteristics of this process, including defensiveness, irritation with friends, becoming angry with friends, the development of unreasonable resentments, and overwhelming feelings of anger. His description of these characteristics highlights the cognitive distortions that accompany relapse. For instance, when describing the resentments of a client during relapse, he writes that:

> The patient felt severe anger with the world in general and his inability to function. This anger was sometimes generalized; at other times focused at particular scapegoats; at other times turned against himself. Episodes of anger, frustration, resentment, and irritability increased. Overreaction became more frequent. Often the fear of extreme overreaction to the point of violence seriously increased the level of stress and anxiety.

For some recovering persons, the return of irrational anger serves as an obvious cue for impending relapse. The therapeutic goal here is to help clients identify their anger so that they can use it as a warning marker. Clients gain two very important opportunities from anger awareness. First, awareness gives them a chance to deal with their anger productively and hence to improve the overall quality of their lives. Secondly, they can help themselves lessen the risk of relapse by treating their anger as an early danger sign.

Of course, in and of itself anger will not "make" anyone drink or take drugs. Rather, it is important to recognize the role of anger as part of a broad relapse pattern that may also include other factors, such as isolation from support networks, depression, anxiety, etc. Recognizing the anger and dealing with it appropriately can help individuals renew their commitment to abstinence. On the other hand, failure to address or resolve anger concerns may encourage and accelerate the entire relapse process. For example, a recovering woman who decides to nurse a secret grudge against her partner may quit talking to him, lose trust, and look to condemn his actions. This only fuels her anger, which in turn isolates her. Eventually, as her general mood deteriorates, she becomes more likely to seek solace and understanding from her intoxicants than from her partner or other persons. Thus, unresolved anger triggers dissatisfaction and despair, which in turn facilitates relapse.

Relate the Client's Anger to Codependency and Dysfunctional Family-of-Origin Themes Where Relevant

Many individuals treated for chemical dependency need help with various codependency problems. Depending on client needs and the philosophy of the treatment facility, codependency concerns may be handled concurrently with addiction treatment or addressed sequentially. The rationale for the former approach is that pervasive codependency issues prevent certain clients from concentrating on their own recovery. The argument for a sequential approach is that premature focus upon codependency distracts staff and clients from the essential task of commitment to abstinence.

A common complaint among angry, codependent clients in early recovery is this: "I work so hard now to do things right but nobody appreciates me. It really makes me mad when they don't notice all the good things I'm doing." Sometimes such individuals have made significant changes in their behavior, which are going unnoticed and unrewarded. At other times, the recovering person believes his actions have changed radically because he feels so much better about himself; however, these changes are primarily internal—his external behavior remains unchanged and irresponsible. In either case, the client's personal dialogue is such that he says to himself that he has a right to get angry if others don't immediately appreciate him. The lack of a well developed inner self, which is the hallmark of codependency, exacerbates the problem and feeds the person's sense of rejection and abandonment.

Many recovering persons have trouble focusing on their own wants and needs. Individuals who are both chemically dependent and codependent may eventually become bitter that others don't or won't meet their needs. Anger, hostility, and resentment gradually develop. This heightens the appeal of mood-altering substances, both as a compensatory way to feel good and as a retaliatory attack on those who are perceived as having ignored or mistreated them.

Additionally, many recovering persons carry tremendous rage with them as a result of being raised themselves in alcoholic or other strongly dysfunctional families. These concerns also need to be addressed, both in order to minimize relapse potential and to help people live better lives. Therapists must walk a tightrope here, encouraging patients to face their anger while refusing to let them use their family-of-origin problems as an excuse to drink or take drugs. "Yes," the therapist must say to these individuals, "you certainly have been injured and I can see how rageful you are. Still, it's *your* anger now and *your* responsibility to deal with it appropriately." It is crucial to keep in mind, when working with anger from the family of origin, that merely ventilating the anger will probably do little long-lasting good. The goal is to release the anger as part of becoming freed from the past, and this implies a cognitive grounding as well. Those who cling indefinitely to their resentments are likely to be those whose view of the world is cynical and whose capacity for joy is severely constricted.

Forgiveness may be part of the process of working through anger about the past. This concept can be offered to those clients who seem ready and eager to leave the past behind them. Although no one *must* forgive another, we find that those who do are often better able to proceed in their lives without excessive anger and hatred. Forgiving should always be offered as an option, not an expectation — something that individuals do when they are ready and primarily for their own gain. It is best viewed as a process rather than a one-time event. Forgiving is something done over time, piece by piece, and often erratically. It is not unusual for a recovering person to be full of hate toward a parent one day, partly forgiving the next, seeking reconciliation the next, and then simply confused. Lewis Smedes (1984) seems to have captured the nature of this gradual process in his book entitled *Forgive and Forget*.

Refer to an Anger Management Specialist if Significant Anger or Aggression Issues Remain After Treatment for Chemical Dependency or Codependency

Many individuals who complete chemical dependency treatment (including aftercare) will still display significant problems with anger or aggression. Some of these persons will not define their anger as a personal issue, nor will they connect habitual anger or aggression with an increased risk for relapse. Little can be done with such persons except to provide them the information about concerns identified by the staff and to offer them the option of returning in the future to deal with these issues.

There are others who recognize that they have definite problems with anger. They may be quite concerned about their ability to handle their anger once chemical dependency treatment is completed. These clients may willingly accept a referral to community counselors who specialize in anger management.

Other clients may recognize an ongoing anger problem and yet be reluctant to deal directly with it at the present time. They may be out of energy or money. They may still be minimizing their anger or hoping it will eventually disappear with continuing abstinence. A stronger shove toward therapy will be necessary, perhaps facilitated by family intervention. The selling point for these persons is that they can best keep the good things they have gained during early abstinence and continue to move toward stability, responsibility, and serenity by working on anger management and anger reduction.

Anger specialists are frequently associated with programs to prevent spouse assault or child abuse. Parenting educators may also have valuable information on anger management, as might assertiveness trainers. Many unaffiliated therapists are also trained in anger management techniques. Therapists with behavioral or cognitive therapy training are especially likely to be proficient in anger management.

The ideal anger therapist would be one who has worked through his or her own anger issues; has no intrinsic bias toward or against anger ventilation, reduction, or management (and so can focus on specific client needs); is neither particularly afraid of nor attracted to anger; and has enough patience to work over long periods with clients as they gradually learn how to wrest control of their lives out of the hands of their rage. In addition, counselors with an understanding of addictive patterns may be especially useful for recovering clients and for those whose anger seems to be addictive or compulsive in nature. However, any therapist can be helpful to many chronically angry persons just by utilizing such basic skills as empathy and nonhostile confrontation.

EXERCISES

8-1 *Assessing Mood-Altering Anger*

Some persons with chronic anger problems use anger regularly as a way to alter their moods, through biochemical changes in their bodies and psychological changes that produce a sense of power or well-being. Some develop a high tolerance for experiencing anger, partly a result of their efforts to "get high" on anger. Here is an "anger addiction assessment" tool to use with clients who need to examine their use of mood-altering anger.

Anger Addiction Assessment

Circle the numbers of those questions to which you answer "yes."

1. Do you ever look for reasons to get angry?
2. Do you get bored with your life if you have not had something to be angry about for a while?
3. Have you ever tried to get help for your anger?
4. Does "having a good fight" have a real appeal for you?
5. Do you sense that at times your anger is controlling you instead of you being in control of it?
6. Do you use anger to avoid other issues in your life?
7. Have you had any job difficulties because of your anger?
8. Have you had relationship difficulties because of your anger?
9. Do you feel really good in the middle of an argument?
10. Have you had any legal difficulties or near-difficulties because of your anger?
11. Do you get angry more often than you used to?
12. Do you have to get angrier than you used to in order to feel good?
13. Has your anger ever led you to enjoy hurting someone else?
14. Have you ever made promises to yourself about controlling your anger that you have been unable to keep?
15. Has your need to get angry led you to spend time in places and with people you ordinarily would not choose?
16. Are you concerned about how much time you spend angry?
17. Have you ever tried to stop doing what you perceive as "wrong" in your expressions of anger?
18. Does getting angry help you feel less anxious?
19. Do you think obsessively about your reasons to be angry?
20. Has being angry become a substitute for other kinds of feelings with your partner, your children, or other people?
21. Have your productivity, choices, or concentration decreased as your anger has become more compulsive?
22. Do you feel better when you are always angry with someone about something?
23. Does getting angry over small things seem irresistible to you at times?
24. Has your anger harmed the welfare of yourself or your family?

25. Do you feel guilt, shame, remorse, or depression before an anger high?
26. Do you feel guilt, shame, remorse, or depression after an anger high?
27. Do you forget the things you say or do when you are high on anger?
28. Does getting angry give you a nice feeling of power?
29. Do you feel helpless about your anger these days?
30. Do you lose control when you are angry in ways that violate your own values?

Rating scale: Respondents with 5 or more "yes" answers on this assessment are likely to be using anger compulsively to alter their moods. The higher the score, the more serious the addictive potential and the stronger an indication that anger is more important to the client than relationships.

8-2 *Addictive Anger Signals and the Problem of Denial*

Statements like "I need my anger more than I need you," and "I know I'm driving you out but I just can't stop," are powerful indicators of being hooked on anger. "I need my anger more than I need you" indicates that having a constant supply of anger has really become more important than human relationships, something that spells addiction. And "I just can't stop" is a clear indication of loss of control. No one really wants to admit addiction to a substance. Nor do people easily admit to anger addiction.

Ask clients to list ways in which their behavior might be showing them or someone close to them that they need anger more than they need others or that their anger is getting out of control. In a group discussion, ask how they would interpret these behaviors themselves, and how rejected or abandoned they themselves might feel if they were treated in these ways.

8-3 *Teaching the Anger "Addiction" Model*

The following handout can be used to facilitate individual and group discussion of the anger "addiction" model.

ANGER PHOBIA

Addicted to avoiding anger; denial of anger

Fear loss of love/relationship

Sacrifices self-identity

Feels guilty if ever angry

May drink to relieve anger or for release from this role temporarily

May have periodic "blows"

Primary solution is acceptance of self; must deal with early messages about anger and learn that self-care is not the same as selfishness

ANGER IN MODERATION

Mostly ignores trivial invitations to anger

Recognizes significant problems through awareness of anger

Expresses that anger directly without blame to others

Accepts responsibility for own feelings; uses "I" statements

Goal is solution of problem in a manner that respects both parties

Lets go of anger as soon as possible

ANGER ADDICTION

Anger chokes out other feelings; it is solution for all problems

Increased tolerance for anger; needs more and more

Gets pleasure from anger

Anger followed by guilt and remorse but does not change

Eventually anger is unmanageable; no choices

Primary solution is abstinence from anger binges; must learn other ways to express feelings

8-4 *The Anger-Relapse Connection*

Use the following Anger-Relapse Connection Form to help the angry, chemically dependent clients examine their potential relapse behavior and set goals to avoid relapse.

Anger-Relapse Connection

1. Check the connection(s) between anger and alcohol/drug use that most apply to you.

   __I use because I want my anger to go away.
   __I use because I want to let my anger out.
   __I use to get back at other people when I'm angry.
   __I use because when I'm angry I don't care about anything.
   __I use in order to hurt or punish myself with my anger.
   __Other (what?: _____)

2. Give three examples from your past for each connection you checked above.

3. Now list the three or four situations that most commonly trigger your using alcohol/drugs and relate to your being or becoming angry.

   (a)
   (b)
   (c)
   (d)

4. Based on the above, write the story of "your next relapse"— predict how it might happen.

5. List the signals you need to watch for in light of what you predicted above.

6. List what you need to do to prevent a relapse if/when these signals occur.

8-5 The Shame-Rage Connection*

Explain to participants that shame is a feeling of being defective, worthless, or inadequate. Ask them to identify some experiences when they were criticized that left them feeling very small, only "about this big" (demonstrate with finger and thumb about an inch apart). Ask them how big they feel when they get angry. Point out that shame makes one focus on one's own defects, whereas anger keeps one's focus on the defects of others. Help them identify times when, because they felt incompetent themselves, they chose instead to criticize others. Ask them to identify times when, because they did not like who they are, they chose to criticize others angrily instead. Role play an example or two and help participants identify and practice more appropriate alternatives.

This connection is particularly vital to make with individuals who may have turned to alcohol or drug use when feeling ashamed. Their use of such substances may have fueled the conversion of their shame into rage.

8-6 The Feelings Collage

The feelings collage is an assignment intended to stimulate awareness of a range of feelings. It is frequently used in treatment centers to help clients recognize and express feelings. Clients are given a list of basic emotions: anger, hurt, sadness, fear, shame, guilt, loneliness, and happiness. They are asked to find three or four magazine pictures which they feel relate to *each*

*Also see exercise 6-5.

feeling, and to cut out letters spelling each feeling. Then they collage a poster with the materials they have gathered, putting the pictures and words for each individual emotion together in a particular area on the poster. Each client then presents his/her poster in a group therapy session, sharing three personal experiences of each feeling.

8-7 *The Anger Box*

The anger box is especially useful with clients who appear to be chronically angry and acting out, who seem to show *all* feelings through the expression of various types of anger. For this exercise, clients are given a cardboard box, with top and bottom flaps intact, and helped to unfasten the box so that it lays flat out, completely.

Now clients are asked to collage the outside surface of the box with pictures, words, and drawings representing their anger and angry acting out. Ask them to collage the inside surface with words, pictures, and drawings representing the feelings they cover, defend against, or mask with their anger and/or angry behavior. Have each client present this collage in a group session and then fold the box up again. In the future, when clients find themselves being angry, they can look into the box to see if they can identify what they are *really* feeling.

9

SELECTED TREATMENT
CONSIDERATIONS

For every chronically angry individual there is a particular set of behaviors and beliefs that exacerbates the problem. Present or past use of mood-altering chemicals additionally complicates therapy. As a result, no single treatment strategy will be effective with everyone.

Nevertheless, three themes are generally helpful: (1) helping clients learn how to contain their anger before they explode into harmful acts of physical or verbal aggression; (2) addressing certain thought processes that promote irrational or excessive anger; and (3) dealing with long-term resentments that hinder a general recovery process. These issues and suggested treatment tactics within each area will be described here.

CONTAINING EXPLOSIVE ANGER

Chronic anger is a deeply entrenched way of feeling that is characterized by certain habitual behaviors. These behaviors include observable actions, such as speaking loudly, walking right up to and standing within inches of another person, talking loudly or in a higher pitch, breathing rapidly, etc. Furthermore, these patterns tend to follow a predictable pattern for each indi-

CASE STUDY: A Man Who Explodes at His Wife

Anger explosions tend to follow a wave-like pattern. The three stages in these waves are the buildup stage, the explosion, and the relief/remorse stage. One wave often leads to another, in a repetitive pattern.

The *buildup* stage consists of a chain of behaviors, thoughts, and feelings that leads toward an angry outburst. Each link in the chain leads toward the next in what eventually becomes a quick, smooth, and mostly unthinking habitual process. Here is an example of a man named Harry, whose anger builds up toward physical violence in a situation where his wife has gone to a movie with a girl friend and returned 60 minutes later than planned:

Thought #1. "She is five minutes late. No problem. Don't get excited."

Feeling #1. Despite this thought Harry notices a twinge of anxiety in his gut.

Action #1. He gets busy by doing the dishes (even though it is not his turn) as he attempts to lessen his anxiety.

Thought #2. "Hey, she's 15 minutes late. Maybe something's wrong. Maybe she's had car troubles."

Feeling #2. A more specific feeling of fear replaces his vague anxiety. As Deschner (1984) notes, fear is often an important component of the total rage response.

Action #2. Harry begins to work more frantically, almost breaking a plate as he throws the dishes into the cupboard.

vidual. For example, someone may begin by tensing her stomach muscles, then start to pace, then clench her fists, and only after all these signs actually start yelling or threatening others.

Awareness of these observable actions can be utilized to help clients monitor their anger. Early signs of anger can serve to warn clients that they are in danger of losing control of their emotions and actions. Individuals who learn to recognize these

CASE STUDY: continued

Thought #3. "Hey, now she's 30 minutes late. Maybe she's met someone after the film and she just forgot to call. That's not very thoughtful of her."

Feeling #3. Anger starts to creep into the scene. Harry is beginning to feel hurt and offended by his wife's so far unexplained behavior.

Action #3. He begins to pace around the house nervously.

Thought #4. "She's 45 minutes late. I'll bet she's doing this on purpose just to piss me off. She can't do that to me. Just wait till she gets home."

Feeling #4. Harry's anger is accelerating toward rage. This strong feeling interferes with clear thinking, increasing the probability that his future thoughts will be irrational.

Action #4. He turns the radio on—loud—to some heavy rock station. This might be relaxing in other circumstances but now it further agitates his nervous system.

Thought #5. "She's almost an hour late. Maybe she's met another man. Maybe she'll never come back. I feel humiliated. I won't let her do this to me!" Harry can no longer think straight. His worst fears and self-doubts take over.

Feeling #5. Just short of a full rage. But note that even this far along Harry could stop himself before he hurts himself or his wife. He needs to take a "time-out" to collect his thoughts and feelings.

early signs can begin to break their anger habit by responding effectively to them. They can then initiate relaxation techniques to keep their anger from accelerating, challenge irrational thought processes, or communicate in nonthreatening ways with others.

Unfortunately, most chronically angry persons seem rather unaware of their own anger patterns. Some prefer to believe that anger "just happens" to them, as if they were struck by lightning, which may be a way to avoid responsibility for their own actions. After all, anybody could be struck by lightning. Other chronically

CASE STUDY: continued

Action #5. He begins talking to himself, half yelling over the noise of the radio. Harry is preparing for battle, thinking that he has every right to defend himself against his wife's outrageous behavior.

Thought #6. "Aha. Here she comes. Now she's going to get it good."
Feeling #6. An extremely dangerous combination of strong fear, anger, and indignation.
Action #6. Harry explodes at his wife as soon as she comes in the door. He accuses her of being totally thoughtless, selfish, unfeeling, interested in other men, etc. He shoves her around and threatens to strike her, ignoring her attempts to explain why she is late. ■

angry persons don't notice their first, early signs of anger, paying attention only to the later, more obvious cues. One reason for this is that they may be feeling annoyed so frequently that "normal" and "angry" may become virtually synonymous body states. They don't realize that they could alter their behaviors because those actions (and accompanying thoughts) seem to appear automatically. The point is that most chronically angry individuals need to become more aware of how they become angry. Only then will they be able to take responsibility for and then change their actions. Indeed, "how I get angry" is usually a more important question for chronically angry persons than "why I get angry."

Lenore Walker's (1980) description of the typical anger/aggression explosion curve is quite helpful to many chronically angry persons. She identifies three main stages in the process: (1) the buildup stage; (2) the explosion itself; and (3) a period of remorse and/or relief that follows the explosion.

The buildup stage is most important in the *prevention* of aggression. This period consists of three components: thoughts, feelings, and actions. A valuable therapeutic task is to help clients link each angry thought with an angry feeling and an angry behavior. For instance, just before an individual attacks another, he may think, "I can't stand this anymore. I won't let him do that to me." The accompanying feelings may be a sick sensation in the stomach and a facial blush indicative of shame. Meanwhile, he takes action by striding toward the other and waving his fist. An anger explosion then consists of a predictable accumulation of gradually more intense feelings, thoughts, and actions. These can be visualized as interlocking links, as in a chain link fence.

Clients can intervene upon their anger by addressing any one of the three areas. They can begin to contain their anger with whatever focus fits them best. That may be feelings for one individual, who initially interdicts his anger by taking a few deep breaths to relax. Another person will emphasize altering her thoughts, perhaps in this situation by reminding herself that the other person is really on her side and not an enemy. A third will concentrate on behavior, disciplining himself to sit down and speak more softly when upset.

The initial goal is to help clients gain control of their immediate situation. Once this is accomplished, they can then begin to develop longer-range management techniques. Most clients will need to change in all three areas to promote permanent alterations in their lifestyle.

Many chronically angry individuals are relatively unaware of their early anger cues. This is particularly evident early in therapy, when clients may frequently lose control of their anger and become aggressive. When questioned about this behavior, their responses will often indicate their low level of self-awareness: "I don't know what was going on"; "Gee, I didn't think I was that angry, until I exploded"; "I don't even remember what triggered my throwing that chair." It is important for therapists to address awareness with clients. This is best done by having clients begin at the point of explosion and work their way backwards toward earlier anger symptoms. Asking clients such questions as "What happened to you right before you exploded?" "What were your thoughts just before you threw the chair?" "What was going on inside you (feelings)?" "What were you doing?" can help them retrace their steps as far as possible. Keep in mind that it is almost always easier to break the earlier links in the chain than the ones that immediately precede an explosion. Clients can effectively change their excessively angry or aggressive behavior when they learn to retrace their chain of thoughts, feelings, and actions to a point early in the process. Later they can recognize when they experience phenomena that signal the start of another anger cycle and develop alternatives.

Some clients will claim ignorance, of course. They may state that they suddenly become enraged, seemingly without warning or any identifiable buildup phase. Or they may say they agree with the theory but were too intoxicated to remember what happened. It is worth challenging these claims rather forcefully, since this information is vital in terms of planning any useful intervention tactics. When pressed, most clients will be able to recall at least one of the three final components of the anger buildup chain: their last feeling, thought, or action prior to the explosion. If they cannot or will not, they may be willing to let the counselor gather this material from family members or other significant informants.

Therapy is directed at helping clients learn to anticipate and eliminate aggressive outbursts. They can learn to become increasingly aware of the indicators of their anger, as well as to undertake new behaviors and ways of thinking and feeling.

Taking a time-out is the only tactic which works when an individual has worked up to an explosion. At some point many chronically angry individuals begin to lose control of their anger. Under these circumstances taking a time-out is a responsible action which prevents irresponsible ones. The angry individual must physically leave before he or she damages property, others, or self. Rather than "losing it," individuals who take appropriate time-outs establish to themselves that they can indeed control their anger enough to get out of trouble. They learn that a time-out is a constructive behavior that any angry person might reasonably employ, something that adds to their sense of self-worth rather than a loss of face.

A good time-out entails more than just walking away from a bad situation for a few minutes. Walking away, if the client has not formulated additional plans to manage his anger, may be unproductive or even harmful. For instance, one very angry man took time-outs that consisted of pacing rapidly and repeating to himself phrases such as "She better watch it. I'm really mad at her now. If she does that again, I'm gonna. . . . " After about 15 minutes of this, he would return to the situation in a worse mood than when he'd left.

Positive time-outs occur when clients: (1) leave before an explosion, not after something bad has happened; (2) use their time-out to do things that distract them from their rage; and (3) make and keep a commitment to return to the person and issue that triggered the rage, but only after they have regained control.

At first, many clients will have only a few seconds to act, a brief interval between when they begin to lose control and when their anger has taken over. They may suddenly feel their face flush or think of saying something hurtful that they know they don't mean. This is the time they must immediately leave, perhaps telling others, "I'm sorry but I can't keep talking right now. I've got to get out of here right now. I'll be back in a while." Family and friends should be informed that this might happen, so that they will not follow after the retreating individual, preventing a necessary exit. Later, as the client gains greater awareness, time-outs can be taken with less of an emergency nature: "I'm getting worn out by this conversation and I'm starting to feel myself getting angry. If we can't figure this out soon, I'll have to take a time-out."

There are many tactics angry individuals can take during their time-outs that will help them calm themselves. These include meditating, going to a self-help meeting, taking a brisk walk, reading recreational material, or talking with people who will help them relax. We don't recommend participation in highly competitive sports, other aggressive or sexually stimulating activities, watching violent movies, or doing anything else that might continue to be overstimulating. We caution clients to be selective about spending time with others during a time-out, in particular those who might encourage their anger; it is not helpful to speak with people who "throw fuel on the fire" during a time-out.

Individuals who take time-outs must be committed to returning to issues that need to be handled. Otherwise time-outs become simply another manipulative device, something used to avoid responsibility. The goal is to take a few minutes off, regain composure, and return. However, it is possible to return too hastily, before the individual is really ready, in which case arguments are likely to be renewed. An important question here is this: "Can I now return and talk quietly with _____ even if he or she is still angry with me?"

It is important to emphasize the difference between issue avoidance and time-outs. A time-out is taken so that a concern can be addressed rather than getting lost in personal attacks, defensiveness, and rage. Time-outs should not be used to evade problems or as a weapon against others. They should be used only after clients have attempted to communicate and tried other means of anger management. In other words, they are a last resort tactic, designed to prevent catastrophe. The more individuals practice other anger management tactics, the less they will need time-outs. However, time-outs are especially useful early in treatment, when clients have few other resources.

From an addictions perspective, the explosion and relief/regret parts of the cycle reflect the themes of powerlessness and unmanageability. One parallel with alcohol or drug consumption is that many persons feel strong, exhilarated, and in control of their lives when intoxicated. Yet they do things during these times which later they regret tremendously. Similarly, while physical outbursts or verbal tirades momentarily ventilate one's anger, producing temporary relief, frequently the aggressor feels great remorse later, as he realizes the damage he has done to himself and others. Deep shame and guilt follow, especially when such individuals have promised themselves they would not do these things and have been unable to keep this commitment. The person who explodes in rage may buy a minute or an hour of power, but pays for that with days or weeks of regret. In addition, negative consequences might include loss of family, job, and friends, as well as court appearances if rage has resulted in physical assault.

Unfortunately, not all exploders feel remorse. Some truly enjoy their rages, perhaps feeling better during a rage than at any other time. They reap benefits through intimidating others. In addition, certain individuals, especially those with strong narcissistic or antisocial characteristics, have little ability to empathize with their victims, using denial, minimization, and rationalization to justify their behavior. Appealing to self-interest is the most useful strategy with these clients. They need to be shown that their uninhibited use of anger causes them more problems than they realized and that it might make sense for them to curtail some or all of that behavior.

For example, a man going through a bitter divorce entered therapy. He was incapable of empathy or understanding of his ex-wife's situation, wishing only to "make her hurt so bad that she'll give me the kids" and stating that what he wanted most was to reap vengeance. This resulted in continuous fighting between them about the children, over the phone and even in court, where this man consistently blew up and screamed at his wife and her attorney. He would not consider altering his behavior in the name of forgiveness, respect for others, or concern for the children. However, when shown how he was hurting himself in court by acting out his rage, he was quickly able to control this behavior. Then, when he realized that his wife was tracking his irrational behavior and that she might use that against him later (in their next court battle), he was able to alter his behavior around her and with their children.

It is important for therapists to realize that not all exploders are physically violent and that someone who explodes is not nec-essarily a batterer or child abuser. Many explosions are verbal, a simultaneous display of being in and out of control. Nevertheless, explosion containment is a necessary part of anger management, whether or not physical violence ensues. Most clients first appear because of this need, and it remains a priority consideration throughout treatment for chronic anger.

CHALLENGING NEGATIVE THINKING

Chronically angry individuals frequently think in ways that promote their anger. They do so in several ways. First, they may believe that they are intrinsically angry persons, fated to go rage-fully through life. Second, they may be convinced that the world is a bad and dangerous place in which they must be constantly on guard. This extremely vigilant perspective contains elements of paranoia and easily leads to a hostile attitude in which others are viewed as enemies. Third, chronically angry individuals make too many negative assumptions about others, often because of failure to empathize. Fourth, they tend to magnify problems by converting annoyances into tragedies and treating trivial concerns as very serious problems. Finally, chronically angry persons may turn their anger on themselves, calling themselves harsh names that only increase their total anger and irritability while lowering their self-esteem.

For example, a woman told on short notice to attend an important business meeting could view this as a fortunate opportunity to demonstrate her skills and a possible step toward promotion. However, a chronically angry person would not take this perspective. Instead, she would probably react with suspicion, doubt, annoyance, and resentment. She might wonder why she was told to attend, look for hidden motivations in others, feel irritated that others are once again imposing on her, and dwell on what seems to her an obviously unfair attempt by her boss to take advantage of her. This is a typical response pattern among chronically angry individuals, who tend to begin each interaction from an assumption that there must be something wrong and that they have a right to get mad.

Chronically angry persons display systematic styles of dysfunctional cognition (Shapiro, 1965), not just specific angry or inappropriate thoughts. The entire cognitive style must eventually be challenged to accomplish lasting change. Chronically angry individuals must learn to think differently about themselves and the world. A general repatterning effort is described clearly in the works of Aaron Beck (Beck, 1988; Beck et al., 1979), whose writings on anger are valuable for both therapists and clients. While such ambitious undertakings may be beyond the scope of counselors whose connection with a client is specifically focused upon recovery from alcohol or drug concerns, here are a few related strategies which can be immediately useful to many clients.

The Concept of "Anger Invitations"

Each person receives at least a few invitations to become angry every day. Most of these invitations are about relatively trivial matters. For example, somebody cuts a driver off as he is driving to work in the morning; children go about their play noisily;

spouses purchase vanilla ice cream instead of chocolate. Other anger invitations are far more serious, such as discovering that one's spouse has lied about a significant matter or has been arrested for drunken driving. Each of these episodes, large or small, presents an opportunity for anger. It is as if the world says, "Here's your chance to get angry. Now what?"

Most individuals realize that they cannot afford to accept many of these invitations. They know they would be angry all the time if they did. They learn to be selective, accepting only those invitations that are truly significant. They can sort out those few anger invitations to accept from all the less significant ones, so that they only respond angrily when appropriate to do so.

Chronically angry persons, however, tend to accept almost every anger invitation that comes along. They blast their horns at the "idiot" drivers who cut in front of them. They scream at their children for being too noisy, never noticing the contradiction. They stew over mistakes their partners make, perhaps silently refusing to eat the vanilla ice cream and waiting until later to bring it up as evidence that their partners don't love them. Furthermore, they may treat these offenses as if they were tremendously important, rising up in such moral indignation and exaggerated outrage that reasonable resolutions of the issues become impossible.

Many chronically angry persons do not even recognize that they actually can make choices about which anger invitations to accept or decline. Saying "No, thanks" does not occur to them because they are mentally geared toward opportunities to become irritated, annoyed, and irate. Some might consider it cowardly to pass up these invitations. They may feel honor bound to defend themselves against every perceived affront to their pride. The result is that chronically angry individuals are continually finding reasons to become and stay upset.

We regularly ask clients to keep a logbook of the anger invitations they receive every day, how many they accept, and how they respond. Just keeping this record for a few days if often enough for clients to realize that they are constantly overresponding to stimuli that others simply ignore. It also helps them begin to understand that they have the right to choose if, when, and how to get angry. Freedom and empowerment are then defined at least partially from the framework of "Nobody has the power to make me angry" instead of "I'm only tough if I stand up to every insult."

Anger invitations are just that—invitations. Chronically angry clients can be helped to break the habit of anger when therapists teach them how to recognize and sort through them with care and common sense.

Disappointments vs. Disasters

Albert Ellis (Ellis & Harper, 1975), the creator of rational-emotive therapy, points out that people often exaggerate the significance of negatively perceived events. They "awfulize" these incidents, making them far worse than they really are. They go from "X did something I don't like" to "What X did is horrible—totally unfair and humiliating!" Then they decide that: (1) X must be bad; and (2) the situation is unendurable. Ellis notes that one irrational belief that often leads to anger is "Others must always treat me considerately and kindly and precisely the way I want them to treat me, and, if not, they should be blamed and punished" (Ellis & Harper, 1975).

Chronically angry persons tend to convert disappointments into disasters. *Disasters* are great misfortunes, calamities that severely affect a person's life. They are infrequent occurrences that necessitate emergency responses, often including anger and rage. Examples of disasters are the discovery that your child has been sexually abused, that a partner has intentionally mishandled a large sum of money, or that someone's neglect has caused a serious injury.

Disappointments occur more often and are less serious than disasters. Frustrations develop when we fail to achieve our hopes, desires, and expectations. For instance, a woman may plan to go out with her friend to a play only to receive a phone message from her that she is sick in bed and cannot attend. The chronically angry individual may become incensed because her friend hasn't kept her promise. Furthermore, she may even decide not to attend the play herself "since I'm so mad now I couldn't enjoy it." A less angry person would know that the other person's illness

CASE STUDY: "Mama Told Me about Men"

Brenda is just 25 years of age, a homemaker and part-time cook with three small children at home. Her husband Jack works long hours as an automobile firm parts manager but comes home as often as possible to be with her and the kids.

The trouble is that Jack never does anything right, at least according to Brenda. For instance, a few nights ago he forgot to pick up milk and formula for the infant on his way home. "You see," she told me, "that's just the way men are. You can't trust them to do anything. They are like babies that you have to watch over." Her mouth formed a deep frown as she spat out these words with visible contempt.

Why this hatred? Yes, Jack had his faults, but he certainly wasn't awful. He had never had an affair, he didn't drink, he had a steady job, he was at least adequate in bed, and he cared deeply for Brenda and the children.

The answer emerged whenever Brenda discussed her mother, whose two husbands had been alcoholic and abusive and had abandoned her. It was mother's voice that spoke through Brenda. She hated all men. Not a day passed when she hadn't told Brenda that men were wicked, evil, nasty creatures who would use you up and throw you away.

Therapy with Brenda was repetitive. Every time she blindly attacked her husband we looked at his behavior. Brenda had to admit that her accusations had nothing to do with his actions. She began to see that she had been brain-

was not intended personally. She would realize that disappointments are not disasters and that her life has not been significantly damaged.

"No big deal" is a valuable phrase for persons who regularly turn disappointments into disasters. "Easy does it" is another and has the advantage of being well-known in the recovering community. Particular clients may also gain by learning how to gradate the things that bother them, perhaps by ranking them from one to ten on a "disappointment/disaster thermometer."

washed by her mother. Most importantly, she realized that she was an adult now and that she had the right to make choices about her beliefs. We worked from certainty ("Of course that is what all men are like") through doubt ("Well, that's what Mom said. But maybe she was exaggerating sometimes. Maybe.") to choice ("This doesn't make sense. Jack's always been good to me. I'm going to quit treating him like a jerk."). As her mental expectations changed, so did her behavior. For the first time, she allowed herself to experiment with trusting her husband with her inner thoughts and feelings. Intimacy began to replace hostility at the foundation of her marriage. ■

These clients may begin by placing almost every item high on the thermometer, since they characteristically exaggerate the significance of their frustrations. A useful question to ask, if this situation occurs, is: "What do you think it means that almost everything you mention is at least a [7, 8, etc.] on your list?"

The overall goals with this material are to help clients recognize how they exaggerate their problems and to help them begin to gain control of their anger by maintaining some perspective on their frustrations.

Replacing Anger-Promoting Thoughts with Anger-Reducing Thoughts

Certain general beliefs that promote anger have been described previously. These include: the contention that the world is a bad or dangerous place in which one must always be on guard; an insistence by the client that he or she is "naturally" excessively angry; and the conclusion that, because of past injuries, one has the right to stay angry indefinitely. Beck (1988) argues that these thoughts have an automatic character, controlling a person's thinking because they take place so quickly and at the edge of conscious awareness.

Automatic thoughts may come directly to the surface of a client's awareness, although they usually remain at the edge of conscious ideation. They may also influence more specific interpretations of particular individuals and situations. For example, the subliminal automatic thought, "No one could ever love me," could push a client toward irrational jealousy: "Julie's talking with Frank. She has no right to do that to me. That really makes me mad." Both the underlying automatic thought, if it becomes conscious, and its more immediate byproducts feel normal, natural, correct, and obvious to the person who thinks them. Unfortunately, because they reflect a selective and distorted perception of the world, they promote antagonistic attitudes and unproductive behaviors toward others.

Here therapists have three tasks. The first is to help clients identify their automatic thoughts. The second is to challenge the presumed correctness of those concepts. Third, clients must be given some ideas about how to think differently.

Repeatedly asking clients about their basic assumptions can help them identify their patterns of automatic thinking. This is especially valuable when they make seemingly exaggerated, distorted, or irrelevant statements that hint at their world view. For instance, a client who suddenly says, in the midst of describing her partner's positive traits, "Well, that just shows you can never trust men," is possibly articulating a deeply held but fundamentally destructive automatic thought. This allows therapists to address the more basic concern.

Clients need assistance in challenging their automatic thoughts, since they are so firmly entrenched that mere recognition of them is insufficient in itself to guarantee change. W. W. Meissner (1986) suggests an approach to working with "paranoid process" individuals which is quite effective in challenging automatic thoughts. Instead of directly telling clients they are mistaken, and probably encountering immediate resistance, counselors should, he suggests, take a more neutral stand. For instance, "You may be right, so what's your evidence?" is followed with, "You make some good points. But are there any other ways to look at what happened or any contradictory evidence?" The goal is to help clients learn how to sift through their layers of assumptions about the universe without ever specifically discrediting their old ways of thinking. In the case of the woman mentioned above, further inquiry revealed that her hostile, suspicious impressions of men had been given her by her mother, an angry and bitter divorcée. Simply calling her attention to these thoughts did not, however, produce immediate change. She responded that her mother had been correct, since this was also her experience with men. Only after carefully reviewing her husband's behavior over the course of their marriage and recognizing that he was indeed fundamentally trustworthy was she able to question her assumptions about men.

Ultimately, clients must choose to think differently. They can then be given concrete suggestions about how to substitute anger-reducing thoughts for anger-promoting ones. This is a three-phase process itself, beginning when a person recognizes an old automatic thought, such as, "I can't take this anymore," "Never believe a woman," or "Why is everybody out to get me?" Next, clients must at first literally tell themselves to stop thinking that way, either out loud or subvocally. However, such thoughts won't just disappear without a fight. Because of this, it is crucial that clients actually replace those thoughts with new ones that have been consciously chosen. For example, the woman in the above situation had to wake up in the morning reminding herself that her husband could be trusted, articulate that idea to herself several times a day (whenever the old automatic thoughts appeared), and discuss this substitution with her husband and in therapy. Although such new concepts may never be as strong or compelling as the older ones, eventually they will become more deeply rooted, perhaps taking on semiautomatic characteristics themselves.

RESENTMENTS AND FORGIVING

Many chemically dependent individuals and affected family members build up tremendous reservoirs of old, hardened anger. Because of the addict's denial of reality, problems develop and remain unresolved. The children of alcoholics may dwell on countless broken promises to go places and do things; spouses may become so angry with addicts that they divorce them after they've gone through treatment because "I can't live with him anymore. It was just too bad for too long." Meanwhile, substance abusers may decide they want nothing to do with those members of their families who are too rigid to accept their "lifestyle." The chemically dependent family is a perfect breeding ground for the generation of resentments. In fact, they are so common that the A.A. Big Book (1976) devotes several pages to the subject, admonishing its readers to let go of their resentments or risk returning to drink.

We have written elsewhere about the development and resolution of resentments (Potter-Efron & Potter-Efron, 1991). The following material is a summary of the main points of that discussion.

Resentments gradually grow stronger over time. They usually begin with a specific injury, such as a wife being told despairingly by her husband that she did something wrong, perhaps not balancing the checkbook. If the critic attacks in public, thus humiliating his partner, resentments develop more quickly and may be more profound. They will also be strengthened if the critic adds a generalization, such as, "You are always doing stupid things like that!" to his assault.

A resentment is unlikely to develop if the initial injury is addressed immediately and appropriately, even if the complaint has been presented poorly. This is particularly true if the criticizer apologizes for any harm done to the other person. Again, this is consistent with the A.A. program, which urges recovering persons to review their behavior "and, if we were wrong, to promptly admit it."

Persons with unrelieved wounds may begin to distrust those who have harmed them. They feel victimized and respond either by attacking the other (which may lead to two angry individuals both building resentments) or by physically or emotionally withdrawing (which makes it more difficult to communicate). Gradually, immediate pain hardens into firm resentments. These resentments are characterized by the conviction that the other has intentionally attacked, repeated searching for and review of other injuries ("You know, he does that to me all the time"), and a focus not only upon the other's specific active insults but also upon any alleged omissions. Thus, the resenter becomes attuned both to *commissions*, perceived hurtful behavior that others have in-

flicted upon them, and *omissions,* the potentially positive things
that others fail to do. This list of omissions can be endless, since
omissions are far more common than commissions: "He never
brings me flowers anymore"; "She always forgets my son's birthday"; "He could have asked me first before he did that"; "She
doesn't seem to care about me any longer." The whole resentment process accelerates once clients concentrate upon omissions.

Shortfalls comprise a third class of injuries that contribute to
the growth of resentments. Shortfalls are occasions when others
do something good that is interpreted as "not enough" by the
injured party. For example, a woman concluded that her husband was thoughtless and self-centered because, when they were
first married, he frequently came home late from work without
calling ahead. Consequently, whenever he did something nice or
generous, such as taking the children to the park so she could
have some privacy, she responded with, "Well, if you had done
that five years ago, when we were first married, I would have
appreciated it. But you didn't. Now it's too little, too late." In
fact, she felt all the more injured because of his "inadequate"
behavior. She believed that since she had been victimized by his
selfishness for years, he "owed" her more than he was doing.

Shortfalls occur frequently in chemically dependent families:
"Now he apologizes for having all those affairs. What good does
it do now? It just makes me think about them all the more."

Resentments can eventually turn into hatreds. The key to this
movement is the development of the desire for revenge against
the offender. Resenters want to make the other person suffer,
preferably in the same way they themselves suffered. They believe they will only be able to get on with their lives after justice
has been done, and this can only be accomplished through the
pain and suffering of the original offender.

Therapists need to emphasize to clients that *the power to end
a resentment is in the hands of the resenter, not in the control of
the person who originally offended them.* Only the resenter can
choose to abandon the quest for revenge; only the resenter can
quit searching for more evidence of omissions; only the resenter
can lay to rest anger about the original offense.

There may be many ways to end a resentment. The process of

CASE STUDY: The Adult Child Who Wouldn't Forgive

Perry hated his father. The man had been dead for 12 years and he had visited his grave only once, literally to spit upon it. Whenever he talked of that brutal alcoholic who had terrorized his family, Perry's eyes narrowed and his voice took on a high-pitched, threatening tone. Perry had watched his father come home in drunken rages, beat up his mother, and then line up the children for two-hour rambling lectures in the middle of the night. He had been beaten, too, until he was 16. That was the year he had knocked his father to the floor and run away, never to return.

Perry blamed his father for everything that went wrong in his life. His father was responsible for Perry's estrangement from his nine-year-old son Daniel (after all, Daniel looked just like his grandfather). His father caused Perry's anxiety attacks, his periodic outbursts, his low self-concept. His father was even the reason for Perry's abstinence, since he feared that he would turn into a monster like his father if he touched a drop of liquor.

Perry had been in therapy, off and on, for all his adult life. He challenged each therapist to make him better. He would then take several sessions to describe at length the endless attacks of his father, an exercise in hatred that never failed to impress his therapists. Then he would drop out of therapy because he "felt better for getting that off my chest." Unfortunately, the pain and rage would return within days or weeks, at which point he would conclude that he needed to seek out another listener.

forgiving, a process described by Smedes (1984) and Flanigan (1989), is especially valuable. However, counselors must refrain from telling clients they "should" or "must" forgive others. Forgiveness is an option. Obligatory forgiveness may actually foster the growth of new resentments alongside the old ones.

Important points about forgiving include:

Finally, Perry wrote an eight-page letter to his father. Eight pages of loathing, disgust, and revulsion were ended with this phrase, "Love, Perry."

Perry brought the letter to his counselor, expecting to read the whole thing through in full fury. Instead, his counselor looked at the document, noticed its ending, and focused upon that. "What does this 'Love, Perry' mean, Perry? I'm surprised to see it here." Within minutes, Perry was sobbing. Finally he could admit that he had desperately longed for his father's love all these years, that his apparent hatred was partly a cover for his neediness. His father had indeed been a tyrant, but he was also his father, and a child needs his father's love. Perry began mentioning all the times he had tried to do things to please his father, the occasional successes and the frequent failures. He even recalled one day when his father had introduced him to his friends as "My son, a real hell-raiser." That was as close to a compliment as his father ever came and Perry had clung to that memory.

Now Perry could forgive his father. He knew he needed to visit his grave again, to tell his father about both his hate and his love. He saw that he had gifts to give his son, who was in the process of becoming quite a hell-raiser himself. Finally, he could be relieved of his personal curse and get on with his life. ■

- Forgiving is a choice that must be made freely for it to have value.

- Forgiving is an act of generosity to the forgiver, not to the person forgiven. Persons who forgive benefit by being able to get on with their lives instead of being stuck in resentment.

- Forgiving is a gradual process, not a one-time event.

- Forgiving involves changing one's attitudes *and* actions toward another. It is useless to say that someone forgives another if his/her behavior remains the same.

- However, forgiving does not always lead to reconciliation. Frequently, the person to be forgiven is unknown, deceased, still dangerous, or unavailable. Forgiving may lead to reconciliation, but that does not have to be a goal. "Letting go" of thoughts and feelings that have trapped the client in unnecessary bitterness is a more crucial theme (Flanigan, 1989).

- Forgiving is not condoning, excusing, or forgetting another's behavior; these decisions might increase one's risks for future victimization, since they involve neither a commitment from another not to injure the condoner again nor a decision on the victim's part not to be revictimized. Forgiving should never be used as a substitute for necessary behavior change.

- Clients may have to forgive themselves as well as others. Often, the two processes occur together. Individuals who begin to forgive others may find that they have been condemning themselves as well, perhaps for acting so nastily toward the offender.

There are several exercises which can help clients understand and begin or continue the forgiving process. A few of these follow.

EXERCISES

9-1 *Anger Analysis*

Anger explosions usually result from the buildup of anger-promoting thoughts, feelings, and actions. The format below can help clients break their anger into its developmental components. Often it is easiest for clients to work *backwards,* beginning at the moment just before the explosion.

Anger Analysis Sample Format

Stage 1 (early)

Thought: _____

Feeling: _____

Behavior: _____

Stage 2

Thought: _____

Feeling: _____

Behavior: _____

Stage 3

Thought: _____

Feeling: _____

Behavior: _____

Stage 4

Thought: _____

Feeling: _____

Behavior: _____

Stage 5

Thought: _____

Feeling: _____

Behavior: _____

Stage 6 (right before the explosion)

Thought: _____

Feeling: _____

Behavior: _____

9-2 Anger Cues

Bring a rubber ducky to group. Explain to the members that you will need four or five volunteers to role play a family. Establish by participant preference who will role play the parents and the children, allowing the "children" to choose their "ages."

Now ask the family to conduct a family discussion/argument about what time of day each family member gets to use the rubber ducky. Ask each person to allow him/herself to begin to get angry at some point in the discussion, and then to back off and relax.

Following the role play, which can be ended in ten minutes or so, ask the entire group to discuss the anger clues and cues they experienced and/or saw occur during the course of the role-played argument.

First, focus attention on the anger cues—physical symptoms that indicate a buildup of tension toward a boiling point, such as increased tension in the neck, shoulders, back, hands, feet, jaw, eyes, stomach or head. Secondly, examine the mental clues which increase the potential tension—words or thoughts that indicate negativity, not caring, justification for anger, or even self-congratulations for being "extra" patient. Finally, ask the participants and observers to describe any *action* clues to getting more upset and needing a time-out, such as foot tapping, finger biting, pacing, moving closer, frowning or glaring.

Now ask group members to identify for themselves which clues in each category apply to them in particular, and to make a personal list of these clues.

Finish this exercise by having the group suggest some ways to help relax again in each area. Present a short visualization of a time-out that includes cues for physical and mental relaxation, as well as slowing down and cessation of tense actions. At the end of the visualization, have group members congratulate themselves on a successful time-out.

9-3 *Anger Invitations*

Encourage angry individuals (or a couple) to examine an area called "invitations to anger." Give them some of your own examples to begin, something like this:

Just the alarm ringing this morning invited me to get angry, because I was still tired. When I got into the bathroom there was old toothpaste stuck to the sink, and it offered me an invitation to get angry—and to take my tired irritation out on my husband and the kids (whoever left the darn toothpaste there). But I decided not to. It was too early to go to an anger party. Then the Post Toasties were gone. That's my favorite cereal, and the only one I really wanted today.

Then ask the clients to discuss their own anger invitations for the day, pointing out that an anger invitation can occur anytime. Note that invitations are encouragements that we can accept or decline, and ask clients how many "anger parties" they want to attend each day and with whom. Point out that too many anger parties equals too little work done, and that anger takes all our time and attention, eating away at us.

Finally, ask clients to be aware for the next week of when they get anger invitations, when they choose to accept them, and how much they want to be angry each day.

This awareness exercise often leads to an increased awareness of choice, including a better ability to choose not to be angry all the time.

The following form may be used to explain the assignment.

ANGER NOTEBOOK/ANGER INVITATIONS

One of the ways to learn about your anger is to keep track of the times you are or could get angry. It is important that you keep a good record of these "invitations."

You will need to get a looseleaf or spiral notebook. Whenever you find yourself getting angry *or* you might have gotten angry enter that episode on the paper. Each entry in the notebook should include:

- Date
- Time
- Brief description of what happened
- Your thoughts
- Your feelings
- Your actions
- Your *choices*. This part of the notebook is very important. Notice in each situation that you always have choices: whether or not to get mad, how to express your anger, etc. Take some time here to notice the choices you have and the choices you make.

At the end of a week look over all your entries and write down your general observations about how you experience your anger.

9-4 *Disappointment/Disaster Seismograph*

The Human Richter Scale below can be useful in aiding clients to evaluate life events.

Instruct clients as follows: List the events that seem to "shake up" your life on the Human Richter Scale, being as thoughtful as possible about which events are "slight damage" disappointments and which are really "devastating" disaster. Use your list to get feedback from peers and counselors. Make adjustments to your scale, making sure that you're not turning disappointments into disasters.

Now make a list of reasonable ways to handle the disappointments and of resources to use if your Richter Scale registers any real disasters.

HUMAN RICHTER SCALE

8.5
(Devastating)
8.0
(Extensive)
7.5
(Severe)
7.0
(Serious)
6.5
(Localized)
6.0
(Distressing)
5.5
(Minor)
5.0
(Mild)
4.5
(Slight Damage)

9-5 *The Burden of Anger*

Ask the angry, resentful individual to list his resentments toward another person verbally, and then write them down for him, so you both have a record of what they are. Count the items on the list and give the client — or have him purchase — one potato (fist-sized or larger) for each resentment.

Instruct the client that his assignment is to carry the potatoes with him wherever he goes, keeping them always in the room with him. The potatoes may be disguised in any way, since resentments are often disguised. They may be carried in a knapsack, purse or briefcase, sport bag, or pocket. Carrying them everywhere often makes an individual aware of the weight and burdensomeness of his anger.

Potatoes are discarded (not eaten) as each resentment on the list is worked through. Note that when the person carries his potatoes too long before addressing his issues, they will get rotten, much like his anger. In such an instance, wrapping them in plastic protects the environment while giving the individual still carrying the burden an object lesson in what happens to anger and resentment nurtured too long.

9-6 *Forgiveness Visualization*

Here is a short visualization that a resentful client can use over time to check his or her progress in letting go of resentments. Prepare the client with a little relaxation and breathing.

> In your mind's eye, imagine the person that you would like to forgive. See her [or his] face, hear her voice or feel her presence. Get her firmly in mind. Then let go of her.
>
> Now think of yourself receiving the things that make you truly feel good, feel happy. Perhaps a breeze kissing your face, the hug of a child, a nice check in the mail, a feeling of satisfaction at work well done. Enjoy getting these things that give you pleasure.
>
> Now imagine that person you want to forgive, again. Imagine her receiving all these things, and feeling very good about herself. See how many of these good things and feelings you are able to offer her and how you feel about her receiving them. Don't worry if things aren't perfect. Just notice what you are and are not ready

to do, and how much you are willing for her to get good things and good feelings right now.

Following the visualization, discuss the results. Sometimes the client discovers that he is not ready to give the other person anything good yet. Others find that they are able to present the other with good things, but not to allow the other to "feel good" about those things yet. Have clients do this visualization several times over a period of weeks or months to help them measure their progress in letting go of resentments and learning to forgive the other person.

10

CHRONICALLY ANGRY
COUPLES and FAMILIES

The focus, until now, has been upon the chronically angry individual. However, when we remember that angry people come from and live in angry families, the need to broaden our perspective becomes clear.

This chapter describes several aspects of angry families, including their characteristics, symptoms commonly found among "adult children" from chronically angry homes, survival issues for those who live with angry individuals, and treatment suggestions when working with mutually angry couples and families. We will also present two documents we have found useful: Fair Fighting Rules for families and a Partners' Bill of Rights.

Characteristics of Chronically Angry Families

Pragmatically, a chronically angry family is one in which one or more members are excessively angry. More abstractly, a chronically angry family is one in which anger is a predominant emotion around which the family is organized. Such families support this system with beliefs that encourage the display of anger through a mutual anger-promoting training process.

Many chronically angry persons vividly remember an endless stream of fights, insults, hostile interactions, and general nastiness within their families of origin. They recall not just single incidents but a pervasively ugly mood in their homes. "You could feel the tension in the air," they might say, adding that they could always count upon somebody getting angry even when things seemed to be going well. Sometimes only one person, usually a parent, would play the role of angry person. But other families were totally angry, with each person bitter or explosive in his/her own way. Mother might yell, father sulk, the older child hit, and the younger one throw tantrums.

Parents often model the behavior their children develop. The father who throws things around when he gets angry may have a child who does the same. The young man who smashes holes in the wall may have frequently witnessed his parents smashing objects or hitting people in rage. "You think *I* have an anger problem," they might say, "You should see my *dad.*"

Chronically Angry Families Are Those in Which Anger Has Become a Major Problem-Solving Technique for at Least Some of Its Members

Children receive such messages as, "Stay away from your mother today. She's really in a bad mood," and, "Just do what you want. I'm sick of your complaining." Anger works in these families, so that those family members who act more reasonably tend to be ignored. Children learn that it pays for them to get angry.

G. R. Patterson (1985) studied the "microdynamics" of angry and physically abusive families. He found that troubled families have great difficulty stopping bothersome behavior before it escalates into attack. Instead of ignoring a child's insults, teasing, or complaints, parents are likely to do or say something negative, which in turn leads to more angry exchanges, thus forming a chain of negative interactions. It took less than 30 seconds for families in Patterson's study to break into hostilities. His main point is that "anger is not just within the individual or within his or her perceptions of the setting. Some of the determinants may actually be in the social environment" (Patterson, 1985, p. 97).

Larry came into my office covered with bruises. Once again, he told me, he had had a few drinks and then challenged everybody in the bar to a fight. He usually won these brawls because he'd go into a blind rage and fight for his life. This time, though, it was a draw. True, he had sent two men to the hospital, but the rest had beaten Larry to a pulp. Besides, one of the guys he challenged was his own brother. Maybe, he thought, it was time for a change.

We worked together for several weeks, discussing both Larry's anger and his drinking. Although he wouldn't attend A.A., he did agree to quit drinking entirely, since both his father and grandfather were recovering alcoholics. He's been sober now for about five years, and he still hasn't gone to A.A., although he calls himself an alcoholic.

During those first weeks, I'd send anger management materials home with Larry. His wife Linda read them all. Pretty soon she was sending questions to me through Larry: "I think I might also have an anger problem. What can I do?" "How come Larry's getting all the attention around here? What about me?" Since Larry complained about her anger a lot, saying she was sabotaging his progress by trying to pick fights, and since he was willing to share time, we began anger-oriented couples counseling.

Linda had her own problems with alcohol, and so she also agreed to abstain from all mood-altering chemicals. Her

Chronically angry families are not necessarily violent; nevertheless, their high levels of negativity and tension can easily lead to aggression. Many are simply loud, mean, or unhappy groups of individuals who turn to anger partly because they don't know how else to handle their concerns and anxieties. They then use anger so frequently that they have few opportunities to learn how to resolve their problems in other, more productive ways. So much of their mutual energy is directed into anger that little is left for play, love, or positive communication efforts.

anger was more slow-burning than Larry's, but it culminated in child-like tantrums that were just as nasty but less physical than Larry's.

Larry was jealous, shame-prone, short-tempered. He took pride in his aggression, seeing it as manly and virile. Linda was far too independent for his comfort. How could he protect her from harm when she insisted on working and leaving the home without always telling him where she was going? On the other hand, Larry was too old-fashioned to suit Linda. He wanted her to depend on him, but how could she do that when he was always getting into ridiculous arguments that might get him fired at any moment?

Safety was the first concern. Would they both take time-outs when they needed them? Could one person ask for a time-out and not have the other chase after saying something like "Oh, sure, go ahead. Run away. Again. See if I care, you stupid moron!" Fortunately, after a few botched efforts they did learn to take appropriate time-outs.

Secondly, could they make a commitment to quit fighting all the time? This was a couple who fought from morning till night, over everything, sometimes just to be fighting. What would hold them together if they weren't attacking each other? Was anger the "glue" that held them together? If so, what would replace it if they quit fighting? This issue was gradually settled, as both individuals opted for a truce

Chronically angry families often develop belief systems that support anger displays. Two beliefs are prevalent in these families: Excessive anger is normal and expected, and people will only be listened to when they demonstrate anger.

Excessive Anger Is Normal and Expected

Families, like individuals, can build up a tolerance to anger. Then they say things like, "Oh, that's just dad letting off steam in the battle, and then a series of peace conferences, and then a permanent end to hostilities. Mutual love and respect emerged as the new adhesives, stronger and more flexible than the old glue.

Larry and Linda decided to get better together. They both realized that their relationship was doomed if they kept drinking and fighting *or* if only one of them quit being so angry. They now go entire days without arguing, instead of hours. Most importantly, they see their arguments as a problem now, not something that all couples do as part of a relationship. ■

again. He does that all the time"—even when dad is completely out of control and perhaps dangerous. These families do not treat anger as a temporary condition or as a signal that something is wrong and needs attention. Instead, they view anger episodes as "ventilation," something that people do when they become overwhelmed with feelings or problems.

It is amazing to see what some families in treatment do *not* take very seriously. Even obviously violent episodes are dismissed because such behavior is considered normal and inevitable: "Sure, little Angie bit her brother but that's OK—she was mad and you know she has a fierce temper just like the rest of us."

Nobody Listens Until You Get Angry

Families with this belief act on it; members only attend to each other when someone yells or threatens to lose control. The family communication rule is "I better act awfully mad or nobody will even notice me." Furthermore, the parent or child who seems the angriest will indeed be the one who receives a disproportionate amount of family attention. Family members believe that people always get angry when they are serious about an issue. Someone who is not angry, then, is someone who need not be taken seriously.

This belief/rule, especially when linked with the first, may lead to continuing escalation of anger and aggression. Today's level of "real" anger becomes tomorrow's clue to the family that the individual is "only a little mad" and therefore ignorable. Yesterday's tantrums become today's normal behavior. The adolescent who had to stomp his feet for attention last year notices that now nobody even begins to listen to him until he threatens to hit his brother. Meanwhile, his brother graduates from talking loudly to swearing at the world to cursing his parents.

Anger is associated with attention, power, and control in these families. This creates a special problem in early recovery, especially if only one member attempts to be less angry. This person may discover that the family promptly disregards everything she says or does, at least for a while. Rather than being reinforced for this behavior change, the less angry individual feels punished. In fact, the family colludes, consciously or not, to force that person back into old behavior. These individuals may need much therapeutic support to maintain their new actions in the face of familial disapproval and disorganization.

Rigid roles and family structures, many of which parallel those seen in alcoholic/chemically dependent families, are frequently displayed in chronically angry families. For example, "scapegoats" (Wegscheider-Cruse, 1976) are common, that is, members who are the first to be labeled as angry and identified as a problem. For instance, an adolescent may be reported as "out of control" because of his habit of punching holes in walls when he gets frustrated. However, the family ignores his father who yells when he doesn't get his way, his resentful mother who "cold shoulders" others for days at a time, and a difficult sister who has mastered the art of blaming her brother for causing every disagreement.

"Placaters" (Satir, 1967) are relatively sensitive individuals who just want the fighting to stop. Their solution may be to anticipate problems, solving them before others are even aware of them, in order to keep others happy. Alternatively, they may step into the middle of arguments, attempting to calm people down. Then they risk becoming triangulated (Kerr & Bowen, 1988), sometimes incurring the wrath of the others. Still, placaters often believe they must intervene: "I can't just let mom and dad fight.

The last time I did dad beat her up." Unfortunately, they lock themselves into this role all the more every time they assume responsibility for regulating the arguments of others.

"Lost children" (Wegscheider-Cruse, 1976) flee the family anger and chaos. These are the children who run to their rooms, turning the radio on loudly whenever their parents fight; adolescents who stay away from home until past midnight; and spouses who go fishing or working or shopping instead of facing their partner's daily rages. These individuals may shut down emotionally, especially if they cannot physically escape.

Clients need help understanding their roles, and even more assistance escaping from rigid family configurations that "lock in" their anger. Whole family work is particularly useful here, since family members left out of therapy may resist change by insisting that others perform their traditional roles and tasks.

Paradoxically, it seems that chronically angry families are ill-suited to handle normal developmental themes around which anger is common. For example, a four-year-old child, terribly frustrated because her brother has the toy she wants, suddenly bursts into tears and shouts "I hate you" at her mother as she runs to her room. This child has been overwhelmed by emotional distress. Her world has fallen apart and she will probably need her parents to help put it back together.

Most parents realize that "I hate you" simply does not mean the same thing to a child as it does to an adult. Here it probably translates to "I am so mad at you right now I don't know what to do"—not "I despise you forever." Many parents will be hurt by this statement and yet not take it to heart. They are not insulted because they know children are not adults. They don't take this attack personally. As Parens (1987) notes, parents in this situation can help their children learn how to express their anger without hurting themselves or others.

Unfortunately, members of chronically angry families may make two unproductive responses to the child's "I hate you!" First, they may ignore it completely, since everybody says such things all the time, never recognizing the child's real pain. Secondly, they may overrespond, actually believing that the child hates them. They cannot model reasonable, modulated responses. They may not know any, or they may know other responses but do not make them because they are so habitually angry themselves.

Adolescence often brings with it a surge of moral anger, expressed best in the phrase "It's not fair!" Members of chronically angry families often do not handle adolescence very well. The children may treat their parents with great disdain and contempt. Meanwhile, parents view their children's insults as opportunities to counterattack. They may have difficulty allowing their children the right to make choices, seeing that as a challenge to their authority. Allowing the expression of difference, for instance in the selection of clothes, may also be difficult. Instead of helping their children learn how to connect choice-making with responsibility, these parents attempt to maintain control by disallowing choice. Adolescence becomes war under these conditions instead of a phase of life.

"ADULT CHILDREN" FROM CHRONICALLY ANGRY FAMILIES

The term "adult child" (Woititz, 1983) is a useful shorthand phrase which refers to the experience of adults who grew up in various kinds of dysfunctional families. Since it is commonly utilized and understood in the field of substance abuse counseling, it is used here to refer to those adults who grew up in chronically angry homes, which may or may not also have been affected by alcohol or drug dependency. The effects of this anger on adults may include a variety of characteristics such as a distrust of one's own thoughts, loss of trust, low self-esteem, vigilance, helplessness, unresolved feelings, boundary inadequacy, problems in parenting, and self-hatred (P. Potter-Efron, 1990).

Certain thoughts and behaviors seem to occur with regularity among adults who grew up in angry families. None occurs with everyone and some individuals may not demonstrate any of these characteristics. Still, we have found this list useful as a preliminary assessment tool.

- A belief that excessive anger is normal and expected.

- The erratic occurrence of child-like tantrums.

- A "hair trigger" temper and unexpected outbursts.

CASE STUDY: The Boy Who Punched Holes in the Wall

Paul was an angry adolescent with the habit of punching holes in his basement bedroom when he got fed up with his parents. Although I was seeing the entire family, there was no doubt in anybody's mind that Paul was the problem.

But why Paul? Dad was himself an angry man a lot of the time, very demanding and continually needing attention. Mom was the silent type who might not speak to you for days when she became upset. Sue, the 18-year-old daughter, was openly defiant and told us that "I'm mad, I like being mad, and I'm never going to change." Little Alan, the baby, was already in training and could throw a tantrum that would exhaust any parent. There was even an oldest child who had been expelled from the home for drug use and hadn't been heard from for two years.

Why Paul? When asked, Mom said because he would never change, and the others all agreed. Besides, Dad said Paul was so loud that he couldn't sleep. Sue called him a whiner and a tattle-tale.

And so family therapy began. All of them were given instructions on fair fighting. *Only Paul listened.* Each was told what to do to be less angry. *Only Paul changed.* No more holes in the walls. No more endless screaming. Polite requests for food at the table.

"So, how's Paul doing?" I would ask each session. "Terrible," the others agreed. "He's just the same as always." The

- "It's my turn now" — the adult as angry individual making up for helplessness experienced as a child.

- "I'll never be like them" — attempts to disown anger.

- Attraction to chronically angry people.

- Oversensitivity to anger in others.

- Intimacy problems.

CASE STUDY: continued

family was absolutely convinced that Paul would stay the scapegoat in this family. His real behavior was apparently irrelevant.

Paul needed an ally, and so therapeutic neutrality was temporarily abandoned. As family therapist, I insisted that the others recognize Paul's changes. Paul was lavishly praised for his efforts, and his parents were challenged to acknowledge and praise them. Only then did the total family picture emerge. Paul's "problem behavior" was the only thing the parents discussed together without fighting. Without his sacrifice, the family risked dissolution.

Now it was the parents' turn to deal with their issues. Lack of intimacy was a major problem here. Carl, the husband, preferred marijuana and television to family activities. Helen, his wife, had a significant problem with bulimia and compulsive overeating. Sex was an infrequent event and an excuse for arguing. Their addictive tendencies had been screened from view by their son's behavior. Now they would have to deal with them directly.

Family counseling was supplanted by couples work with the parents. Even though the children didn't attend sessions, each continued to improve. Paul's school performance improved and he fixed the holes in his walls. Sue moved out of the house in order to stay angry, then returned

Belief That Excessive Anger Is Normal and Expected

Adult children may not be angry all the time. However, they may still believe that persistent anger is a normal part of daily life. Therefore, they may allow others to act irresponsibly in this area. They might not intervene when their partners rage at their children. They may think that their families, friends, and employers have the right to verbally abuse them.

These individuals may be quite uncomfortable with their anger. But even if they recognize that others would consider the level of when that didn't work. Alan gave up most of his tantrums on schedule.

Carl and Helen were seen periodically for several months. They had to address their addictions, both as individual concerns and as a replacement for mutual intimacy. They became gradually growing closer now once they could distract themselves from their own issues. ■

anger they experience or endure to be excessive, they have learned since childhood that people in families are usually angry. Their belief systems and world views do not give them permission to alter their situations. They feel their anger is uncontrollable, or they sense that others simply get angry a lot and that one must put up with it as a routine relationship expense. Cognitive therapy (Beck et al., 1979) can be helpful here, by challenging the client's assumptions of helplessness and choicelessness.

The Erratic Occurrence of Child-Like Tantrums

Adult children from chronically angry families may exhibit a curious alternation between controlled and uncontrolled behavior. They will do very well for long periods of time, then suddenly suffer a "tolerance break" (Smalley, 1988), in which they explode into infantile, irrational outbursts. At these times higher thinking processes seem to shut down temporarily. These rages can be alarming to all, including the raging individual, and they may include dangerous acts of aggression toward others or self.

These rages seem to occur for at least two reasons. First, one or both parents modeled loss of control, demonstrating that parents periodically "lose it." Secondly, some adult children learn to dissociate during family fights, defending against overwhelming feelings by entering a kind of trance state. At these times, they quit thinking and start yelling or fighting, perhaps mimicking their parents' words and actions. On one occasion, for example, a client began yelling at his fianceé that she must never call his mother "ma." She reported that his eyes seemed to glaze over as he did so. Only later, in therapy, did he remember that he himself had been severely beaten by his father for using that expression with his own mother (he still does not know why it was a bad thing to say).

"Hair Trigger" Temper and Unexpected Outbursts

Another pattern displayed among adult children from angry families entails frequent, sudden anger, sometimes over trivial annoyances. Again, this behavior usually has been modeled by at least one parent. As a child the affected adult learned to respond with anger quickly and unthinkingly to a multitude of situations. This behavior is automatic, in that the anger represents the person's first reaction to any sort of stress. Underlying thoughts that promote this anger include the ideas that "anything new is dangerous," "don't trust anyone," and "that's the way we are in this family—quick to anger."

Some individuals with hair trigger tempers also pride themselves on how quickly they cool off. Therapists may use this occurrence to emphasize the irrational nature of such persons' outbursts: Their anger dissolves so quickly because it is not based on significant problems in the first place. In general, it is not helpful to accept someone's definition of themselves as quick-tempered, especially if there is evidence that this behavior was learned in the family or origin. What may appear to be "hair trigger" temper is quite treatable. Many individuals can develop the skills, including patience, which allow them to change their specific actions and their self-concepts.

"It's My Turn Now"—Becoming the Aggressor as an Adult

Angry parents are powerful persons even if they are not physically assaultive. Their children may have cowered and hated this anger. Simultaneously, they may have identified with the parent-aggressor, concluding that they, too, could use anger to control others. Thus, as adults they may find themselves becoming un-reasonably angry with their own children whenever they don't get their way. They deal with their own pain and fear by transfer-ring it to the next generation of victims. In this way victims become victimizers (Neilsen, 1990).

"I'll Never Be Like Them—but I Am"

Many adult children have made solemn vows never to act like their angry parents. They have sworn to raise their children with kindness, respect, praise, and gentleness. Many succeed, becom-ing excellent parents and breaking the generational pattern. Some adult children develop the opposite problem, becoming anger avoidant in their need to disown even legitimate anger. These individuals so fear the raging monster inside themselves that they shun any sensations of anger. They conclude, with absolutist thinking, that even a trace of anger demonstrates that they are really like their parents.

Sadly, many adult children engage in excessive anger despite vows to parent without anger or aggression. It is stunning to see adults who know that they are hurting their children with their sarcasm, criticism, or physical aggression, deeply capable of em-pathically understanding the pain they are creating and guilt-ridden about it, yet who apparently choose to continue a genera-tional pattern of emotional and physical abuse. Such individuals seem to alternate between appropriate adult states of awareness and more desperate, immature periods in which they feel over-whelmed by standard parental responsibilities. One minute these parents help their children deal with petty jealousies; the next they attack with their own. They may even report that when they become irate they feel more like one of the children than an adult. Spouses who witness these events often validate that impression, expressing amazement that their normally mature partners can become so "infantile" when angered.

Attraction to Chronically Angry Individuals

The phrase "You're just like my father (mother), the way you get mad at me so much" is something heard routinely in counsel-

ing. Indeed, some adult children from angry families seem mag-
netically attracted to deeply angry persons, who become their
friends, partners, and employers. They then repeat the same patterns of coping with anger that they learned with their parents.
This may be part of a repetition compulsion, in which adult
children attempt to undo damage through repeating the past
while trying to alter the results in present experience. They may
consciously recognize this pattern, even acknowledging that they
hope to heal old wounds by curing their current partner or associate. If they could only take that person's anger away, somehow
they could then deal with the old feelings of helplessness in
another, less painful manner.

On the other hand, this attraction to angry people can sometimes be explained on the basis of ingrained behavioral and cognitive habits learned in childhood and carried into adulthood.
In this case, the individual's cognitions are often deterministic,
centered around the conviction that one's fate in life is to be
surrounded by angry people. Happiness is not the issue here;
these individuals may be miserable but unable to conceive of a
life in which their partners are not angry.

Oversensitivity to Anger in Others

Many adult children are quite alert to anger cues in others. They
are particularly vigilant for nonverbal indicators, such as a slightly
tightened jaw or lowered eyebrows. Furthermore, they quickly and
automatically respond to these signals with coping mechanisms
they may have learned in childhood. Their goal is to anticipate and
cut off another's anger *before* the other person becomes aware of
it. Consequently, they may "know" that someone is angry, even
when the other person would completely deny it.

Conversations with these vigilant adult children may sound
like this: "I know you are really mad at me, aren't you?" "No, I
don't think so. Why do you say that?" "Oh, I can tell just by the
way you look at me. I can always tell when you are angry."

One problem with this behavior is that these individuals tend
to pick up and react to isolated anger indicators out of context.
Furthermore, they may overinterpret these cues, transforming a

little frustration into a sure sign that an associate is really quite angry with them (or soon will be). Additionally, the very fearfulness that drives these individuals to search for anger may keep them from noticing any other emotions. Their understanding of the affective worlds of others may contain only the two states of "angry" and "not angry."

Intimacy Problems

Adult children from chronically angry families may have difficulty expressing "soft" feelings such as love, caring, and interest in others. Anger may have displaced these emotions in the family of origin. These feelings were perhaps not expressed because people were too busy being angry. Or they may have been expressed in a distorted and damaging fashion, as when a parent pinches or mercilessly tickles a child as an alleged sign of affection. Parents who severely discipline their children "so they don't get spoiled" or because "it's a tough world out there and they better be ready for it" provide further examples of this pattern. Children may indeed recognize their parents' attempts at intimacy, but it is certainly confusing when a parent follows critical or abusive attacks with touch, hugs, and apologies—only to return to being unpredictably angry. These individuals may bring similar habits into their adult lives, becoming confused when confronted by others who do not understand the positive meaning of their apparently hostile actions. "But that's how my parents showed they love me. What's wrong with what I'm doing?" they may complain. Some become adults who believe that love invariably hurts and that a relationship is not "the real thing" unless it is painful, angry, and destructive. These are adult children who repeatedly choose chaotic, angry, distant, or impossible/incompatible partners and end relationships that could be calm, nurturing, and productive.

With help and determination, adult children from chronically angry families can change the patterns noted above. The first phase of this process is to provide them with new information about what they can do when they encounter individuals who are chronically angry.

COUNSELING CLIENTS WHO LIVE
WITH ANGRY INDIVIDUALS

It is difficult for anyone to live with those who are frequently irrationally angry. Rewards may be few and praise virtually non-existent in such situations. There may be a danger of violence, perhaps unpredictable and unexplained.

The following suggestions are designed for individuals in this situation, to help them survive physically and emotionally. Counselors can introduce these suggestions to their clients as they are presented below.

- Protect your physical safety first.

- You have the right to be treated with respect.

- Don't accept responsibility for someone else's anger.

- Don't get hooked by becoming excessively angry yourself.

- Get support from others.

- Observe what the angry person achieves with his or her anger.

- Learn how the other's chronic anger has affected you.

- Consider how you handle anger. Are you anger avoidant or chronically angry?

- Consider leaving when a chronically angry person cannot or will not change.

If physical danger is a concern, therapists should help their clients design appropriate plans to minimize this risk. These plans may include leaving the scene at early signs of trouble or going to the home of a friend or a shelter facility. If flight is impossible, clients should stay as calm as they can, using a steady voice, making relatively slow movements, maintaining physical distance, and utilizing neutral (non-emotional) language to lessen the confrontational tone of the interaction. Clients should also be advised to report any physical abuse, whether directed at them or their children, to the police.

Clients can only utilize these plans when they believe they have the right to be treated with respect. By defining and giving examples of physical, sexual, and emotional abuse, therapists can help clients understand the meaning of interpersonal respect. It may be valuable to focus on the concept of shaming communications (Potter-Efron & Potter-Efron, 1989a), defined as verbal or nonverbal behavior that diminishes the recipient. Examples of shaming statements include swearing at people or calling them names, ignoring them, being overly critical, and saying or implying that the other is inferior. Long-term victims of shaming interaction may need to learn from counselors and new peers that such behavior is not normal or inevitable.

It is important that recipients of chronic anger "detach" from this anger, not taking it too personally, since its source is in the habits of the chronically angry individual. They can learn to do so in several ways. First, clients can reject taking responsibility for another's anger. This means refusing to accept the argument "You make me angry" as a valid excuse for angry or aggressive actions. Clients who have heard such claims repeatedly need to recognize them for what they are: attempts by chronically angry individuals to give away responsibility for their own behavior. Angry persons must learn to expect everyone, including themselves, to be accountable for their own actions.

Second, clients need to make a personal commitment not to respond to anger with anger. Instead, they must learn to substitute selective inattention and calm assertiveness. Selective inattention refers to the practice of ignoring anger-provoking statements, the "anger invitations" previously described. One useful analogy (at least in Wisconsin, where fishing is a popular hobby), is to compare such invitations to bait on a hook. The goal is to see the bait and pass it by. Assertiveness training (Alberti & Emmons, 1986) may also be helpful with those who live with or around chronically angry individuals. Initially the gains may be more theoretical than practically useful, since the chronically angry person is unlikely to cooperate in establishing a mutually assertive environment. Still, the mere knowledge that assertiveness is possible can be quite empowering, giving the recipient of anger a choice of responses.

Counselors should emphasize the value of getting support

from others to break the sometimes overpowering influence of chronically angry persons on those around them. Clients will often be remarkably affected by meeting a few times with less angry individuals, just realizing how much of their time and energy has revolved around another's anger. Support groups also provide encouragement for efforts at detachment and motivation to pursue long-term goals in the face of immediate failure or despair. Developing a support groups is particularly important in instances of spouse abuse, since many abusers systematically attempt to isolate their partners.

A principal goal of family therapy is to help clients gain objectivity (Kerr & Bowen, 1988) about the nature of their situation. This is essential for clients involved in the detachment process from chronic anger. Objectivity is fostered by helping clients observe what the angry person achieves with anger, noticing how they have been personally affected, and considering how they handle anger themselves.

In Chapter 6, we discussed several possible gains from chronic anger, such as power and control, emotional distance, a defense against shame, and exhilaration. Therapists can review these possibilities with their clients, assisting them to identify what others are achieving with their anger displays. This often breaks through client denial or a naive belief that angry persons just "get mad" without cause.

It is also important to foster clients' awareness of how their lives have been affected by another's chronic anger. One way is to have clients answer the following questions:

- How do your feelings change when the other person gets angry?

- How do you alter your behavior to try to keep someone from becoming upset?

- What long-term changes have taken place as a result of being around an angry person?

- How has your self-concept been affected?

- What have you lost or gained as a result of this experience?

- How has your thinking been affected?

- Have there been any related spiritual or religious changes?

Pointing out how the client's beliefs about the world and themselves have changed as a result of their relationship with a chronically angry person addresses the brainwashing process victims of chronic anger and abuse endure. So does the metaphor of being a hostage for those whose angry partners/parents isolate them. It is relevant to note that hostages, since they are dependent upon their captors for survival, may become very caring, caretaking, and loyal to those who are dominating them. They may adopt the world view of the person upon whose good will their survival appears to depend, abandoning their own real and centered understanding of the world.

Therapists should be aware that a client may respond strongly to the above questions, perhaps becoming quite angry or depressed. Such responses can be framed as a positive indicator that the individual is finally recognizing the devastating effects of living with or within the influence of a chronically angry person. Once a certain level of emotional release is achieved, clients can be helped to begin the more objective process of planning how to alter their future behavior.

Clients also need to assess how their own anger has been affected. Individuals may gradually move toward either extreme, becoming more anger avoidant or irrationally angry. They may view this as an inevitable reaction to their situation: "I've got to really watch myself so I don't ever get angry. That's the only way I can keep my sanity around him." "Wouldn't anybody get angry after living with her for a few years? Wouldn't you?" The therapist's task here is to help clients regain control of their own emotions, especially if there was a time when they had a more moderate approach to anger.

Reviewing a list of fair fighting rules will remind some clients of skills they regularly used to utilize but have abandoned under the pressure of constant conflict. Fairly often, a person who has reacted to chronic anger with anger can effect significant system changes by fighting fairly him/herself over a three- or four-month period. As the recipient of the anger remains calm, states feelings, and refuses to be "hooked" into reacting with anger, the chronically angry person may eventually respond by behaving with less anger than before.

Finally, counselors should discuss with clients the possibility of their leaving the chronically angry person. This alternative is necessary to consider if it appears that the angry person cannot or will not change. The need to look for signs of change should be emphasized, however, since the entire process may be rather slow and positive movement may be difficult for the client to recognize. Though patience is very important, for both helper and client, exit may be the ultimate effective strategy. When this is the case, the therapist can help clients to accept this choice, deal with any ensuing guilt, and take active charge of their lives.

THERAPY WITH CHRONICALLY ANGRY COUPLES AND FAMILIES

Therapy with chronically angry couples and families is difficult, interesting, and energetic work. It is seldom boring. The most common problem is keeping the energy level in check. The first process goal of the counselor is to *stay in control of the situation* without taking on the role of judge or policeman. This is best accomplished by limiting anger displays in the office or group room to a few minutes, just long enough to establish negative patterns of behavior. Therapists can then ask clients to predict how what has just been seen would continue, if not contained, through the stages of buildup and explosion.

Another possible impediment to growth is that many chronically angry individuals considerably distort reality to fit a world view in which others spend most of their time purposely upsetting them. This is one reason we suggest seeing couples and families together if possible. When the client is seen alone, it is more difficult not to ally with his or her misperceptions, even if every effort is made to maintain neutrality. We must *identify and confront two distinct distortion sets* when both partners are chronically angry, either of which, if left untreated, will seriously undermine system change. We believe the treatment of choice is couples or family therapy, unless there is evident physical danger to one or both partners.

Therapists need to *distinguish different variants of chronic anger*. One couple may be mutually combative, continually at war with each other. These individuals seem to be constantly arguing or physically fighting, at home and in the office. Mutual hostility defines the relationship itself. Therapy with this couple may not even be possible, if there is a continuing risk of violence or if the commitment toward mutual annihilation is too strong. Such spouses need immediate behavioral help, with an emphasis on the ways they trigger and increase both their own anger and that of their partner. Although both clients and counselors may view the therapeutic potential of these couples as limited, they do have a chance to break through their anger impasse. Indeed, they are frequently astounded to discover that they can contain their anger through the use of such relatively simple tactics as actually listening to what the other person is saying. Suddenly free from mandatory argumentativeness, they may remember the positive aspects of each other that brought them together initially. Perhaps more with these couples than others, it is important for the therapist to serve as a champion and spokesperson for the marriage (Solomon, 1989).

A second couple type features one aggressor and one resenter. The aggressor continually ventilates anger toward the other, who initially may seem calm but is storing his or her anger for future use. This person develops resentments, which may be demonstrated through the use of cynicism or sarcasm, nonverbal gestures of disdain, and a"cold," icy anger that more than matches the partner's "hot" anger. The timing of anger expression is a common problem with these couples. The more explosive individual may become angry quickly, ventilate, feel relief, and think the entire issue is over; meanwhile the resenter slowly simmers inside and then finally erupts, to the complete surprise of the partner, whose reaction may then be to become angry again, but now over the partner's unfairly bringing up old business. This pattern will occur during therapy and can be quite frustrating to the counselor who believes an issue has been settled only to discover that the resenter has only begun. It is vital to help these couples recognize the differences in how they experience and

express their anger, and while doing so to define each style positively. If possible, the participants need to learn how to "stretch"
toward each other; quick erupters must slow down their anger
and tolerate the resenter's need to talk about seemingly old issues; resenters need help addressing their concerns more immediately and understanding their partner's "short fuse."

A third pattern features one obviously angry person with a
passive-aggressive partner. The passive aggressor may appear in
a martyr role, absorbing the partner's wrath without doing anything. But that inactivity is a powerful weapon. The "victim"
frustrates the partner with forgetfulness, irresponsibility, and indifference. This is a difficult pattern to interrupt, since passive
aggressors rarely label such behavior as angry or aggressive. Their
therapeutic response tends to be "Yeah, but . . . ," as they frus-
trate the counselor with the same mechanisms they use with
their partners. Homework assignments are often undone or forgotten by the passive aggressor, triggering "You just must not
care about me" messages from their partners—to which the passive aggressors can take offense and feel misunderstood. Progress
with such couples is normally slow and tedious, but not impossible. Emphasis must be placed upon helping passive aggressors
feel more in charge of their own lives. It is probably wise to begin
in areas in which their partners have patience. For example, they
may be given responsibility for initiating sexual contact, provided
that a mutual time frame for the experiment is understood. Success should be defined as the passive aggressor's making a sincere
effort to complete the assignment, not as total behavioral enact-
ment. Small movements toward initiative must be praised; the
counselor should avoid falling into the trap of expecting anything
specific from the passive aggressor.

Family therapists must work diligently to *join the family*
(Minuchin & Fishman, 1981) when working with very angry families in which there is an abundance of hostile and even dangerous
behavior. Many negative interactions will have to be ignored in
order to concentrate upon the most immediately significant or
modifiable ones. Counselors must be adept at making temporary
alliances with members who are willing or able to change at a
particular moment, without becoming permanently bound to
them. It is important, however, to notice which family members

seem most capable and interested in change and to consistently support their efforts and hopes.

The starting point with most couples and families is *calling a truce*. This provides a temporary breathing spell while helping to break negative communication spirals. We usually ask each person in the couple or family to agree to cease using one of his/her weapons, such as swearing or sneering at the others. The very act of cataloging each person's weapons provides needed information about family interactions and may also remind members of their power to hurt each other and the responsibility that goes with that power. It is vital to include a clear message that the use of violence is not acceptable under any circumstances.

It is valuable to help family members *assess how anger has affected the relationship*. Examples include lessening mutual trust, excessive amounts of time and energy spent fighting, mutually lowered self-esteem, mutual guilt, the development of resentments, loss of optimism, feeling sick, trapped or hopeless, and a sad awareness that love is being lost in the fog of anger. Even a few minutes reflecting on the tragic aspects of the latter may help strengthen the resolve of family members to stop the anger that is destroying the family unit.

Positive goals must be set, since simply ending the anger will just create a vacuum. Since a vacuum can readily be filled with other problematic behaviors, it is essential to focus therapeutic effort on the creation of positive interactions. Besides, just trying to end negative behavior may turn counseling time into endless "look what he did to me" sessions. The general theme is to replace angry and shaming interactions with those based in respect (Potter-Efron & Potter-Efron, 1989a). More specific goals can be contracted for with each family at the beginning of therapy and later as more information about the group is obtained. The *Partners' Bill of Rights* provided in Table 5 is helpful both in finding areas of disrespect and in providing positive direction for angry couples and families.

Praise is usually in short supply in chronically angry families, often because members are often overly competitive, fighting among themselves for any remnants of respect or appreciation. Additionally, angry persons concentrate on what others are doing wrong, if only to perpetuate and justify their anger. We *encourage*

TABLE 5
Partners' Bill of Rights

1. *My partner has the right to feel good about him/herself in spite of me and my problems.* Just because I feel miserable, that doesn't mean my partner should feel that way, too. And my partner doesn't always have to be oriented toward fixing things for me.

I have the right to feel good about myself in spite of my partner's problems. I care about how my partner feels, but I am not expected or obligated to fix his/her problems for him/her, or to feel badly just because s/he is feeling badly.

2. *My partner has the right to express his/her feelings and share his/her pain.* I do not have to take his/her expression of feelings personally and feel guilty, at fault, or blamed.

I have the right to express my feelings and share my pain. I will do so respectfully. And my partner does not have to take what I say to him/her personally and feel guilty or at fault, or accept blame just because I give it.

3. *My partner has a right to his/her dislikes and doesn't always have to please me or to sell him/herself short.* It is all right for my partner to have his/her own tastes, whether they are the same as mine or not.

I have the right to my likes/dislikes and don't always have to please my partner or to sell myself short. It's all right for me to have tastes that are different from those of my partner.

4. *My partner has a right to pursue his/her own interests and hobbies.* It may be necessary for us to negotiate time and money issues together.

I have a right to my own interests and hobbies and the right to pursue them. It may be necessary for us to negotiate time and money issues together.

5. *My partner has a right to be whoever s/he is and doesn't have to change to pacify me.* This includes a right to do his/her tasks in his/her own way without being discounted. I can learn to tolerate and appreciate his/her differences from me, rather than to have to convert him/her to my way of thinking, doing, and living in every way.

I have the right to be whoever I am and don't have to change to pacify my partner. This includes a right to do my tasks in my own way without being discounted by criticism that I am stupid, inefficient, or the like. My partner can learn to appreciate my differences from him/her, rather than to have to convert me to his/her way of doing things.

6. *My partner has a right to say "no" to things that violate his/her values and deep needs and to things s/he feels infringe on his/her rights as a person.* If I disagree strongly on these issues, I will use fair fighting rules and honest expression of feelings over time to work them out, rather than trying to use power, manipulation, and pressure to get my way. I understand that difficult issues need time to work out smoothly.

I have a right to say "no" to things that violate my values and deep needs and to things I feel infringe on my rights as a person. If my partner and I disagree strongly on these issues, I have the right to be treated fairly and with respect, and to have the time I need to work through these issues with him/her.

7. *My partner has the right to be human and make mistakes.* In fact, his/her mistakes can help me recognize that we are both human, and that I make mistakes, too. I will do my best to leave his/her past mistakes in the past.

I have the right to be human and to make mistakes. I do not have to be perfect to be lovable.

(continued)

TABLE 5
Continued

8. *My partner has the right to be treated with respect.* S/he does not deserve to be yelled at, sworn at, called names, put down, discounted, or criticized. If I should feel discounted, I will not respond by doing the same thing back, but look carefully at my own behavior first. Only after I am very sure that I am not discounting or disrespecting him/her verbally or nonverbally will I respectfully challenge the behaviors I feel s/he uses that are disrespectful to me.

    I have the right to be treated with respect. I do not deserve to be yelled at, sworn at, called names, discounted, or criticized. I have the right not to tolerate abuse if my partner fails to treat me respectfully on a regular basis.

9. *My partner has a right to be listened to and taken seriously.* I will not dismiss what s/he has to say as the "same old thing," or stop listening in the middle of a discussion. I will not interrupt or spend the time just thinking about what to say back to make my point. I will take a "time-out" if I need one, but not just leave or ignore my partner.

    I have a right to be listened to and taken seriously. However, I will not expect my partner to be perfect. If I feel I haven't been heard, I will find an appropriate time to respectfully restate myself without attacking.

10. *My partner has the inherent right to feel worthwhile and valuable.* I will not discount who s/he is, but spend my time looking positively for his/her strengths so that I can point them out appropriately and appreciatively. I will find times to praise my partner without diluting my praise with criticism.

    I have the inherent right to feel worthwhile and valuable. I will not discount who I am, but spend my time looking positively for my strengths, rather than depending on my partner to support my sense of self. I will find times to praise myself without diluting my praise with criticism.

praise specifically by teaching chronically angry couples and families how to give each other positive affirmation of their behavior and identities. See the description of the Praise Circle in the exercises for a tool that we use for this purpose.

    Another useful practice is to *study the mutual escalation process* in the couple or family. This can be done simply with a "First you do this and then you do this and then what happens?" format. It may be helpful to role play scenes from arguments in a playful manner, especially when working with young children. Behavior should be placed in the context of each individual's feelings, thoughts, and assumptions about the others. Identifying "trigger words" and behaviors that cue couples and families to initiate hostilities is an essential aspect of this task. This also provides an opportunity to examine how the escalation process might be curtailed through the choices that individual family members make about their behaviors.

The *relationship between anger and control* needs to be established. Many times the expression of anger is both an attempt to dominate others and a symptom of underlying feelings of powerlessness and helplessness. Tasks here are to help individuals locate how their anger may be a sign of their lack of power, to identify needs they believe are in danger of not getting met, and to provide alternative ways for them to express these needs. Assertiveness materials (Alberti & Emmons, 1986) may be useful in this situation, as part of a process of converting hostile and unproductive communications into more positive interactions.

Fair fighting is a skill that can be described and taught to families. In exercise 10-6, a simple fair fighting list of "dos and don'ts" is provided for use with both couples and families.

Rigidity is a serious problem in many chronically angry families. Individuals think in "black or white" terms, behave in "either/or" ways, and moralize in "good or bad" dichotomies. Excessive anger occurs among these individuals as they clash over apparently irreconcilable viewpoints. Members of these families are unable to accept each others' perceptions as anything but morally corrupt. Consequently, we stress the need for *acceptance of difference* among family members. Family members must begin to tolerate and respect their different approaches to life's problems. Practically, this respect can be encouraged through utilization of empathy-building exercises, such as role switching and asking partners to "put yourself in the other's shoes."

Many troubled couples and families do learn to free themselves from the bonds of chronic anger. Counseling is usually a frustrating process, with periods of gain alternating with plateaus and occasional backsliding. At times it may appear that the therapist is the only person in the room on the side of the marriage (Solomon, 1989) or family. However, this is not often the real situation. Usually, the very anger that is so evident is a sign of intense investment in the relationship, an investment that can be constructively channeled toward love and respect.

EXERCISES

10-1 *Learned Beliefs About Family Anger*

Present the following list of statements. Have participants circle those statements that apply to their family of origin and check each statement that applies to their current family of procreation.

In a group, use this list to discuss core beliefs and myths about anger they learned in the families into which they were born, and whether they are currently passing any of these beliefs or myths on to their own children.

1. The only way to get attention is to get angry.
2. To solve a problem, you have to get angry.
3. Anger is the only feeling it's safe to share.
4. People try to make problems for each other.
5. Everything that happens is somebody's fault.
6. People will give in if you complain long enough.
7. People expect the worst from each other.
8. If you don't get somebody back, they won't respect you.
9. Getting mad is just part of everyday life.
10. Everybody needs to get their anger out — it's good for you.
11. If you're serious about something, you show it by getting mad.
12. People in this family just have hot tempers.

10-2 *Anger Incident Diary*

Have persons living with individuals who are chronically angry keep an "anger incident" diary, especially noting when they get "hooked" or accept their partners' invitations to get angry. Point out how they have fallen into "playing the game" when they get hooked, and explore alternative strategies for dealing with their partners in each situation, including ideas for using selective inattention and clear assertiveness.

Maintain the anger incident diary over several weeks so that clients can look back and see how they have grown in learning how "not to get hooked."

10-3 *Looking at the Changes*

Have persons who live with someone who is chronically angry examine some of the damage to themselves — and pierce their denial — by assigning them to answer the following questions:

1. How do your feelings change when _____ gets angry?

2. How do you alter your behavior to try to keep _____ from becoming upset?

3. What long-term changes have taken place in you as a result of being around an angry person?

4. How has your self-concept been affected?

5. What have you lost or gained as a result of this experience?

6. How has your thinking been affected by this experience?

7. Have there been any related spiritual or religious changes?

10-4 *Inner Circle of Anger Recipients*

Ask those members of a group who have been in the role of the scapegoat (or the person most often blamed for things), to form a small circle within the larger group. Any other persons who feel that they have been "shame and blame" carriers for their families may also join. However, the inner circle should probably not become larger than five people.

Ask the participants in the inner circle to share with each other how it feels to be a target of anger. Encourage them to discuss the immediate and long-range effects this has had upon them. To minimize self-pity and hopelessness, also have them discuss how they have survived and even grown healthy despite this situation.

Since victims of anger often learn to be victimizers as well (Neilsen, 1990), have them discuss their own appropriate or inappropriate uses of anger.

In a chemical dependency treatment setting, inquire as to the effects of the scapegoat role upon their use of mood-altering substances.

10-5 *Hard Eyes and Soft Eyes*

Explain to participants that people can look at each other with "hard eyes"—critical, judging vision—or with "soft eyes"—curious, accepting vision. Role play simple life situations, such as a child lying to a parent, a partner making a mistake, or an error on the part of a waiter. Have participants look at the same error through "hard eyes," explaining what they see, think, and feel while seeing this way. Then ask them to look again at the situation, this time with "soft eyes." Again, have them describe what they see, think, and feel. Ask them in what manner they themselves would like their actions seen. This exercise can be especially useful for teaching empathy and tolerance of others within a family context.

10-6 *Use of Fair Fighting Rules*

Fair fighting rules are especially useful for angry couples and families. When offered for the first time, each rule must be carefully examined and explained. It is not true that angry people always know what it means to "listen" or how to "stick to one issue." The more concrete the counselor's explanation, the better. For example, in explaining the "Stick to one issue" rule to clients, one could say, "That means that if Sid brings up the fact that I consistently forget my keys and have forgotten them again, we must finish discussing that issue. I don't get to respond by telling Sid that he forgets to give me phone messages. I have to deal with my responsibility and Sid's feelings about my forgetting my keys first. Then, when that is all over, if I need to also talk to Sid about a problem, I can." Or I might suggest that to "listen means to hear the words and try to understand what they mean. When I am preparing a response in my own head to what the other person is saying, then I am not listening. I am assuming I already know what the other person means instead of trying to figure out what he means in this situation. To listen I must give the other person my complete attention for a moment. I may still not agree with him, but I have to make a sincere attempt to understand what he is saying."

Angry people do much better with these rules if (1) the rules are explained in detail, as above, no matter how intelligent the people; (2) they are asked to put a copy in prominent places at home and also carry copies in their wallet or purse to refer to; (3) they are taught that change is not immediate and no one is perfect, but that their job—*their only job*—is to monitor their *own* compliance to these rules. They are not to monitor their partner's compliance, point out their partner's violations, or fight over the fair fighting rules in any way. Their goal is to use the fair fighting rules themselves so that they can respect their own behavior. Participants are given the information that when one member of a couple or some family members consistently comply with the rules instead of getting drawn into nasty fighting, at first it will be frustrating for them. They will be angry because it will feel like those who are not obeying the rules are "getting away with something." They are asked to use time-outs to help them be patient with family members who refuse to fight fair. In fact, the system as a whole almost always changes to become considerably more fair within a few weeks, with even those who are "refusing to fight fair" altering their behavior in many small but interesting and helpful ways. Fair fighters are asked not to point these changes out unless they are asked to validate them, but to simply "mind their own business" by continuing to fight fair themselves.

Fair Fighting Rules

DON'T	DO
Mimic or mock others	State feelings
Hit, push, pinch, shove, restrain etc., or threaten to do so	Stick to *one* issue at a time
	Sit down and talk
Stand up and yell	Take time-outs as needed
Make faces	Listen
Name-call	Focus on behavior, not the person as a whole
Get stuck in the past	Make regular eye contact
Run away from the issue	Be flexible—have the option to change your mind
Say "forget it," "tough," "I don't care," "so what," etc.	Breathe calmly
Get the last word in	Be open to negotiation
Have to win	Be responsible for what you say
Say "always" or "never"	
Interrupt	

10-7 Fair Fighting Training

Individuals in group and family group therapy, as well as angry individuals in work settings, can be taught to fight fairly with ease and a high level of acceptance using the following format:

1. Individuals are asked to find partners to practice with, but not to partner up initially with members of their own family.

2. Individuals are then asked to look at their rules sheet and to circle the three "Don'ts" that they do most (are "best" at), and then to circle the three "Do's" that they need to practice most. When individuals have done this, they are told that they are going to practice "fighting" and to start by practicing "unfair fighting." They are cautioned that they may not actually be

physical or leave the room, but can act these habits out by pretending to threaten verbally or by turning their backs on their partners.

3. Partners are then offered a topic to "fight" about: for example, "who is going into therapy," "where we are going to go to dinner," or "who blew the budget." They are told to go ahead and fight as unfairly as they wish with their partners. The response to this instruction is ordinarily a roar of noise and many people laughing, as they all act out their worst fighting habits. The unfair fight is allowed to continue for three to five minutes, with participants being encouraged to "be creative." At the end of that time, partners are asked first to talk the experience over with each other, and then to report in the large group what happened, what if anything was resolved, and what they noticed about this kind of fighting.

4. Next partners are asked to fight again, on the same topic, but this time concentrating on the "Do" list, and especially working hard on the three items they have circled that they need to practice most. At the end of three to five minutes they again are asked to give each other feedback and to comment to the larger group on what happened, what if anything was resolved, and what they notice about this kind of fighting.

5. The next training step is to help family members and couples use the fair fighting rules to practice on actual issues in group or individual sessions, with the group or therapist providing monitoring functions for the couples. Again, it is important to caution the related pair to monitor only their own learning, and not each other's performance.

10-8 Praise Circle

This exercise was originally printed in Shame, Guilt, and Alcoholism (Potter-Efron, 1989). It operates on the principle that shaming or angry individuals need to substitute positive behaviors for negative ones they abandon. Here the goal is to help individuals and families learn to exchange praise for criticism.

A family is asked to join hands (the therapist should be included in the circle to demonstrate that he has joined the family and that he is not afraid to share caring feelings). Then a parent is instructed to begin the process by specifically praising one other individual in the family. This gives the therapist an opportunity to observe how comfortable that parent is in giving praise and emphasizes the importance of parental leadership in this task. Vague statements ("Oh, I guess I like you a little, but I don't know why"), phony praise ("I just like everything about you"), refusals ("I can't think of anything about him I can praise"), and hidden criticisms ("Well, I did like it when you took out the garbage, once, weeks ago [but you haven't done it since, so you are bad]") are disallowed. The individual who receives praise then must select someone else in the family to give a positive message. This process is repeated until everybody receives and gives two or three statements. Receivers are monitored to ensure that they actually hear the praise they are given and they are challenged when they attempt to discount those statements. Giver and receiver must make eye contact while interacting.

After the praise circle is completed, we ask participants to share their feelings. This usually leads to a discussion about how the family has lost the habit of praise over time, partly as an effect of drinking. Normally, members express grave doubts about the family being able to give each other praise at home. This negative attitude is realistic, given the thousands of episodes of criticism family members have exchanged. Nevertheless, the counselor can lend hope, pointing out that they have just succeeded in changing that pattern if only for a few minutes and that they probably all feel better because of it. The therapist can then assign homework tasks such as having the family try the praise circle at home or instructing each person to "secretly" give praise to someone else. I generally follow up these assignments by repeating the circle in the next family session.

Recovering alcoholics and their families benefit greatly when they substitute praise and respect for shame messages. This creates a positive atmosphere in the present that frequently contrasts sharply both with the recent past of that group and with the alcoholic's family of origin. Shame from the past is more likely to be resolved when an individual lives in a situation where respect for one another is modeled and practiced.

11

SELF-DESTRUCTIVE ANGER

Self-destructive anger is another kind of anger commonly exhibited by clients reporting addiction and/or having been affected by addiction or abuse in family relationships. Self-destructive anger is anger directed toward the individual's own self. It is seen in both simple and complex forms related to chemical dependency. Chemical use itself can be an expression of self-destructive anger. So can eating disorders, accidents, promiscuity, excessive self-blame, suicide attempts, and self-mutilations such as cutting, burning or sticking oneself with pins. There is no single relationship established between any given drug and self-abuse or self-destructiveness. Many different relationships are found, partly depending on the function of alcohol or drug use for the client.

Those who exhibit self-destructive anger coincident with chemical use also exhibit anger against the self when they are not using chemicals, though perhaps at a less significant level. An individual who self-mutilates or makes suicide attempts when intoxicated often has, can, and may do the same when not using. A sober attempt at self-mutilation may have less physically severe consequences, if the drug is being used partly to anesthetize pain. However, the individual who is self-destructive with anger will almost always be found to be a self-hater in attitude and orientation or a manipulative threatener of the self when angry, even when he is not intoxicated. It is also possible that the drunk who makes a sloppy, unsuccessful attempt at suicide can make a more successful one when he gets sober if he has the determination and energy for it. The counselor needs to be alert to each situation.

Many addicts use alcohol or drugs as an excuse to become angry, a way to obtain angry "excitement" in life, or simply a disinhibitor of anger expressed toward others. However, a significant number of persons addicted and affected by addiction have substantial anger, but such strong prohibitions against expressing it toward others that even disinhibition through intoxication will only allow them to express that anger toward themselves. When abstinent, these persons tend not to express anger outwardly, but to maintain a pattern of anger and aggression kept in. This is sometimes observable in self-hating thoughts or behaviors, such as verbal self-condemnations or self-neglect. Occasionally it is not observable at all, and the individual with internalized anger is seen as selfless and usually unruffled. When this pattern is found in affected family members, they have often played family roles of "lost" children or caretakers. Lack of self-care can also be an expression of self-destructive anger.

SOURCES OF SELF-DESTRUCTIVE ANGER

Sources of self-destructive anger are varied. Identification of the source of self-abuse and neglect is very important in choosing an appropriate treatment strategy. Personality anger, biologically or chemically related anger, familial anger, and social rage all contribute to the formation of deep pockets of aggressive unrest that persons can direct against themselves. Self-destructive anger as evidenced in the behavior and cognitions of addicts and affected family members often stems from a mixture of these sources.

Depression is a common component of the lives of self-destructive clients. It may be biologically inherited, chemically created, or caused by situational stress. Children in angry/addictive families may be taught to hate themselves and may develop patterns of internalized anger and self-rejection in cognition, emotion, and behavior. Others have been taught that they do not belong in the family because of familial rejection of certain characteristics they possess, such as homosexuality, disliked gender, or disability of some sort. Because anger brings even greater rejection or punishment, they have learned that it must be turned inward in order for them to survive in a hostile environment.

Several conditions in alcoholic and dysfunctional families help to create individuals who are self-destructive. Abuse, which cripples the self-concept, leaving an individual blaming himself for family problems, is a primary contributor. It becomes especially powerful in creating self-destructive anger when the individual has blamed himself, deciding that he is a jinx and inherently harmful and dangerous to others. To be bad or harmful in oneself is to deserve punishment. If the pattern of being abused by others stops or the individual leaves the original home environment, necessary punishment will often be meted out by the individual to himself, since the figure he has depended upon for punishment is no longer available. Brainwashing, which leads a person in a family to feel that he is especially responsible for the problems of all others or that he is unlovable and a self-creator of the abuse he receives, is especially influential in the establishment of patterns of self-abuse. The victim who sees himself as more powerful than the abuser, believing that it is his own evil or inadequate character that causes the bad behavior of others, has a negative self-concept which is grandiose—it may decree that only he can provide appropriate punishment for himself. Brainwashing also contributes to self-destructive behavior when a victim joins the rest of the family in viewing himself as contemptible or disgusting, rejecting himself in much the same way that those who have actually held power and control reject him.

In addition, the experience of learned helplessness in an angry family can give rise to self-destructive behavior. One learns that one is helpless when no response in life improves one's position; then suicide or self-abuse for anesthesia may appear to be the only possible solution when difficulties seem overwhelming. Traumatic events create a fragmentation of the self. Sometimes this encourages the construction of character patterns in which a person hates and wants to destroy the weaker parts of himself, which he holds responsible for his having been treated violently. The individual here is attempting to eradicate the vulnerable aspects of himself in order to erase the potential for being hurt so badly again. In effect, he takes over the role of the abuser or persecutor himself, with reference to his own body and soul. The self-abuse represents the destruction of the part of him which is most easily hurt by others.

Other causes of self-destructive anger include family shaming, rejection, and social influences such as racism, gender bias, homophobia, strong social judgment and peer ridicule. Peer abuse and social condemnation, overt or covert, seem to have a more potent effect on persons whose familial background has already been rigid, critical, and rejecting. The person who has already learned to blame himself for others' problems finds it much easier to blame himself for his own and to judge himself unacceptable and punishable.

Those adult children who live with survivor guilt from the family of origin sometimes also adopt a self-destructive attitude in the face of peer or other social criticism, as a method of reinforcing the appropriateness of self-punishment. Survivor guilt may be especially connected with self-destructive expression of anger when the survivor of abuse has had his own aggressive desires that the most abused family member be hurt or punished. Survivor guilt may be very strong in the experience of a person in recovery who took on a placating or helpful role, choosing to dislike the victim and encourage the abuser in order to stay safe himself.

Self-destructive anger results in acute and often chronic self-abuse and self-neglect. Certain internal positions of those who accumulate anger and have difficulty expressing it appear to lend themselves to the development of self-destructive anger. Some of these positions are:

- I hurt myself because I am bad.

- I hurt myself because I do not want to hurt you.

- I hurt myself to hurt you.

- I hurt myself to feel something.

- I hurt myself because I am ashamed and afraid.
- I hurt myself to get your attention.

I Hurt Myself Because I Am Bad

Self-abusers who take this position as a result of dysfunctional social relationships may be addicts. They are very often also children of addicted or chronically angry and abusive parents. These individuals usually have internalized poisonous messages from others through the process of introjection. They have accepted negative statements by others about themselves as a part of their core belief system. They may hurt themselves because they have been scripted to do so, thus verifying a parental/family belief that there is something wrong with them, and fulfilling the needs of other members of the family system. Or they may become self-abusive because in a critical system where they perceive themselves to be just as bad as they have been judged, self-punishment is the only way of maintaining autonomy and independence — the only way they know for sure that the punishment that is meted out is under their own control. This is a way of preserving their own identity rather than being engulfed by the violent self of others.

Self-destructive chemical use may fulfill either or both of these functions, at least at first. Even when chemical use is out of control, the choice of hurting oneself through chemicals has power itself. It is a statement that the individual himself has decided how he will punish himself and no one else's choices will be allowed to supersede his own. It is his autonomous choice of how to expiate his badness while acting it out.

I Hurt Myself Because I Do Not Want to Hurt You

Individuals who take this position have learned that the expression of anger is dangerous and harmful. They have usually made a deep internal decision that they must not and will not echo the abusive behavior of another member of the family, often that of a parent, stepparent, or older sibling. They are likely also to have an exaggerated sense of their own power to influence others, and may feel that they are a bad influence on others, or a jinx—someone whose closeness will automatically harm others. This fear of closeness protects them from expressing angry feelings toward others while enabling them to preserve a sense of having power in their lives—whether they really have any power or not.

Whether from an overdeveloped sense of responsibility, a grandiose sense of importance or a belief in their thorough badness, or because they regard anger as a weapon too dangerous to use, these persons retroflect their anger, turning it on themselves. When another person is angry with them, rather than becoming angry in return, they are likely to become angry with themselves, and to consider themselves bad for having created angry feelings in someone else, or in need of a purification or purging so that they do not in turn become angry and harm others.

Chemical use for these clients fulfills at least two functions: a feeling function and a control function. The first is either anesthesia of feelings or exaggeration of feelings. They anesthetize the anger that they would otherwise have toward others, drinking or using indiscriminately and self-destructively. Or they may use in order to evoke anger in a specific place or manner that will not harm the person with whom they are really angry. The individual who drinks in order to get into fights that he will inevitably lose, choosing his opponents at a bar far away from home (where he got upset in the first place), is a good example of the person who both displaces his anger and punishes himself in the way that he chooses to ventilate it.

I Hurt Myself to Hurt You

Persons who are self-destructive in order to hurt others may be chronically angry as well. Probably they do turn a substantial amount of their anger outward. They are quite likely to have grown up in or developed symbiotic relationships with others, and to lack an adequate sense of the real boundaries between individuals. They are likely to have both high internal and high external anger. When others do not respond to their outward show of anger in the way they want, it is fairly easy for them to switch to self-abuse. They express and experience their self-destructiveness as revenge against the person they feel has injured them. Such persons are often as dangerous to others as to themselves, though not always.

Chemical use here commonly occurs as part of a fight in progress or as a relapse to get back at someone. It is generally either passive-aggressive in nature or intended to lead up to a grand gesture of self-harm of some kind.

I Hurt Myself to Feel Something

Persons taking this position are desensitized and/or have regular dissociative states which they may experience as almost a cessation of being. Anger is often the last feeling remaining to these desensitized, traumatized individuals; they use this anger to prove to themselves that they still exist. Self-destructive anger is a method they have learned to verify status as a living individual. Even if they cannot produce emotions in themselves, they may be able to evoke physical pain. If they cannot evoke emotional pain in themselves, they can still draw blood. Chemical use is an attempt to obtain feelings of some sort; however, it often evolves into just another opportunity to obliterate consciousness. Such individuals have commonly been traumatized at a prior time in their history and have developed a ritual to verify their existence in spite of the trauma. Paradoxically, the most self-abusive parts of the ritual, including self-mutilation, may be conducted during blackouts and not remembered at all.

I Hurt Myself Because I Am
Ashamed and Afraid

Persons raised in a family situation in which the expression of anger is shameful may develop what Gershen Kaufman (1985) refers to as an affect-shame bind, connected to anger. When the expression of anger itself is repeatedly and powerfully shamed, the individual learns to use self-destructive anger internally to ensure that no situation arises that would call for the expression of anger outwardly. For this shamed person, to feel shame may be the equivalent of feeling like wanting to die. It is to be avoided at all costs. Self-destructive anger substitutes, for the sensation of shame, a noisy, patronizing and persistent critical parent angrily stating the individual's worthlessness. This voice alleviates the fear of being angry at someone or shamed publicly because one is angry. It is not a pleasant choice, but for individuals who believe that anger is the worst thing they can express, it is a better choice than being angry with anyone else. Chemical use in such cases is generally an attempt to make the anger go away. If chemical use disinhibits the anger instead, so that it is displayed, the shame felt later reinforces the affect-shame bind itself, and intensifies the problem.

I Hurt Myself to Get Your Attention

Persons experiencing these feelings may have poor social skills, so that they cannot effectively gain the attention they want. Or they may be so highly self-conscious that even if they know how to get what they want, they cannot bring themselves to be open about it. They may have an impaired or inadequate sense of identity that prevents them from indicating to others what they want or need in an acceptable manner, so that others will understand and respond. This kind of self-destructive anger may occur in the form of direct action against the self or in the form of self-neglect.

Caretakers who fail to care adequately for themselves, while they suffer physical or emotional pain as a result of their sacrificial caretaking of others, may be self-destructively seeking attention. Individuals who act out directly and manipulatively, engaging in self-harm in order to obtain another's attention, obtain what they need but not always in the form that they prefer. They can control the acts of self-abuse, but not the responses of others — responses which can range from nurture and guilt to anger or shaming. Still, their acts of self-destructiveness have gained them attention and reinforced that they are important to others.

Chemical use in this case is direct and to the purpose, designed to draw attention from others. The harder it is to get those others' attention, the more self-destructive the chemical use is likely to become. Interestingly, caretakers may elicit the same kind of attention from others for the same general purposes, but be unwilling to acknowledge that there is any anger in their lack of self-care or in their creation of guilty feelings in others. Chemical use in the caretaker who needs attention tends to be hidden, since it is the dependent attention of others that the caretaker desires. Prescription drug or hidden alcohol abuse is common among caretakers in this category.

ASSESSING SELF-MUTILATING ANGER

A few words need to be said about the assessment of self-destructive anger. Some chemical abusers and dependents are relatively straightforward about the fact that their use is self-destructive. Although others may deny this, the counselor can often see clearly the role of chemicals in acting-out anger.

Some individuals use chemicals as part of a self-destructive ritual in which other behaviors take prominence. Here chemical use is adjunctive to a ritual which is self-harming or self-destructive. The kind of self-mutilation observed in those who cut, burn, or otherwise physically mutilate themselves is an example. When alcohol or other drugs are only a part of a larger ritual in which the individual takes out anger on himself, some guidelines are helpful to the chemical dependency counselor both in assessing the immediate danger inherent in the situation and in determining the role of the drug chosen.

An important part of assessing such a behavior is for the counselor to remain thoughtful and in touch with his own feelings. Overreacting may lead the client to hide the behavior in the future and to hide its connection to a ritual event that occurs repeatedly. The client may feel that if the counselor cannot tolerate the external behavior of cutting, his reaction to how she thinks and feels and uses a cutting ritual will be even worse. However, a person who is cutting herself is also clearly stating that there is something very wrong in her life, and that violation of her own body boundary is possible, relevant, and meaningful to her—so that suicide attempts certainly need to be viewed as a possibility.

Dismissing the behavior as "attention-getting" is an error. It is shaming to a client, who is doing what she can to communicate. Dismissing the behavior often ends a client's openness as well, and is a dangerously indifferent strategy. An attention-seeking client using this kind of behavior needs the attention she seeks.

Assessing the severity of the actual, observable behavior on a rational basis helps keep the counselor and the client centered. Since safety is a primary consideration, it is important to ask to see the cuts that have been made or, if they are not readily accessible, to verify that a doctor has seen them. Questions relevant here are: "Is the client safe right now?" "How severe is the cutting?" and "Was this cutting intended and/or tending toward serious self-injury or suicide?" Every instance of cutting is not a suicide attempt. Light, superficial slashes near blood vessels and deeper slashes into fatty tissue where there are no arteries are intended to convey a different message and/or to provide a different kind of relief than deep slashes in areas where arteries can be hit or severe self-injury done. One serious slash on the wrist may signal a far more angry, self-destructive intent than several deeper cuts in the fatty tissue of the thighs.

The state of mind of the individual, the depth of depression or severity of anxiety, and the relationship of the self-injury to issues of separation are significant as well. In general, the more hostile the attitude, severe the depression, frightening the anxiety, and intense the separation issues, the more dangerous the situation. Individual differences in ritual, intent, and perseverance of cutting are important to note. One client cut herself two or three times each night in order "to go to sleep." This ritual remained "successful" for her until long after she had been sober and its meaning had been identified (a replication of nightly child sexual abuse from years before). The message in the nightly cutting was: "Now you have already been violated and you can sleep safely the rest of the night." Another client drank to anesthetize herself to the pain and found she could not cut so deeply or destructively when sober. Thus, the times she was drinking were the times when intent became seriously suicidal. Sober "scratching" at her wrists was a signal that depression was worsening and she was beginning to feel desperate. In the first case, the alcohol was adjunctive, and the self-destructive anger needed to be dealt with separately. In the second case, alcohol was an integral part of the ritual of self-injury and increased the likelihood of suicide significantly.

Any cutting done in a condition of blackout, whether the person has been using chemicals or not, is to be regarded with great seriousness; treating it as such will sometimes help to in-

terrupt the patterned ritual and move the individual toward recovery, possibly because many self-mutilators are looking for a
kind of control in their own lives, and blackout, because it re-
moves the sense of control, defeats the ritual at the conscious
level.

Alcohol and other drugs can also be part of a self-destructive
ritual in other ways. The man who gets drunk in order to pick a
fight and get beaten up is echoed by the woman who gets drunk
in order to put herself in sexually dangerous situations or to
be promiscuous in an age of sexually transmitted diseases. The
educated IV drug user who risks AIDS by sharing needles with
an active prostitute may be self-destructively angry instead of
simply in denial.

PRINCIPLES OF TREATMENT

The treatment process with self-destructive anger is quite vari-
able, since each basic position must be addressed from a unique
perspective, as well as the more general one. Nevertheless, there
are some useful principles to remember in the identification and
treatment of self-destructive anger:

- Safety comes first, even before counselor control.

- Validate that self-destructive action occurs because a
  person is in pain.

- Determine whether chemical use is primary or adjunctive.

- Define the responsibilities in the therapeutic relationship.

- Identify the sources of self-directed anger.

- Define appropriate behavior and establish clear boundaries.

- Enlist clients in helping to determine the internal position they are taking and the statement this makes.

- Respect clients' right to be angry and confirm that human beings can survive each other's anger.

- Help clients deflate an exaggerated sense of the power of anger.
- Determine the relationship of chemical use to self-destructive anger.

Safety Comes First, Even Over Counselor Control

If a person uses self-destructive anger to get "attention," let him or her "win" on a temporary basis by providing attention. To refuse to do so can be to ignore a significant message asking for help.

Validate that Self-Destructive Action
Occurs Because a Person Is in Pain

Often the sources of that pain will not be immediately apparent. Deal with self-destructive anger without shaming the client. Most clients with internalized anger directed at the self already have significant shame issues and will withdraw further, feel worse about themselves, and possibly escalate behavior when shamed by a judgmental counselor.

Determine Whether Chemical Use Is
Primary or Adjunctive

The therapist needs to examine whether the chemical use is the primary act of self-destructiveness or an adjunctive behavior connected to other self-aggressive behavior. If it is connected to a ritual, determine whether the connection exists in order to inhibit or disinhibit self-oriented anger. Some individuals use in an attempt to make the anger go away (inhibition) and others to allow the anger to emerge (disinhibition). Find out what the components of the ritual are and how it is conducted. Does chemical use make the ritual easier to perform, such as providing a sexually ashamed and ordinarily prudish person with sexual boldness? Does it allow for escalation of the ritual, such as anesthesia to allow more severe self-mutilation? Or is it an attempt to halt or ameliorate angry action against the self, such as smoking marijuana or drinking in hopes of falling asleep rather than being self-abusive? How does the chemical use compound the prob-

lem? In other words, what is its result in the actual practice of
the self-destructive ritual? How might sobriety affect this ritual if
the person stops using? If sobriety were to end the ritual, what
could the person put in its place that is less self-destructive?

Define the Responsibilities in the
Therapeutic Relationship

Be clear about exactly what you will do and when you will do
it, in terms of helping the client deal with the self-abusive anger.
Be clear about what the client's responsibilities are; state explic-
itly that ultimately the client has responsibility for his or her life.
Use the relationship as a partnership in order to help the angry
person defuse anger against the self, not as a dictatorship in
which you give the advice—which may further anger the client
or leave him dependent on you.

Identify the Sources of Self-Directed Anger

Work to identify the sources of self-directed anger in the client's life and to help the client gain insight into the most relevant
issues. Severe depression warrants an evaluation for medication.
Social anger directed at the self, such as homophobia or rage
over disability or weakness, often requires small group work in a
safe setting to defuse or learn to target expression differently.
Self-directed anger from abuse and family or relationship problems demands work on self-concept and new assertiveness skills.
Awareness of the issues may not result in immediate ability to
act appropriately in the self-destructive client, but it is the beginning of the process of acceptance, which *will* lead to changes.

Define Appropriate Behavior and
Establish Clear Boundaries

Establish clear definitions of appropriate and inappropriate
behavior, as well as clear boundaries for the client. Distinguish
between anger at self and aggression toward self and set behavioral boundaries for the client to follow. To combat the cynicism
and hopelessness, prohibit self-abusing clients from discussing

ways to hurt themselves with each other, by invoking a sense of mutual responsibility for each other.

Enlist Clients in Helping to Determine
the Internal Position They Are Taking,
and the Statement this Makes

Encourage them to be as specific in understanding themselves as possible. "I hurt myself" to get *whose* attention or *what kind* of attention? "I hurt myself to feel" *what* event or feeling? *How* is this feeling important to me? *What* event am I commemorating, if any? I hurt myself because I do not want to hurt you *how*? I hurt myself to hurt you by making you feel *what*? Whenever a question of specificity can be answered thoughtfully and clearly, a path opens to look at other practical options for accomplishing the same objective. Often, the counselor and client who have identified the client's goal can brainstorm other ways to accomplish it better.

Respect Clients' Right to Be Angry, and
Confirm that Human Beings Can
Survive Each Other's Anger

Demonstrate this respect by modeling assertive behavior with others yourself. Clients with self-destructive anger may need to know that you can tolerate and trust an expression of their anger without falling apart or rejecting, shaming, or punishing them. If they become openly angry with you as a part of their recovery, it may be relevant to let them know that you do not expect or desire that they punish themselves.

Help Clients Deflate an Exaggerated
Sense of the Power of Anger

This may need to be done in two ways. First, the power of others' anger which frightened them so deeply in the past needs to be put in context—children are often very frightened by adult anger, and what may seem overwhelmingly powerful to a child may not be so to an adult. What frightened them terribly in the past would not have had such a big impact on them if it had first occurred when they were larger, when they were adults. For instance, a client can, as an adult, be in control of his father's glare by purposefully doing some small thing to evoke it on an intentional basis—and he can survive this. His anger, expressed without accompanying aggressive behavior, can be powerful without being harmful. Tests can be done and experiments conducted to verify this reality. Anger needs to be demystified and unmasked as a simple and survivable emotion.

Determine the Relationship of the Chemical Use to Self-Destructive Anger

Making clients aware of the function of their chemical use and its relationship to their anger is highly significant in gaining their interest in beginning to resolve their problems. For the client, feeling that one really understands how one works is the beginning of a sense of power in the decision-making process. Is the chemical use a part of the self-destructiveness itself; that is, is the self-destructively angry person drinking or using drugs as a primary means of demonstrating self-hatred? Is the using an attempt to inhibit being angry with others that backfires badly, resulting in unsatisfying outcomes? Does the chemical use allow the expression of anger and aggression against the self in a manner that greatly increases physical and/or emotional danger to the individual? How is chemical use part of a ritual process of self-destructive anger? Does the person actually accomplish what he intends with his chemical use?

Much of the time, the counselor will be able to demonstrate clearly that the chemical use is not helpful even in terms of the individual's short-term objectives. In cases where an individual maintains a decision to use self-destructively, understanding the process better may increase uneasiness prior to the event of using and make the decision to use more difficult.

In addition to the suggestions above, we advise following the recommendations of Mary Louise Wise (1990) regarding therapeutic responses to self-injury. Wise notes three *unhelpful* ways to respond to self-injury: (1) with disgust or judgment; (2) viewing self-injury strictly as client manipulation; (3) focusing primarily on "reducing" or "managing" the extent or amount of self-injury and thus ignoring the client's deeper messages within the pain.

Wise suggests ten helpful ways to respond to self-injury: (1) affirming the reality of the pain to the client; (2) conveying respect for the survival value of the client's self-injuries (helping him/her survive otherwise unbearable distress); (3) acknowledging the need of the client to retain this pattern; (4) linking current self-injurious behaviors with similar ones in the past; (5) recognizing that a temporary increase of self-destructive behavior may accompany a client's retrieval of memories about past abuse; (6) focusing on the meaning of the behavior to the client; (7) having faith that the client will develop new patterns for survival over time; (8) when a client injures self, responding with concern both for the injury per se and for the client's total experience; (9) encouraging a client to make time-limited decisions not to self-injure as he/she develops sustained relationships with counselors and peers; (10) exploring with the client, in a safe context, the feelings and needs previously denied, betrayed, or neglected.

EXERCISES

11-1 *Self-Neglect, Self-Abuse and Self-Sabotage*

Use the exercises below to help self-destructive individuals understand the many ways in which they can and do take out their anger on themselves. Each exercise also challenges clients to commit to making changes in behaviors they identified as harmful.

1. Self-neglect violates the principle of humanity, because when we neglect ourselves we are not treating ourselves as persons worth loving or caring for. Some of us are aware of our self-neglect, but some deny it. We say "I'm too busy to take care of myself," or "It's too much work to take care of myself," avoiding the real implications of our behavior.

(a) Check anything on the following list that you neglect for yourself. Use the extra lines to add any other ways you neglect yourself.

_eating regularly   _exercising as you need
_eating nutritionally   _taking time to relax
_going to the doctor   _getting enough sleep
_going to the dentist   _caring for self when ill
_caring for appearance   _working reasonable hours
_buying items you   _keeping physical environ-
   really need   ment comfortable

_____   _____

(b) Make a commitment to change one of these behaviors, and work on it. Write here how it feels to give yourself something you

2. Self-abuse violates the principles of humanity and humility— that we are persons worth caring for, and that we are no worse than others. Use the following checklist to evaluate whether you are abusive to yourself. Add any other specific ways you can identify self-abuse.

_drink too much   _pinch, hit, or bite self
_use drugs   _work to exhaustion
_eat until painful   _suicidal thinking
_starve self   _burn, cut, or tear self
_take dangerous risks   _binge, purge, or use laxatives
_pick sores   _chew fingernails to the quick
_put self down with others   _put self down internally

_____   _____

Make a commitment to change one of these behaviors.

Behavior:
How I will change it:
How can I fit this change into my life?
One person I will share my change with after I make it:
One person I will call if I need support:
One place I will go to help stop my self-abuse if I need to:

3. Self-sabotage violates the principles of autonomy and competence. We sabotage ourselves when we fail to act on positive options, when we undermine our own success, and when we lack follow through to make important changes for ourselves.

  (a) How do you sabotage yourself? Be specific.

  (b) What happens to your self-concept when you sabotage yourself?

Starting today, make a commitment to quit all acts of self-sabotage for the next 24 hours. Write about how you do feel when you choose not to sabotage yourself.

4. Some deeply shamed persons become entangled in relationships with individuals who regularly hurt and shame them. This increases their shame even more but at the same time feels "right"—they believe they deserve to be treated with contempt. Look back to a time when you felt really bad about yourself. See if you can remember any actions you took then that you now realize invited someone to hurt you. A few examples are taunting someone until he/she physically or verbally attacked you, making "mistakes" or forgetting your responsibilities so often that your employer had to reprimand you, and choosing to go out with critical or cruel people when more positive choices were available.

  (a) How did this behavior affect your life?
  (b) What did it do to your shame?
  (c) Are you still doing some of these actions?
      If so, can you make a commitment to quit setting others up to hurt you?

11-2 *Self-Acceptance*

A self-destructive individual is often a despairing person with a traumatic background. Numbness is often a way of preserving the self from intolerable pain, including the painfulness of shame. Often, there is a hint of oppositionality in this person, which she has adopted to keep herself from being vulnerable to and swallowed up by another needy human being, as may have occurred in her family of origin (where a history of abuse most often begins).

Direct reception of positive support is unusual for this person. Most often, she is an expert at deflecting, declining, and neutralizing positive information about herself, and very suspicious of the motives of the person complimenting or reinforcing her strengths.

An indirect method which enables her to begin to support herself better is to have her identify with a physical object she can relate to on her own when she is entirely unthreatened by the presence of other people. A natural object with some flaws, such as a shell which has a small blemish in it, is an appropriate object. A geode, with its rough exterior and lovely interior, also makes an appropriate object. Keep a small bowl of such objects available on your desk, and when it is relevant, ask the client to allow one of these objects to "choose" her. Tell her she will know if she is "chosen" because either the object which is "choosing" her will immediately jump to her attention, or it will "choose" her more quietly, by drawing her attention back to itself again and again.

When the client has been "chosen" by an object, ask her to tell you how the object is like her. As she makes initial connections, you can reinforce them by noting the trauma which formed the rock or the heavy pressure of the water under which the shell survived and then comparing these events to her difficult experiences growing up.

When the client seems to have adequately identified the object with herself, point out its beauties as well as its flaws. Indicate that it looks like a "keeper" (something worth keeping around) even though it is not perfect. Ask her what she thinks. If she agrees that she would keep this object herself, then request that she indeed do this by carrying the object in a pocket or purse and spending 10 minutes or so every day just looking at it. Suggest that she need not analyze it, but that it has chosen her because it has something to teach her about herself. Her own self will usually then take over the process of reinforcing some of her beauty and strengths in a quiet, unobtrusive way through use of the right brain. Check in on how she is doing with her "magic" object once every few weeks.

11-3 Survivor Guilt

Survivor guilt as a cause of self-destructiveness is often hidden, sometimes even from the person who is experiencing it. One means of helping the client to identify it is by telling a story such as the following:

> Once there was a little boy who lived with his mom and dad, and his three puppies. The little boy and the puppies all had lots of energy and liked to play hard all day. Sometimes they even played when the little boy was supposed to be doing chores, or when his parents were still asleep in bed, and sometimes accidents happened when they played. Once the puppies tore a sofa cushion when they were playing, and once the little boy and his puppies woke up his parents way too early. When things like this happened, the little boy was always the one who got punished.
>
> One day all four were playing happily in the living room. Everything was going fine, but then they got a little too bouncy. They rolled over and over on the floor and bump! Someone rolled right into the leg of the end table. Mom's favorite plant toppled off. Crash! The pot broke and dirt spilled all over the rug. When Mom found out, she was very angry and spanked the boy hard. The puppies all felt very sad. They all did different things. The biggest one pulled and pulled on Mom's pants as if to say, "Stop! Don't hurt my little boy!" The middle-sized puppy ran over to lick the boy's hands and face to make the spanking hurt less. The littlest puppy was scared, and ran all the way under the table. She curled up in a tight ball, sad about the little boy's spanking, and too scared that she would be spanked too!

The client is then asked, "If this story had happened in your family, which puppy would you have been like?" Use the client responses for a basis for discussing different sources of survivor guilt and examining the inappropriateness of destructive self-punishment.

11-4 Toxic Shame

When a client needs to look at the connection between her shame and her self-destructive anger, the concept of toxic shame can be introduced, as follows:

> Toxic shame is created when a child or adult is given messages that tell her that her very being is irrelevant, defective, deficient, or worthless. People can receive these messages verbally or non-verbally in either gestures (sneering or coldness) or actions (ignoring or hitting). Abusiveness violates personal boundaries, as does emphasis on family image and keeping secrets.

Encourage clients to identify how they give themselves the following deficiency messages:

- I am no good.
- I am not good enough.
- I am not lovable.
- I don't belong.
- I should not exist.

Ask them how they originally got these messages, and from whom. Whose voice talks so critically in their head? Whose anger are they acting out against themselves?

It may be important to note that a parent who is supportive now may have been an angry person in the past. "I" may be the "old" parent the client needs to challenge internally.

Learning to talk back to the voices of the past often decreases self-destructive behavior.

12

ANGER ISSUES of THERAPISTS

Counselors occasionally become angry with particular clients for reasons we examine in this chapter. Guidelines are also presented to help professional counselors decide when and how to express their anger.

Some therapists need to address their own tendencies toward anger avoidance or chronic anger. Here we reexamine anger avoidance from the perspective of how its presence among counselors hinders effective therapeutic intervention. Excessive anger is approached in a similar manner. Anger avoidance or excessive anger intrudes on a helper's ability to empathize with certain clients, making appropriate confrontation difficult. For example, one therapist may find himself intimidated by his clients' rage, while another periodically explodes at her clients in an "unprofessional" manner that endangers her continuing employment. While many therapists encounter their own anger issues sporadically, others discover they have consistent and predictable problems in this area.

It is crucial that counselors be aware of their intrinsic biases about anger. Is anger something to be encouraged, explored, accepted? Is anger a "negative" emotion to be reduced or eliminated as quickly as possible? Is an angry person "healthy" or "sick," "normal" or "abnormal"? Is it ever appropriate for a counselor to feel anger toward a client? To express that anger? Most therapists have internal, automatic responses to these questions, based on their family-of-origin beliefs, personal experiences, and professional training. Answers to these questions inform practice, sometimes interfering with an objective analysis of what particular clients need.

REASONS PROFESSIONALS BECOME ANGRY WITH CLIENTS

Any professional therapist may become angry with a client, even if that therapist has few general problems with anger avoidance or chronic anger. Counselors may be surprised, frightened, disturbed, or pleased with this anger; they may attempt to ignore or utilize it. They are often puzzled by their anger, wondering why it is appearing with this particular client at this time. Although there may be an infinite number of answers to this question, the possibilities below are quite commonly linked to anger toward clients.

The Therapist's Anger is a Signal that Something May Be Wrong in the Therapeutic Relationship

Counselors must be careful not to dismiss their anger as meaningless or totally unprofessional. Instead, that anger should be examined for clues as to what difficulties may have developed in the counseling relationship. Counselors should remember, though, that anger only signals that something is wrong somewhere in an individual's life; it does not provide specific information on the exact problem, which may or may not be relevant to the therapeutic encounter. It is dangerous to assume either that the anger has nothing to do with the current therapy or that it must be connected.

The Therapist's Anger is Frequently a Signal of Frustration and Helplessness

No therapist is universally effective. Certain clients seem unreachable, at least during a specific session or course of treatment. Client resistance often is translated into a sense of personal failure by counselors whose mission is to reach and help their clients. Therapists need to examine their anger at clients to see if they are feeling ashamed of their ineffectiveness.

The entire staff of an agency may join together to blame a resistant client or group of clients. This scapegoating is noticeable in staff meetings when several staff members "badmouth" a client and collectively ventilate their anger. Scapegoated clients may then be dismissed from treatment programs with the label of "uncooperative," or the primary focus may be shifted from therapy to control.

A Therapist's Anger May Be a Signal that Appropriate Boundaries Need to Be Established or Maintained

A demanding and needy client calls her therapist repeatedly every day, while at the same time informing him that she feels cheated when he is not immediately available. The therapist is initially receptive but gradually finds himself becoming angry and resentful at her intrusiveness. Therapists may have similar responses to clients who have a need to be "special" or with those who are interruptive, controlling, or overly accommodating. The anger reveals a need to establish and maintain effective boundaries, without which therapists feel invaded and out of control. The message within the therapist's anger is: "Get back! You're getting too close and asking too much from me. I need some space for myself." Counselors who fail to heed this message may wind up feeling used and then exploding in rage at their clients.

Therapist Anger Can Signal the Presence of Countertransference Issues

Certain clients remind their therapists, not always at a fully conscious level of awareness, of individuals with whom they are angry. For example, a counselor who is herself a survivor of spouse assault may easily become irate with male clients who "act just like my ex-husband." Similarly, therapists may become angry with clients who remind them in any way of their parents or various significant others, including difficult former clients. The relevant question, of course, is, "With whom am I really angry here?" Therapists should examine any instance in which they feel small or young, as well as times when their anger seems grossly disproportionate for the situation, for countertransference themes. If this occurs regularly, therapy for the therapist is strongly recommended. Until countertransference issues are resolved, therapists may need to refer certain clients to their colleagues.

Therapist Anger May Be a Response to "Masked" Anger of the Client

Therapists are generally sensitive to their client's verbal and nonverbal behaviors. They may "catch" hints of their clients' anger, absorbing it into their own experience without identifying its source. This subliminal perception of anger is likely to occur when clients are unaware of their anger about a specific situation or when they are angry about something but don't want to inform the counselor about that anger. Counselors may also be responding to passive-aggressive behavior, as when clients fail to complete homework assignments or show initiative within the therapy session. Most therapists become frustrated after a certain number of "I don't know" responses, perhaps without recognizing the client's passive-aggressiveness contained within that statement.

Therapist Anger May Be a Result of Moral Revulsion

Every counselor has a moral value system, which usually includes a broad acceptance of others. However, particular clients may say or do things that challenge one's ability to accept them: They make specious racial or ethnic attacks, swear or curse excessively, directly threaten or attack their children, display an appalling lack of current gender norms, or deliberately insult or attempt to intimidate the counselor. Therapists might respond with deep moral indignation, so strong that they experience feelings of revulsion and disgust. This anger reflects an attack upon their own value system, as well as a natural desire to defend those values by attacking the transgressor. Therapists must be careful when they are in this position, since it is easy for them to justify aggression against clients with a "Well, she deserved it after what she did to those children" attitude. If this attitude cannot be altered, it may be best to refer the client to a more neutral counselor.

HANDLING ONE'S ANGER DURING A THERAPY SESSION

Since any therapist may become angry during a session, it is advisable to have a method to deal with it. The following steps are helpful in this pursuit.

Counselors must allow themselves to notice their anger, as against disregarding or minimizing it. Since for many counselors it is "not nice" to be angry with clients, initial awareness is itself an important part of appropriately handling one's anger.

It is valuable to realize that awareness of anger provides choices. Therapists may choose to study their anger without directly bringing it into the therapeutic session; they may "bracket" that anger until later, when they can discuss it with colleagues and supervisors; they may act on it by dealing with the client/ helper relationship dynamics; or they may choose to share their anger directly with a client.

Counselors need to search for immediate cues that might help explain their anger, such as a client's loud voice, a therapist's backache, distracting noises from another room, etc. It may be possible to address these issues quickly, with a minimum of effort. For instance, moving one's chair back a few inches may resolve anger that results from the pain of sitting too near a particularly loud client.

When is it appropriate for therapists to share their anger directly with clients? There is no exact answer to this question, given the great variance of therapy situations. Therapists should recognize that sharing their anger is a significant endeavor that may trouble and threaten clients. Therefore, the decision to do so must be made cautiously, with primary consideration given to creating and maintaining a positive therapeutic environment. While occasionally sharing anger may improve the therapeutic relationship, by forcing client and counselor to interact honestly while examining the core of their relationship, the danger of damage to the client and loss of therapeutic trust in therapy must be considered. When tempted to express anger to a client, therapists are advised first to wait at least a few minutes before acting. If, then, the anger is still significant, and particularly if the therapist can see value for the client in stating that anger, the therapist may choose to proceed.

Before a counselor expresses anger to a client, six questions must be considered:

- Does the therapist's anger primarily reflect significant aspects of the relationship between counselor and client, such as boundary confusion, as against being personal to the helper or a result of countertransference?

- Can the therapist take responsibility for that anger without blaming the client?

- Can the therapist present his or her anger in moderation, without verbally or physically attacking the client?

- Is the client stable enough emotionally to be able to handle the therapist's presentation of anger?

- Can the counselor make a commitment of enough time and energy to deal with the client's responses to the anger of the therapist?

- Is there a reasonable probability that the expression of anger may benefit the client?

ANGER AVOIDANCE CONCERNS OF PROFESSIONAL COUNSELORS

Anger avoiders have a basic fear of the experience and/or expression of anger. Anger is viewed as a suspect emotion, one that produces uncomfortable feelings and damages relationships. Anger avoiders generally attempt to minimize conflict through such mechanisms as denial or minimization of disagreement, confusion which prevents taking effective action, excessive accommodation, and too rapid withdrawal from one's anger. Anger avoiders feel best in the complete absence of anger, both their own and that of others.

Some counselors carry this need to avoid anger into their professional interactions. They tend to define a "good" therapeutic relationship as one that is maximally supportive and minimally confrontative. Such counselors may specialize in comforting their clients, never realizing that they have entered into an unconscious contract with them to avoid anger. They like their clients and want their clients to like them. The therapy setting is defined as a refuge from anger. The safety of both client and helper is a primary consideration.

Anger avoidant therapists are likely to be slow to recognize their own anger, even when being tested by clients seeking to discover limits within the relationship. Since they have difficulty recognizing their anger, they cannot utilize it to tell them when to insist that clients maintain proper boundaries, keep their commitments, do their share of the work, etc. Anger avoidant counselors may eventually confront their clients, but they tend to do so with great caution and with a strong desire to confront without any hint of anger. Their confrontations tend to be weak, late, and ineffective.

Counselors who identify themselves as anger avoidant need to recognize several thoughts and behaviors which can undermine the therapeutic mission. These are discussed below.

Failing to Notice or Attend to a Client's Anger

Anger avoidant counselors may fail to observe relatively obvious signs of client anger, such as sarcastic remarks or raised voices. They may literally ignore angry remarks, preferring to comment upon their clients' other feelings and behaviors. Note that these same counselors may be adept at noticing and responding to cues about other affects; they seem unobservant only around the subject of anger. They may be acutely sensitive to signs of sadness in grief, for example, while missing grief-related anger symptoms. Later, these counselors minimize the total amount of anger exhibited during the session, thus distorting the session to reflect the underlying need to avoid anger.

Equating Mental Health with Freedom from Anger

Since anger avoidant counselors are uncomfortable with their anger, they cannot welcome its presence within the therapeutic endeavor. Anger is viewed as something unhealthy, and therefore as a sign of personal immaturity or system dysfunction. Anger avoidant therapists fail to ask themselves this question: "What good is this anger doing right now for the client (or system)?" Instead, effort is concentrated upon eliminating the anger as quickly as possible. It is as if the goal is to argue the anger away rather than to discover the important messages contained within the anger. "Goodness" then easily becomes defined pragmatically as the absence of anger rather than the attainment of a specific positive state.

Assuming that Clients Are Uncomfortable with Anger

Anger avoidant counselors may believe that their clients are as uncomfortable with anger as they are. This assumption is particularly unfortunate with clients who are indeed actually attracted to anger, a group discussed previously. Counselors who fail to recognize the attraction of strong anger may embark on useless discussions with their clients about how to get rid of this supposedly noxious affect; most clients will participate in these discussions, without informing their counselors of their error. Therapists should be certain to ask their clients if their anger ever helps them feel strong, excited, alive, or exhilarated. This important question will be missed, however, when anger avoidant counselors presume that the experience of anger is inevitably painful.

Rushing to Fix Things and to Make Peace

Anger avoidant therapists have difficulty tolerating intense or long-lasting anger. Therefore, they move quickly to restore peace and harmony during therapy. Tension between client and therapist is particularly bothersome; anger avoidant counselors may feel guilty if a client becomes angry with them, believing they are at fault and have failed their mission to relieve pain. They may fail to realize that their clients are testing them with their displays of anger, checking to see if the counselor can handle their anger without crumbling. Therapists may fear the anger of their clients, in particular if they identify those clients with threatening people from their past. Such projections seem to be common around anger and may form the core of a therapist's difficulty with angry clients. If accommodation worked with these powerful historical figures, anger avoidant therapists may find themselves alleviating their clients' anger instead of process-ing it with them. The anger avoidant therapist sends the message "please don't stay mad at me" to the client and does whatever he or she can to bypass that anger.

Automatically Allying with the Less
Angry Client in Couples or Family Counseling

A modicum of bias is inevitable in couples and family therapy, despite efforts to join the entire system or alternate taking sides. However, this problem may be exacerbated when anger avoidant counselors encounter couples or families in which the display of anger is polarized. Since anger avoidant therapists are attracted to clients who also hide anger and are repelled by those with strong anger, they are prone to take the side of less angry persons. They may actively dislike angrier individuals, regularly discount-ing their statements, while being overly sympathetic toward the "victims" of that anger. Anger avoidant counselors may also con-fuse anger with aggression, treating the angry client as if that person were physically assaulting others. The message they give, usually only half-consciously, is that the angry individuals are the cause of the problem just because they are angry.

Feeling Resentful or Used by Clients

These signs, along with being scared of a particular client, may be indicative of a therapeutic relationship that has become distorted through the therapist's anger avoidance. All these internal sensations imply the presence of unaddressed boundary problems within the relationship. As noted before, clients sometimes are very demanding of the therapist's time or attention, and too insistent on a personal, "special" relationship. The counselor buries the anger that might directly signal this problem, because "good therapists never get angry at their clients, no matter what they do." Instead, the anger avoidant therapist gradually becomes resentful of that client, without ever knowing exactly why. Alternatively, the client may become an object of dread, the person whose missed appointments are celebrated with a sigh of relief. Therapists may even derogate such clients to their colleagues, labeling them as particularly uncooperative or as hopeless causes instead of directly speaking with them about their behavior.

What can counselors do to minimize damage within the therapeutic relationship related to their own anger avoidant tendencies?

First, it may be valuable to make a list of clients and/or situations that trigger anger avoidance behaviors. By doing so, therapists may recognize previously hidden behavior patterns, such as avoiding the anger of men who swear a lot or women with long-term resentments.

Next, anger avoidant counselors need to train themselves to observe relatively minor verbal and nonverbal cues of anger that they would normally overlook. Watching taped reviews of sessions may be useful in accomplishing this task, although simple awareness may be sufficient. It may be helpful to ask fellow counselors, such as therapy group co-leaders, for their feedback after sessions as to who was angry and how they could tell.

Thirdly, it is necessary for anger avoidant counselors to begin to notice their own anger signs, particularly with frustrating, scary, or intimidating clients. These cues may be minimal, such as squeezing a pen or pencil tightly, or more obvious to all, such as talking more loudly or at a higher pitch. Once observed, therapists can ask themselves what the anger is about.

Of course, it is not mandatory to express each and every angry feeling. However, anger avoidant counselors do need to consider what to do with their anger once they recognize it. Possibilities include directly telling the client ("Right now I feel angry with you. You made a promise and it seems like you don't care that you broke it"), acting on the anger without directly telling the client (for example, by moving one's chair back with an invasive client), "bracketing" the anger until it can be discussed with colleagues or supervisors, or dismissing the anger as unnecessary or about something irrelevant to the client (this must be done cautiously, however, since it fits the bias of anger avoiders).

Finally, anger avoidant counselors must gradually learn to take more risks with their clients, expressing ideas and taking actions that might result in a client's becoming angry with them. It is necessary to challenge the assumption that anger has no place in a therapeutic relationship. It is also important to realize that both client and therapist will survive the appearance and expression of anger. A therapeutic relationship must be able to withstand a reasonable amount of anger; otherwise, it is likely to be more of a caretaking than truly therapeutic interaction.

THE EXCESSIVELY ANGRY COUNSELOR

Some therapists exhibit an excess proneness toward becoming angry with clients. Usually, these helpers have general problems with anger in their lives; they may be explosive, resentful, habitually angry, or dependent upon using therapy sessions to get an anger "rush." Less frequently, they become inappropriately angry primarily in therapy situations. When this occurs, the anger is more likely to be an outcome of some combination of moral indignation ("I just can't stand these clients—they are so lazy"), deliberate intimidation ("First you've got to gain their attention"), or shame-based anger that reflects the counselor's sense of impotent rage with a client ("Nothing I do seems to work with her. It's like she sits there laughing at me"). As discussed below, the therapeutic milieu is damaged in several ways when therapists are excessively angry.

Clients May Be Traumatized or Re-traumatized

Many clients, particularly in the area of addiction counseling, have been attacked physically or emotionally by parents, part-

CASE STUDY: David, an Angry Counselor of Adolescents

David is not young anymore. He's a man in his forties, very angry, who has been in recovery ten years from his own addictions to alcohol and Valium. His history is a text-book study of an antisocial personality: school suspensions and truancy, a high school dropout, skirmishes with the law from early adolescence, violence, and very early abuse and addiction to "whatever I could get my hands on—booze, dope, glue, anything."

Here's how David got sober. A senior counselor named Wally at a treatment center (the sixth that David had been ordered to attend) screamed at him that he would personally strangle Dave if he ever so much as looked at him funny. Sure, David had heard that kind of stuff before, in prison particularly, and he could easily shrug it off. But Wally re-minded him of his Uncle Fred, the only man in his troubled family of origin who seemed to care about David. Maybe staying sober would be a way for him to honor his uncle. At any rate, David never drank or drugged again. Within two years he had even completed alcohol and drug counseling training and had been hired at a local center for adolescent abusers.

"I know what worked for me," argued David. "You just have to show them how much you love them by intimidat-ing them. The more I shout and scream at them, the better the results." Indeed, David could get anyone to confess to a

ners, and authorities. They have come to therapy for a healing experience, which centers around the creation of a safe environ-ment. This sense of safety cannot be fostered with a therapist who periodically explodes at them with rage or contempt. What-ever the general value of anger, it always carries the risk of re-minding clients of previous times of danger and abuse. Experi-encing danger in therapy is not growth-promoting, especially when the danger is represented by the very individual charged alcohol and drug problem. The joke in the center is that everytime he shakes a kid another bag of dope falls out of their pockets.

David assumes that these adolescents are just like him. He really wants to save them, to keep them from straying down the same path he took. He figures that maybe he can scare them sober. Most of all, he wants them to feel loved, and he only knows one way to do that. Yell at them, threaten them, dominate them, break their spirit. That's what love is all about to David. That's the gift he gives them, the only gift he can give.

But here's what many of those adolescents say: "Sure, I told David I smoked every day, even though I didn't. You would too if he were shaking his fist in your face and screaming at the top of his lungs. He's a joke. How did he ever get to be a counselor? What's his problem?" Secretly, they laugh at him, while giving the appearance of compliance when he's around. His anger certainly scares them, but they don't feel any of David's love or caring.

David might go on like this forever. He thinks he's doing a great job. He just wishes all his colleagues were as tough as he is. ■

with creating a secure environment. These clients may complete therapy feeling more abused than when they entered.

Clients Will Leave Therapy or Display Overcompliance

Many clients will simply disappear from therapy when faced with an excessively angry counselor. Others may stay, perhaps because they must, but resolve the situation through becoming extremely compliant. They obey, just as they have probably obeyed in the past, while searching for opportunities to escape.

Intimidating therapists may allude to these persons as positive examples of the virtue of anger: "All I had to do was yell at them a few times and they settled right down." More likely, these clients will do exactly what the therapist demands while secretly resisting as much as possible. In A.A. terminology, these clients may "talk the talk" instead of really "walking the walk."

Clients and Therapists May Engage in Endless Power and Control Battles

Some clients will react to excessive anger with their own anger. The result is "in your face" encounters between irate individuals battling for control. Whatever original concerns existed are soon forgotten as the therapist tries to "break" the client, while the client invests in "you can't make me do anything I don't want to" oppositionality. The dramatic displays of anger between client and helper may be interesting to watch, but they distract both from the real purposes of counseling. Successful treatment is mistaken for victory when therapy centers around battles over power and control.

The Therapist May Lose Control and Become Physically Abusive

Physical abuse of clients does occur, often after a therapist has become frustrated with a client, begun arguing with that person, and then suddenly become too excited to back away or take a personal time-out. Counselors will usually feel tremendous remorse afterwards, as they become acutely aware that they have violated the rights of their clients and perhaps harmed them physically or emotionally. These incidents make counselors vulnerable to loss of respect from colleagues, job suspensions or terminations, and lawsuits. Needless to say, they cannot be allowed to continue and are cause for immediate institutional action. Therapists who find themselves engaging in physical aggression against clients, or who are strongly tempted to do so, need to get immediate help from their colleagues, supervisors, or personal counselors.

Habitually Angry Helpers May Overinterpret Client Anger While They Are Undersensitive to Other Affect

Counselors who are excessively angry tend to read anger into situations where there is none ("Come on, now. I know you're really mad at him, aren't' you? If I were you, I know I would be."). Simultaneously, they may disregard other emotional states or perceive them as mere covers for the client's anger. These examples of projection distort therapy, as clients are given the anger actually belonging to the counselor. When therapists consistently focus upon anger that is not there or exaggerate the intensity of anger that is present, clients are placed in a "crazy-making" situation in which they are expected to disown their own experiential reality.

Excessively Angry Counselors Act as Poor Role Models

Therapists are expected to demonstrate such standard social skills as listening well, assertiveness, anger control, and empathy. Unfortunately, habitually angry therapists may be unable to do so, at least during those occasions when their anger is triggered. Clients do model themselves after their therapists, frequently copying their counselor's actual behavior rather than his or her stated opinions. Excessively angry therapists encourage their clients to become or stay excessively angry.

Helpers who discover that they have problems with excessive anger can take several actions that will help them.

First, therapists must acknowledge the reality of this problem to themselves and others. This acknowledgment, along with a commitment to change one's professional demeanor, breaks through the denial and minimization that often accompany chronic anger. Taking full responsibility includes refusing to blame clients any longer for one's own inappropriate choices. Counselors should utilize the concept of anger invitations discussed previously to help them gain greater control of their feelings and actions.

Second, supervision time can be used to anticipate those problematic clients and situations that most frequently trigger excessive anger. Therapists should make specific plans to manage their anger on these occasions, informing coworkers if necessary. As with chronically angry clients, it is crucial to substitute positive for negative behaviors, instead of merely attempting to cease negative ones.

Third, therapists with long-term anger issues need to consider seeking professional counseling for this problem, especially if it interferes with their daily counseling functions. This is particularly true for professionals who are themselves working a 12-step program and are still consistently angry. Anger does not just disappear with abstinence or participation in self-help groups, although these practices may lessen some of the negative effects of chronic anger. Recovering counselors may also consider completing a first or fifth step on anger, substituting the concept of anger for one's originally identified addiction or compulsion.

REFERENCES

Alberti, R., & Emmons, M. (1986). *Your perfect right.* San Luis Obispo, CA: Impact Press.

Alcoholics Anonymous (1976) (3rd ed.). New York: A.A. World Service.

Averill, J. R. (1982). *Anger and aggression: An essay on emotions.* New York: Springer-Verlag.

Allen, L. (1980, January). PCP: A schizophrenomimetic. *U.S. Pharmacist*, 60–66.

Barnard, C. (1990). Alcoholism and sex abuse in the family: Incest and marital rape. In R. Potter-Efron & P. Potter-Efron (Eds.), *Aggression, family violence, and chemical dependency* (pp. 131–144). New York: Haworth Press.

Bavolek, S., & Henderson, H. (1990). Child maltreatment and alcohol abuse: Comparisons and perspectives for treatment. In R. Potter-Efron & P. Potter-Efron (Eds.), *Aggression, family violence, and chemical dependency* (pp. 165–184). New York: Haworth Press.

Beck, A. (1988). *Love is never enough.* New York: Harper and Row.

Beck, A., Rush, A. J., Shaw, B., & Emery, G. (1979). *Cognitive therapy of depression.* New York: Guilford.

Bender, S. (1987). PMS and chemical dependence. *PMS Access. 14.*

Black, C., & Bucky, S. F. (1986). Interpersonal and emotional consequences of being an adult child of an alcoholic. *International Journal of the Addictions.* 21(2): 213–231.

Black, R., & Mayer, J. (1980). Parents with special problems: Alcoholism and opiate addiction. In C. H. Kempe & R. Hefler (Eds.), *The battered child.* Chicago: University of Chicago Press.

Bolton, F., & Bolton, S. (1987). *Working with violent families*. Newbury Park: Sage Productions.

Broman, C., & Johnson, F. (1988). Anger expression and life stress among blacks: Their role in physical health. *Journal of the National Medical Association*. 80(12), 1329–1334.

Choti, S., Marston, A., Holsten, S., & Hart, J. (1987). Gender and personality variables in film induced sadness and crying. *Journal of Social and Clinical Psychology*. 5(4), 535–544.

Cloniger, D. R. (1987, April). Neurogenetic adaptive mechanisms in alcoholism. *Science*. 236, 410–416.

Cohen, S. (1985). Aggression: The role of drugs. In S. Cohen, (Ed.), *The Substance Abuse Problems* (Vol. 2). New York: Haworth Press.

Coid, J. (1986). Socio-cultural factors in alcohol-related aggression. In P. F. Brain (Ed.), *Alcohol and aggression* (pp. 184–211). Dover, NH: Croom Helm.

Coleman, D., & Strauss, M. (1983). Alcohol abuse and family violence. In E. Gottheil, K. Druely, T. Skoloda, & H. Waxman (Eds.), *Alcohol, drug abuse, and aggression*. Springfield, IL: Charles C Thomas.

Conn, L., & Lion, J. (1984). Pharmacologic approaches to violence. *Psychiatric clinics of north America* 7(4): 879–886.

Covington, S. (1986). Facing the clinical challenges of women alcoholics: Physical, emotional and sexual abuse. *Focus on family*. 9(3): 10–11, 37, 42–44.

Crowley, T. (1987). Clinical issues in cocaine abuse. In S. Fisher, A. Raskin, & E. H. Ulenhuthl (Eds.), *Cocaine: clinical and behavioral aspects*. New York: Oxford University Press.

Cuber, J., & Harroff, P. (1974). Five types of marriage. In A. Skolnick & J. Skolnick (Eds.), *Intimacy, family and society*. Boston: Little, Brown.

Daigle, R. (1990). Anabolic steroids. *Journal of Psychoactive Drugs*. 22(1), 77–80.

Daley, D., Moss, H., & Campbell, F. (1987). *Dual disorders*. Centre City, MN: Hazelden Press.

Deschner, J. (1984). *The Hitting Habit*. New York: Free Press.

Eberle, P. (1980). Alcohol abusers and nonusers: A discriminant analysis of differences between two subgroups of batterers. Paper presented at the Annual Meeting of the Society for the Study of Social Problems. Toronto.

Elkin, M. (1984). *Families under the influence*. New York: W.W. Norton.

Ellis, A, & Harper, R. (1975). *A new guide to rational living* (2nd ed.). Hollywood, CA: Wilshire Books.

Fauman, M., & Fauman, B. (1980). Chronic phencyclidine (PCP) abuse: A psychiatric perspective. *Journal of Psychedelic Drugs*. 12(3–4).

Finkelhor, D. (1983). *The dark side of families: Current family violence research.* Beverly Hills: Sage Publications.

Flanigan, B. (1989). Workshop on Forgiveness. Madison, WI.

Flanzer, J. (1990). Alcohol and family violence: Then to now—who owns the problem. In R. Potter-Efron & P. Potter-Efron (Eds.), *Aggression, family violence and chemical dependency.* New York: Haworth Press.

Flanzer, J., & Sturkie, D. K. (1987). *Alcoholism and adolescent abuse.* Holmes Beach, FL: Learning Publications.

Gelles, R. J. (1972). *The violent home.* Beverly Hills: Sage.

Gentry, W. D. (1983). Behavioral medicine and the risk for essential hypertension. *International Review of Applied Psychology.* 32(2), 85–94.

Gilligan, C. (1982). *In a different voice.* Cambridge, MA: Harvard University Press.

Gittelman, R., Mannuzza, S., Shenker, R., & Bonagura, N. (1985). Hyperactive boys almost grown up. *Archives of General Psychiatry.* 42: 937–947.

Gorski, T. (1983). *Relapse warning sign assessment.* Hazel Crest, IL: Cenaps Corp.

Grinspoon, L., & Bakalar, J. (1985). Drug dependence: Non-narcotic agents. In H. T. Kaplan & B. J. Sadock (Eds.), *Comprehensive textbook of psychiatry/IV* (Vol. One, 4th ed., pp. 1003–1015). Baltimore, Williams and Williams.

Hallagan, J., Hallagan, L., & Snyder, M. (1989). Anabolic–androgenic steroid use. *New England Journal of Medicine.* 321(15), 1042–1045.

Halliday, A., Bush, R., Cleary, P., Aronson, M., & Delbanco, T. (1986). Alcohol abuse in women seeking gynecologic care. *Obstetrics and Gynecology.* 68(3), 332–326.

Heath, D. (1983). Alcohol and aggression: A "missing link" in worldwide perspective. In E. Gottheil, K. Druley, T. Skoloda, & H. Maxman (Eds.), *Alcohol, drug abuse and aggression* (pp. 89–103). Springfield, IL: Charles Thomas.

Hecker, M., & Lunde, D. (1985). On the diagnosis and treatment of chronically hostile individuals. In M. Chesney, & R. Rosenman (Eds.), *Anger and hostility in cardiovascular and behavioral disorders* (pp. 227–240). New York: Hemisphere Publishing.

Honer, W., Gewirtz, G., & Turey, M. (1987, August 22). Psychosis and violence in cocaine smokers. *The Lancet, 451.*

Jaffe, J. (1985). Opioid dependence. In *Comprehensive Textbook of Psychiatry* (Vol. One, 4th ed., pp. 987–1003). Baltimore: Williams and Williams.

Jesse, R. C. (1989). *Children in recovery.* New York: W.W. Norton.

Johnson, E. (1989). The role of the experience of anger and anxiety in elevated blood pressure among black and white adolescents. *Journal of Behavior Medicine. 81*(5), 573–584.

Johnson, E., & Broman, C. (1987). The relationship of anger expression to health problems among black Americans in a national survey. *Journal of Behavior Medicine. 10*(2), 103–116.

Johnson, R., & Montgomery, M. (1990). Children at multiple risk: Treatment and prevention. In R. Potter-Efron & P. Potter-Efron (Eds.), *Aggression, family violence and chemical dependency* (pp. 145–164). New York: Haworth Press.

Kantor, G. K., & Strauss, M. A. (1986). *Drinking patterns and spousal violence.* National Council on Alcoholism Forum. San Francisco.

Kashkin, K., & Kleber H. (1989). Hooked on hormones. *JAMA. 262,* 3166–3170.

Kaufman, G. (1985). *Shame: The power of caring* (Rev. Ed.) Cambridge, MA: Shenkman Publishing Company.

Keane, T., Fairbank, J., Caddell, J., Zimering, R., & Bender, M. (1985). A behavioral approach to assessing and treating post—traumatic stress disorder in vietnam veterans. In C. Figley (Ed.), *Trauma and Its Wake* (pp. 257–294). New York: Brunner/Mazel.

Kerr, M., & Bowen, M. (1988). *Family evaluation.* New York: W.W. Norton.

Kleinman, C. (1990). Forensic issues arising from the use of anabolic steroids. *Psychiatric Annals. 20*(4), 219–221.

Kübler-Ross, E. (1969). *On death and dying.* San Luis Obispo, CA: Impact.

Labell, L. (1977). Wife abuse: A sociological study of battered women and their mates. *Victimology. 4,* 258–267.

Leonard, K. E., Bormet, E. J., Parkinson, D. K., Day, N. L., & Ryan, C. M. (1985). Patterns of Alcohol Use and Physically Aggressive Behavior in Men. *Journal of Studies on Alcohol. 46*(4), 279–282.

Lerner, H. (1985). *The Dance of Anger.* New York: Harper & Row.

Levenson, J. (1985). Dealing with the violent patient: Management strategies to avoid common errors. *Postgraduate Medicine. 78*(5), 329–335.

Levy, A., & Brekke, J. (1990). Spouse battering and chemical dependency: Dynamics, treatment, and service delivery. In R. Potter-Efron & P. Potter-Efron (Eds.), *Aggression, family violence and chemical dependency* (pp. 81–98). New York: Haworth Press.

Luisada, P., & Brown, B. (1976). Clinical management of the phenylcyclidine psychosis. *Clinical Toxicology. 9*(4), 539–545.

MacAndrew, C., & Edgerton, R. (1969). *Drunken comportment: A social explanation.* Chicago, Aldine Publishing.

Markoff, C. (1984). Cited in PMS and alcohol abuse: Cocktail hour becomes cocktail daze. *PMS Connection.* Irvine, CA: PMS Action.

Meissner, W. W. (1986). *Psychotherapy and the paranoid process.* North-vale, NJ: Jason Aronson.

Miller, M. M., & Potter-Efron, R. (1990). Aggression and violence associated with substance abuse. In R. Potter-Efron & P. Potter-Efron (Eds.), *Aggression, family violence and chemical dependency* (pp. 1–36). New York: Haworth Press.

Minuchin, S., & Fishman, H. C. (1981). *Family therapy techniques.* Cambridge, MA: Harvard University Press.

Morgan, J. (1985). *Alcohol and drug abuse guide for pharmacology faculty.* Rockville, MD: National Institute of Alcohol Abuse and Alcoholism.

Moyer, K. F. (1976). *The psychobiology of aggression.* New York: Harper & Row.

Nakken, C. (1988). *The addictive personality.* Center City, MN: Hazelden Press.

Neilsen, L. (1990). Victims as victimizers: Therapeutic and professional boundary issues. In R. Potter-Efron & P. Potter-Efron (Eds.), *Aggression, family violence, and chemical dependency* (pp. 203–226). New York: Haworth.

Parens, H. (1987). *Aggression in our children: Coping with it constructively.* Northvale, NJ: Jason Aronson.

Patterson, G. R. (1985). A microsocial analysis of anger and irritable behavior. In M. Chesney & R. Rosenman (Eds.), *Anger and hostility in cardiovascular and behavioral disorders* (pp. 83–100). New York: Hemisphere Publishing.

Peterson, R., & Stillman, R. (1978). Phenylcyclidine abuse: An appraisal. Rockville, MD: National Institute of Drug Abuse.

Pickens, R., & Meisch, R. (1973). Behavioral Aspects of Drug Dependence. *Minnesota Medicine. 3,* 183–186.

Pickens, R., Hatsukami, D., Spizer, J., & Suikis, D. (1985). Relapse by Alcohol Abusers. *Alcoholism: Clinical and Experimental Research. 9*(3), 244–247.

Pittman, F. (1989). *Private lies.* New York: W.W. Norton.

Polster, E., & Polster, M. (1973). *Gestalt Therapy Integrated.* New York: Brunner/Mazel.

Pope, H., & Katz, D. (1987, April 11). Bodybuilder's psychosis. *The Lancet.*

Potter-Efron, P. (1990). Abuse in adult children of substance dependents. In R. Potter-Efron & P. Potter-Efron (Eds.), *Aggression, family violence and chemical dependency* (pp. 99–130). New York: Haworth Press.

Potter-Efron, P., & Potter-Efron, R. (1991). Anger as a treatment concern with alcoholics and affected family members. *Alcoholism Treatment Quarterly, 8*(3).

Potter-Efron, R. (1990). Differential diagnosis of physiologically, psychiatric, and sociocultural conditions associated with aggression and substance abuse. In R. Potter-Efron & P. Potter-Efron (Eds.), *Aggression, family violence and chemical dependency* (pp. 37–50). New York: Haworth Press.

Potter-Efron, R. (1989). *Shame, guilt and alcoholism: Treatment issues in clinical practice.* New York: Haworth Press.

Potter-Efron, R., & Potter-Efron, P. (1991). *Ending our resentments.* Center City, MN: Hazelden Press.

Potter-Efron, R., & Potter-Efron, P. (1989a). *I deserve respect.* Center City, MN: Hazelden Press.

Potter-Efron, R., & Potter-Efron, P. (1989). *Letting go of shame: Understanding shame in our lives.* Center City, MN: Hazeldon/Harper and Row.

Potter-Efron, R., & Potter-Efron, P. (1985). Family violence as a treatment issue with chemically dependent adolescents. *Alcoholism Treatment Quarterly,* 2(2): 1–15.

Reid, W., & Balis, G. (1986). Evaluation of the violent patient. In A. Frances & R. Hales (Eds.), *American Psychiatric Association Annual Review* (Vol. 5, pp. 491–509). Washington, DC: American Psychiatric Press.

Satir, V. (1967). *Conjoint family therapy.* Palo Alto, CA: Science and Behavior Books.

Schaefer, S., Evans, S., & Sterne, M. (1985). Incest among women in recovery from alcoholism and drug dependency: Correlation and implication for treatment. In *Alcohol, drugs, and tobacco: An international perspective.* Proceedings of the 34th International Congress on Alcoholism and Drug Dependence: Vol. 2.

Seecoff, X. (1986). Subjective perceptions to the intravenous "rush" of heroin and cocaine in opioid addicts. *American Journal of Drug and Alcohol Abuse.* 12(1–2), 79–87.

Shapiro, D. (1965). *Neurotic styles.* New York: Basic Books.

Siegel, R. (1980). PCP and violent crime: The people vs. peace. *Journal of Psychedelic Drugs.* 12(3–4), 317–330.

Slade, J., Catlin, D., Yesalis III, C., Malone, D., Jr., & Brower, K. (1991). Anabolic Steroids. Presentation at 22nd Annual Medical-Scientific Conference of the American Society of Addictive Medicine. Boston, Mass.

Smalley, S. (1988). *Workshop on codependency.* Eau Claire, WI.

Smedes, L. (1984). *Forgive and forget.* New York: Pocket Books.

Smith, K. C., Ulch, S. E., Cameron, J. E., & Cumberland, J. A. (1989). Gender related effects in the perception of anger expression. *Sex Roles.* 20(9–10): 487–499.

Snell, W., Miller, R., & Belk, S. (1988). Development of the emotional self-disclosure scale. *Sex Roles. 18*(1-2), 59-73.

Solomon, M. (1989). *Narcissism and intimacy.* New York: W.W. Norton.

Spielberger, C. (1988). *State-trait anger expression inventory: Research edition.* Odessa, FL: Psychological Assessment Resources, Inc.

Spielberger, C. D., Jacobs, G., Russell, S., & Crane, R. S. (1983). Assessment of anger: The state-trait anger scale. In J. Butcher & C. Spielberger (Eds.), *Advances in personality assessment* (Vol. 2, pp. 161-186). Hillsdale, NJ: Lawrence Erlbaum Associates.

Spielberger, C., Krasner, S., & Solomon, E. (1988). The experience, expression and control of anger. In M. Janisse (Ed.), *Health psychology: Individual difference and stress.* New York: Springer-Verlag.

Spotts, J., & Shontz, F. (1984). The Phenomonological structure of drug-induced ego states. II. Barbiturates and sedative hypnotics: Phenomenology and implications. *The International Journal of the Addictions, 19*(3), 119-151.

Stearns, C. Z., & Stearns, P. (1986). *Anger: The struggle for emotional control in American history.* Chicago: University of Chicago Press.

Steinglass, P., Bennett, L., Wolin, S., & Reiss, D. (1987). *The alcoholic family.* New York: Basic Books.

Stoner, S. (1988). Undergraduate marijuana use and anger. *Journal of Psychology. 122*(4), 343-347.

Stoner, S., & Spencer, W. (1986). Age and sex differences on the state–trait personality inventory. *Psychological Reports. 59*, 1315-1319.

Tavris, C. (1989). *Anger: The misunderstood emotion* (rev. ed.). New York: Touchstone.

Taylor, S., & Leonard, K. (1983). Alcohol and human physical aggression. In R. Green & E. Donnerstein (Eds.), *Aggression: Theoretical and empirical reviews* (Vol. 2, pp. 77-111). New York: Academic Press.

Tennant, F., Black, D., & Voy, R. (1988, September 2). An anabolic dependence with opioid-type features. *New England Journal of Medicine.*

Thomas, S. P. (1989). Gender differences in anger expression: Health implications. *Research in Nursing and Health. 12*(6), 389-398.

Tricker, R., O'Neill, M., & Cook, D. (1989). The incidence of anabolic steroid use among competitive bodybuilders. *Journal of Drug Education. 19*(4), 313-325.

Ulanov, A., & Ulanov, B. (1983). *Cinderella and her sisters: The envied and the envying.* Philadelphia, PA: Westminster Press.

Vaglum, S., & Vaglum, P. (1985). Borderline and other mental disorders in female alcoholic psychiatric patients. *Psychopathology, 18*, 50-60.

Walfish, S. (1990). Anxiety and anger among abusers of different substances. *Drug and Alcohol Dependence. 25*(3), 253-256.

Walker, L. (1980). *The battered women syndrome.* New York: Springer.

Washton, A., Gold, M., & Potash, A. L. C. (1984). Survey of 500 callers to a national cocaine hotline. *Psychosomatics, 25*(10), 771–785.

Wegscheider–Cruse, S. (1976). *The family trap.* St. Paul: Nurturing Networks.

Wender, P., Reimherr, F., Wood, D., & Ward, M. (1985). A controlled study of methylphenidate in the treatment of attention deficit disorder, residual type, in adults. *American Journal of Psychiatry. 142*(5), 547–552.

Wender, P., Reimherr, F., & Wood, D. (1981). ATT depict disorder (minimal brain dysfunction) in adults. *Archives of General Psychiatry. 38,* 449–456.

White, G., & Mullen, P. (1989). *Jealousy.* New York: Guilford Press.

Wise, M. L. (1990). Adult self injury as a survival response in victim-survivors of childhood abuse. In R. Potter-Efron & P. Potter-Efron (Eds.), *Aggression, family violence, and chemical dependency* (pp. 185–202). New York: Haworth Press.

Woititz, J. (1983). *Adult children of alcoholics.* Hollywood, FL: Health Communications.

Wolf, E. (1988). *Treating the self.* New York: Guilford Press.

Zinker, J. (1977). *Creative process in gestalt therapy.* New York: Brunner/Mazel.

INDEX

265